ENERGY TRADING

ENERGY TRADING

Edited by

Dr. Parag Diwan

Prof. Sharad Goel

PEP
POWERING ENERGY...
PENTAGON ENERGY PRESS

ENERGY TRADING

ISBN 978-81-8274-351-9

First Edition: 2009

First published in India by

PENTAGON ENERGY PRESS
An Imprint of
PENTAGON PRESS
206, Peacock Lane, Shahpur Jat,
New Delhi-110049
Phones: 011-64706243, 26491568
Telefax: 011-26490600
email: rajan@pentagon-press.com
website: www.pentagon-press.com

Printed at New Elegant Printers, New Delhi.

Preface

Energy markets trade in commodities that are quite different in nature. It is helpful to break them into renewable and non renewable commodities and classified into three groups in this volume

1. Fuels—Oil and Gas, other derivatives and by products
2. Electricity-Power
3. Emission

This classification thus suggested corresponds to the historical pace at which these markets were opened up. Fuel market especially Oil and Gas market, opened for competition in the 1980's at the spot-and-cash market levels. Electricity market followed in several countries in the early and mid 1990's. Finally the date 1990's saw the quickening pace of trading in new types of commodities such as emissions.

Energy trading is also unique. A number of energy trading commodities cannot be found in any other market. There are standard products- Futures, Forwards, Swaps and Options; but they also all have unique features due to their predominantly physical nature. They settle differently defined differently as described by the author in the different chapters.

The purpose of this volume on Energy Trading is to describe the Management of Crude oil Trading, Natural Gas Trading, Power Trading and Emission Trading. Authors emphasis is focused on the Managerial and Implementation aspects of 'Fundamental Analysis' to understand the global Energy markets. Each of these energy markets the market participants like Speculator, Hedger, Arbitrager, Producers or end users deals with different set of market drivers which in turn affect the behavior of energy trading. In the energy markets the supply side concern not only the storage and transfer of actual commodity, but also how to get the actual commodity gets out of the ground.

This volume is an attempt to understand and describe market behavior in terms of Economics of Supply and Demand, Price driver, that causes markets to move up and down, Trading Mechanics, Risk Management and the role of Financial Derivatives Instruments in Energy Trading.

Editors has emphasized on all the Trading Platforms i.e. OTC and future markets for all the major globally traded energy commodities. Different 'Futures Contract' of Crude Oil, Natural Gas, Power and Emission on NYMEX, ICE, DME, IPE, MCX and other major global exchanges were also explained in this book.

This book provides extensive glimpses into: the people who trade Energy Commodities and Contracts, the market places where they trade and the rules that governs trading.

This book also presents the Economics of markets, Micro and Macro structures in simple way. This book will help in understanding how Energy markets works and how government and Exchanges regulate Energy Trading.

Energy is the one of the most recent market to be transformed into trading derivatives and risk management. This book aims to provide practical guidance in efficient trading of Energy Commodities, derivatives and their use as tool of risk management. The idea of using derivatives in the Energy markets has been around for many years. The magnitude of the increase in trading in the Energy Markets is reflected by the phenomenal growth in the daily volumes of the global Energy Markets.

This volume is useful to the students, academicians, traders, researcher and working professionals in the domain areas of Oil and Gas, Power and Emissions Trading.

New Delhi
1 June 2008

Dr. Parag Diwan
Prof. Sharad Goel

Contents

Chapter 1

Energy Trading

Introduction

What is Energy? Energy is the Ability to do work.

All of these sources provide us the energy we need to live our busy lives.

It comes in different forms—heat (thermal), light (radiant), mechanical, electrical, chemical, and nuclear energy. Energy is in everything. We use energy to do everything we do, from making a jump shot to baking our favorite cookies to sending astronauts into space—energy is there, making sure we have the power to do it all. There are two types of energy—stored (potential) energy and working (kinetic) energy. For example, the food you eat contains chemical energy, and your body stores this energy until you release it when you work or play. Learn more about these different forms of energy.

All forms of energy are stored in different ways, in the energy sources that we use every day. Refer Table 1.1 these sources are divided into two groups :

(i) **renewable** (an energy source that can be replenished in a short period of time), and

(ii) **non-renewable** (an energy source that we are using up and cannot recreate in a short period of time).

Renewable and non-renewable energy sources can be used to produce secondary energy sources including electricity and hydrogen.

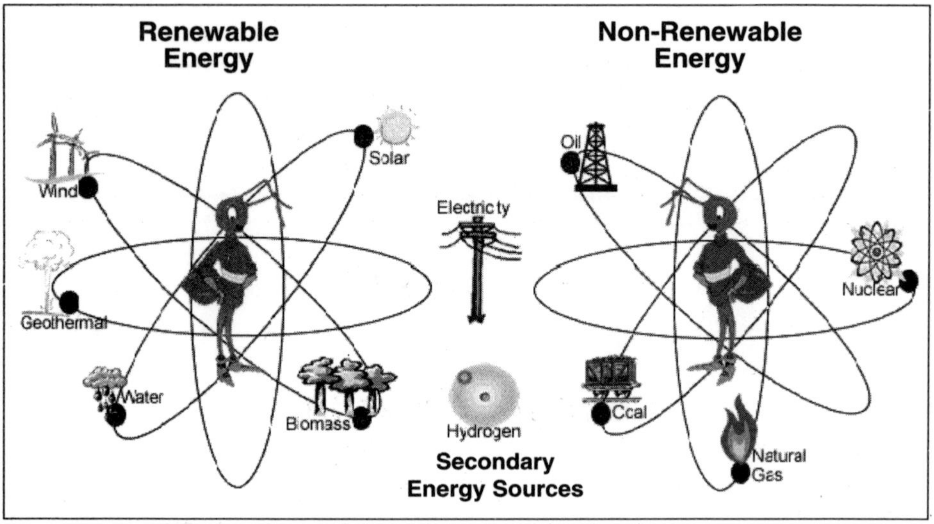

Figure 1.1: Sources of Energy

Renewable energy sources include solar energy, which comes from the sun and can be turned into electricity and heat. Wind, geothermal energy from inside the earth, biomass from plants, and hydropower and ocean energy from water are also renewable energy sources.

However, we get most of our energy from non-renewable energy sources, which include the fossil fuels—oil, natural gas, and coal. They're called fossil fuels because they were formed over millions and millions of years by the action of heat from the Earth's core and pressure from rock and soil on the remains (or "fossils") of dead plants and animals. Another nonrenewable energy source is the element uranium, whose atoms we split (through a process called nuclear fission) to create heat and ultimately electricity.

We use all these energy sources to generate the electricity we need for our homes, businesses, schools, and factories. Electricity "energizes" our computers, lights, refrigerators, washing machines, and air conditioners, to name only a few uses.

We use energy to run our cars and trucks. Both the gasoline used in our cars, and the diesel fuel used in our trucks are made from oil. The propane that fuels our outdoor grills and makes hot air balloons soar is made from oil and natural gas.

Energy Commodities such as Oil and Gas are of paramount importance in economies worldwide. Oil, gas, hydro electricity, nuclear power and coal are the five constituents of primary oil. Oil and gas account for about 60 per cent of the total world's primary oil consumption. Crude oil is a mixture of hydrocarbons that exists in a liquid phase in natural underground reservoirs. Nations struggle to explore for oil, and import it at almost any cost. It is also an important contributor to the export realizations of many countries. In countries like Russia, nearly half the hard currency earnings come from crude oil exports. The figure rises to about 80% for Venezuela and 95% for Nigeria and Algeria.

Oil has many applications and it is hard to imagine the modern world without it. Almost all industries including agriculture are dependent on oil in one way or other. Of the industries, oil and lubricants, transportation (including road, rail, sea and air), petrochemicals (some of the end products of petrochemicals include plastics, synthetic fibers, detergents and chemical fertilizers etc.), pesticides and insecticides, paints, perfumes, etc. are largely and directly affected by the oil prices as several products derived from crude oil are basic inputs in the production in these industries. The impact on these industries would result in spiraling effect on other industries and people. Without oil or its close associate natural gas, urban domestic life will become miserable. Oil light homes and streets and serves as a fuel for cooking. In cold countries, oil or gas is needed for heating homes. Metals are being progressively replaced by plastic, a product of oil and artificial fibers have made inroads into the domain of cotton. The indispensable ropes for agriculture and fishing, hitherto made from jute, are now being made from plastics. Polythene (plastic) bags, sheets and covers become indispensable in modern day's packaging and shopping. A wide range of chemicals, medicines and toiletry items is derived from oil.

There are in fact many products obtained from the processing of crude and other hydrocarbon compounds. These include aviation gasoline, motor gasoline, naphtha, kerosene, jet fuel, distillate fuel oil, residual fuel oil, liquefied petroleum gas, lubricants, paraffin wax, petroleum coke, asphalt and other products. The prices of crude are highly volatile. High oil prices lead to inflation that in turn increases input costs; reduces non-oil demand and lower investment in net oil importing countries. India, which is a net importer of oil, thus is often subject to the vagaries of price volatility in crude. Given this scenario, crude futures will come as a boon to everyone, ranging from the government and corporate to retail users. Crude oil is marketed principally in New York, London and Singapore. Futures are sold promising next-month delivery at agreed amount, price and location, in a minimum of 1000 bbl, and are settled daily. In India Crude Oil is majority marketed in Mumbai through future exchanges like NCdex (National commodity & Derivative exchange) and MCx (Multi Commodities exchange), Oil is priced relative to certain standard kinds of crude. In London, it is Brent blend crude from the North Sea; about 2/3 of the world's crude oil is priced in terms of Brent. In New York, West Texas Intermediate (WTI) light, sweet crude is the standard. OPEC prices its oil in terms of a basket of seven crudes: Saudi Arab light, Emirates Dubai crude, Nigerian Bonny light, Algerian Saharan blend, Indonesian Minas, Venezuelan Tia Juana, and Mexican Isthmus. Individual crudes are sold at a discount or premium, depending on quality and difficulty of transport. Crude oil is a very variable commodity.

World Wide Energy Scenario

In the past four years the world has witnessed oil prices move from low of around $12 per barrel to $70. Presently the oil prices have crossed $112 per barrel, but even at $100 the oil price will be in keeping with the adjusted real price at the time of first oil shock. Within the energy scene, the 20th Century clearly belongs to oil. In this period, the share of oil has increased from practically nothing to as high as 35-40%. This excludes non-commercial energy sources. During 1950-2000, demand for oil grew from 50 million barrels per day to 75 million barrels per day. In the last five years, the estimated growth was another 10 million barrels per day. The large emerging economies in Asia will further push the demand by another 30 million barrels per day—a total of 115 million barrels per day by 2030.

The global population has increased from 1.6 billion in 1990 to 6.4 billion in 2005. The average per capita supply of commercial energy has matched this increase. However, the global mean hides enormous regional and national inequalities. Per capita energy consumption in India is less than one tenth of that of industrialized nations. Consequently, there is appalling loss of economic activity, productivity and efficiency.

Word Energy Demand

The IEO2006 reference case projects increased world consumption of marketed energy from all sources over the next two and one-half decades. Fossil fuels continue to supply much of the increment in marketed energy use worldwide throughout the projections. The total world energy consumption of oil is expected to decline from 37.8% percent in 2005 to 33 percent in 2030, largely in response to higher world oil prices which would dampen oil demand, whereas natural gas's share is expected to increase from 23.6% in the previous year to 26.3% in 2030, as shown in Table 1.1 below.

Table 1.1: World Marketed Energy Use by Fuel Type (1980-2030)

(*quadrillion Btu*)

Year	*Oil*	*Natural Gas*	*Coal*	*Nuclear*	*Renewables*
1980	131	54	70	7.6	18.4
1990	136.1	75.2	89.4	20.4	24.1
2003	162.1	99.1	100.4	26.5	32.7
2004	165.5	102.2	104.4	26.9	34.5
2005	168.8	105.4	108.5	27.2	36.3
2010*	185.6	121.1	128.8	28.9	45.2
2020*	210.8	156.1	160.1	32.9	53.1
2030*	239.1	189.9	195.5	34.7	62.4

Note: *Projections.
Source: www.eia.doe.gov

According to international energy outlook's projections worldwide oil consumption would rise from 83.97 million barrels per day in 2005 to 98 million barrels per day in 2015 and then to 118 million barrels per day in 2030. All the projections have been revised downwards because of the expected higher oil prices path. For many years, it has been projected that natural gas would be the fastest growing energy source; however, higher natural gas prices (linked to oil prices) in IEO2006 make coal more cost-competitive, especially in the electric power sector, and as a result natural gas use and coal use increase at similar rates. Natural gas demand is expected to rise by an average of 2.4 percent per year over the 2003 to 2030 period which is greater than oil and almost equal to the rate of growth of coal.

REASONS FOR EXPECTED CHANGES IN THE DEMAND PATTERN

1. *Environmental Considerations*

In the recent past, increased emphasis on the environment has proved to be one of the major drivers of current and future use of natural gas. The ongoing debate over climate change and how it should be addressed is a prime example of the divergence between concerns about energy supply and the environment, as shown in Table 1.2.

Table 1.2: Fuel-wise Carbon Intensity

Fuel	*Carbon Intensity (Mt C/EJ)*	*Ratio to Natural Gas*
Natural gas	14.4	100%
Crude oil	19.9	138%
Coal	25.4	177%

Source: EIA.

2. *Power Generation*

Natural gas is used internationally as fuel by thermal power plants. The introduction of CCGT, which burn gas for energy, has revolutionized power generation technology. Natural gas contains no sulphur and releases substantially less CO_2 than coal. Though generating electricity from coal-based power Natural gas consumption for power generation is projected to grow by 4% per year in the industrialized countries, compared with 0.1% decrease for oil and 0.9% increase for coal; this would account for 56.3% of the projected increase in total energy for power generation. Natural gas is projected to capture 24% of the power generation market in the industrialized countries and 21% in the developing countries in 2020, up from 14% and 13% respectively in 1999. In absolute terms, gas demand for power generation in developing countries is projected to triple from 0.2 tcm in 1999 to 0.6 tcm in 2020, while in industrialized countries; it is projected to grow from 0.6 tcm in 1999 to 1.0 tcm.

INDIAN ENERGY SCENARIO

The energy demand as shown in Table 1.3 is projected to grow at about 6 to 7% for fuelling the projected demand growth in the country. Hydrocarbon sector will have to play a vital role not only for providing energy security but also have to look after the environmental concern due to global warming. The Hydrocarbon vision document has addressed a variety of issues including enhancing the share of natural gas in the energy basket and improving the quality of petroleum products etc. In this regard the natural gas demand is likely to further grow during the years to come. Large scale import of natural gas in the country have been envisaged both through LNG/pipeline route. The projected share of various energy supplies according to the hydrocarbon vision indicate that coal s share will remain around 53% till 2011-12 before falling to 50% in 2025.Oil's share will fall down from 32% to 25% in 2025 nuclear and hydro will continue to make meager contributions in the entire energy basket and gas's share will rise to 20% in 2025 from the current share of 9%.

Table 1.3: Primary Commercial Energy Consumption in India (mmtoe)

Source	*1999-00*	*2000-01*	*2001-02*	*2002-03*	*2003-04*	*2004-05*
Petroleum products (inc RBF)	110.84	115.53	119.84	120.72	125.29	129.75
Natural Gas	24.2	25.07	25.24	26.96	27.81	27.68
Coal	122.99	126.95	134.39	139.92	148.08	153.75
Lignite	7.3	7.57	8.19	8.59	9.23	10.06
Hydel electricity	6.93	6.41	6.32	5.49	6.35	13.14
Nuclear electricity	3.47	4.4	5.08	5	4.61	3.055
Wind energy	0.12	0.14	0.17	0.21	0.23	—
Total	275.85	286.07	299.23	306.89	321.6	337.435

Source: Ministry of Finance, Economic Survey.

As the above table suggests Commercial energy consumption has grown at a CAGR of 4% from 280 MMTOE in 1999-00 to 327 MMTOE in 2003-04 Coal and lignite form 48% whereas Oil and Gas account for 38.3% and 8.5% respectively of total commercial energy mix.Infact Coal and oil have dominated the energy supply basket during the past five decades with 85-90% of share, leaving natural gas with a small share. This is not in line with the world trend where natural gas occupies nearly 24% share in energy basket. It is only during the last two decades, when large off shore fields were developed and cross country pipelines were laid, the share of natural gas in energy basket could rise but it would still be lower than the world average share of natural gas. In the changing scenario, the focus is on developing and expanding core sectors in which oil and gas industry is at the forefront.

Energy Trading

The original form of trade was barter, the direct exchange of goods and services. Modern traders instead generally negotiate through a medium of exchange, such as money. As a result, **buying** can be separated from **selling**, or earning. The invention of money (and later credit, paper money and non-physical money) greatly simplified and promoted trade. Trade between two traders is called bilateral trade, while trade between more than two traders is called multilateral trade is the voluntary exchange of goods, services, or both. A mechanism that allows trade is called a market. Trade exists for many reasons. Due to specialization and division of labor, most people concentrate on a small aspect of production, trading for other products. Trade exists between regions because different regions have a comparative advantage in the production of some tradable commodity, or because different regions' size allows for the benefits of mass production. As such, trade at market prices between locations benefits both locations.

Trading can also refer to the action performed by traders and other market agents in the financial and commodities markets.

Three Broad Category of Trader

1. Hedger
2. Speculator
3. Arbitrager

1. **Hedger** faces risk associated with the price of an asset. They use future, forward and options to reduce or eliminate the risk.
2. **Speculator** wish to bet on future movements in the price of an asset. Future, forward and options can give them extra leverage; that is, they can increase both the potential gains and potential losses in a speculative venture.
3. **Arbitrager** is in business to take advantage of a discrepancy between prices in the two markets. If for an example, they see future price of an asset getting out of line with the cash price, they will take offsetting in the two markets to lock in a profit.

Oil, Gas and Petrochemical trading has come a long way since OPEC formation. Dramatic growth in the late 1990s was followed by an equally dramatic decline following the collapse of major energy merchants in 2001. With close regulatory oversight, deregulation, and the participation of new players like hedge funds, markets are seeing improved liquidity and better price transparency.

Over the last twenty years oil has become the MAJOR TRADING commodity in the world. During this period, oil trading has evolved from a primarily physical activity into a sophisticated financial market. Oil is fungible and traded in world commodities markets, there is much uncertainty associated with projections of future patterns of oil trade; however, anticipated changes in the world's oil trading patterns—particularly, the shifting regional dependence of importing regions on producing regions—may have important geopolitical ramifications. In the process it has attracted the interest of a wide range of participants who now include banks and fund managers as well as the traditional oil majors, independents and physical oil traders.

Gas is moving closer to being a global industry. The geographical dislocation of reserves to market is being partly mitigated by new cost-effective ways of linking stranded fields and customers. Progress on integrating supply and demand is likely to accelerate and, as economies of scale increase and new alliances are formed, regional markets will continue to develop and coalesce. At the same time, liberalization of markets is heralding new choice for customers, more dynamic, liquid gas trading conditions for gas companies, a changing balance of risk and reward for all players. Indian economy is developing at 9% per annum. In Indian market the demand of gas is increasing because the increasing demand in cement, infrastructure, power sector, Plastic industry and other industries. The depleting reserves of gas are likely to increase the price requiring the betterment of trading activities so trading of gas is becoming a major trading activity.

Forms of Market

The Markets where Trading is done basically classified into two types.

- Physical Markets—Over-the-Counter (Spot and Cash markets)
- Paper Markets—Commodity Exchange (Futures markets)

1. OTC-Over the Counter

Over The Counter means where trading is privately negotiated derivative contracts. The OTC is mostly used in the early days for the trading where two parties do the privately contract and do the trading between them. The OTC have following Characteristics:

- **Forward contract**—The forward means the contract is settled on the forward date with particular specification, on the particular date.
- **Privately negotiated**—The contract is between the two parties with the specification mentioned by them, its price and the time of delivery.
- **Custom made contract**—It means each contract is different from one other its specification changes with the contract size, each contract is different from other as they are specified by two parties who are involved in the contract.
- **No role of clearing corporation**—There is no corporation who settles there contract. It is the basically the trust between the parties

and the contract clears on the trust. There is no corporation who involves in the clearing of the contract.

- **No margin payment**—The Contract is between the two parties and contact Price is specified by the seller to the buyer the buyer pays the upfront amount and obliged to take the delivery on that date. As there is no middle man and there is trust between them so there is no margin came into exists in this payment.
- **No M-T-M settlement**—The OTC the buyer is obliged to take the delivery and what gain or loss is on the date of exercise. There is no daily gain or loss which is provide to it.
- **No Regulation**—There is no regulation and no rules for the trading it is just a contract which is done between two persons for rules and regulation made by them.
- **Settlement in delivery**—In this contract settle in the form of delivery.

Drawbacks

1. **Counter party Risk:** This arises if parties do not discharge their obligations fully when due or at any time thereafter. This has two components, namely replacement cost risk prior to settlement and principal risk during settlement.

(a) The replacement cost risk arises from the failure of one of the parties to transaction. While the non-defaulting party tries to replace the original transaction at current prices, he loses the profit that has accrued on the transaction between the date of original transaction and date of replacement transaction. The seller/buyer of the security loses this unrealized profit if the current price is below/above the transaction price. Both parties encounter this risk as prices are uncertain. It has been reduced by reducing time gap between transaction and settlement and by legally binding netting systems.

(b) The *principal risk* arises if a party discharges his obligations but the counter party defaults. The seller/buyer of the security suffers this risk when he delivers/makes payment, but does not receive payment/delivery. This risk can be eliminated by delivery vs. payment mechanism which ensures delivery only against payment. This has been reduced by having a central counter party which becomes the buyer to every seller and the seller to every buyer.

2. **Liquidity risk** which arises if one of the parties to transaction does not settle on the settlement date, but later. The seller/buyer who does not receive payment/delivery when due, may have to borrow funds/securities to complete his payment/delivery obligations.

3. **Third party risk** which arises if the parties to trade are permitted or required to use the services of a third party which fails to perform. For example, the failure of a clearing bank which helps in payment can disrupt settlement. This risk is reduced by allowing parties to have accounts with multiple banks. Similarly, the users of custodial services face risk if the concerned custodian becomes insolvent, acts negligently, etc.

2. Commodity Exchange

Exchange Trading is trading which done on the exchange. A commodities exchange is an exchange where various commodities and derivatives products are traded. There are many commodity markets across the world that trade energy products and contracts based on them. These contracts can include spot prices, forwards, futures and options on futures. Commodities exchanges, usually trade futures contracts on commodities. Such as trading contracts to receive something, say gasoline, in a certain month. A refiner can sell a future contract on his gasoline, which will not be produced for several months, and guarantee the price he will be paid when he delivers; a large gasoline consuming company buys the contract now and guarantees the price will not go up when it is delivered. This protects the refiner (seller) from price drops and the consuming company (buyer) from price rises.

What are Trading Derivatives?

Trading Derivatives are financial instruments (contracts) that do not represent ownership rights in any physical asset but, rather, derive their value from the value of some other underlying commodity or other asset. When used prudently, derivatives are efficient and effective tools for isolating financial risk and "hedging" to reduce exposure to risk. Derivative is a product whose value is derived from the value of one or more basic variables, called bases or underlying asset in a contractual manner. The underlying asset can be equity, forex, or commodity (crude oil, bullion, agri-products). Derivative contracts transfer risk, especially price risk, to those who are able and willing to bear it. Derivatives allow investors to transfer risk to others who could profit from taking the risk.

E.g. An oil producer may wish to sell his output (yet to be produced) at a future date to eliminate the risk of change in price by that date. The price of this derivative is driven by the spot price of oil which is the "underlying asset". person transferring risk achieves price certainty but loses the opportunity for making additional profits when prices move opposite his fears. Likewise, the person taking on the risk will lose if the counterparty's fears are realized. Except for transactions costs, the winner's gains are equal to the loser's losses. Like insurance, derivatives protect against some adverse events. Because of their flexibility in dealing with price risk, derivatives have become an increasingly popular way to isolate cash earnings from price fluctuations.

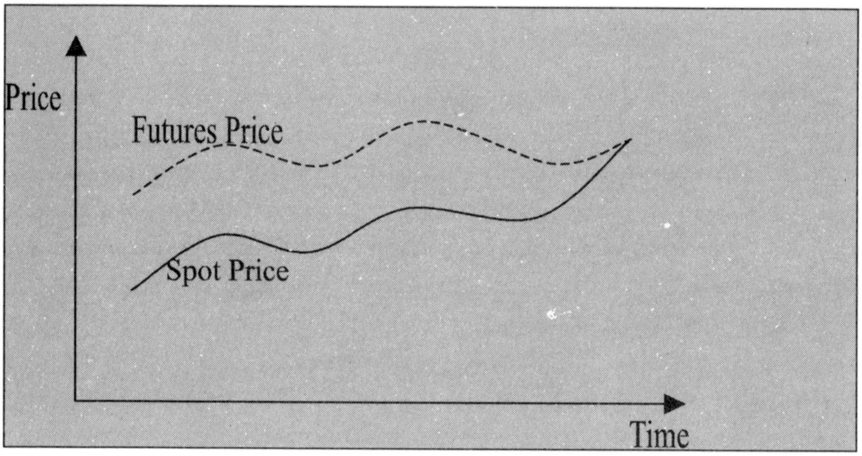

Figure 1.2: Variation of Basis Over Time

The most commonly used derivative contracts are forward contracts, futures contracts, options, and swaps.

Evolution of Derivatives Markets

In 1974, Congress observed that derivatives trading was about to expand from its traditional base in farm commodities into financial futures—contracts based on bonds, interest rates, currencies, and so on. To ensure that derivatives traders received the same protections whether they were trading pork bellies or T-bonds, (P.L. 93-463) created the CFTC to oversee all derivatives trading, regardless of the nature of the underlying commodity. The CFTC was given exclusive jurisdiction: all contracts that were "in the character of" futures contracts had to be traded on a CFTC-regulated futures exchange. There were two major exceptions to this exchange-trading requirement. Forward contracts, where actual delivery of the commodity would take place at the expiration of the contract, were considered cash sales and not subject to the CEA. Second, the so-called Treasury Amendment (part of the same law that created the CFTC) specified that contracts based on foreign currencies or U.S. Treasury securities could be traded off-exchange. Existing markets in these instruments had long used futures-like contracts and appeared to function well without direct government regulation; Treasury saw no public interest in bringing them under the new CFTC.

During the 1980s, a large and active market in OTC derivatives evolved, utilizing swap contracts that served exactly the same economic functions as futures. The first swaps were based on currencies and interest rates; later, OTC contracts based on commodity (including energy) prices were introduced. These OTC markets were well established before the CFTC made any move to assert its jurisdiction, despite the fact that swaps were clearly "in the character of" futures contracts. The potential CFTC jurisdiction, however, created legal uncertainty for the swaps industry: if a court had ruled that a swap was in fact an illegal, off-exchange futures contract, trillions of dollars in outstanding swaps could have been invalidated. This might have caused chaos in financial markets, as swaps users would suddenly be exposed to the risks they had used derivatives to avoid.

The CFTC issued a swaps exemption in 1989, stating that although it believed the CEA gave it authority to regulate swaps, it would not do so as long as they differed from futures contracts in certain enumerated respects. In 1992, Congress gave the CFTC additional authority to exempt OTC contracts (P.L. 102-546). In response, the CFTC modified the 1989 swaps exemption in 1993, and also issued a specific exemption for OTC derivatives based on energy products.

Under the 1993 exemption, OTC energy derivatives would not be regulated if all Trading was between principals whose business involved the physical energy commodities underlying the derivatives, if all contracts were negotiated as to their material terms (unlike futures contracts, where terms are standardized), and if all contracts were held to maturity (rather than traded rapidly, as futures are). This exemption was a matter of regulation, not statute. In May 1998, the CFTC issued a "concept release" that indicated that it was considering the possibility of extending features of exchange regulation to the OTC market. The release solicited comments on whether regulation of

OTC derivatives should be modified in light of developments in the marketplace. Among the questions were whether the existing prohibitions on fraud and manipulation were sufficient to protect the public, and whether the CFTC should consider additional terms and conditions relating to registration, capital, internal controls, sales practices, record keeping, or reporting. The concept release drew strong opposition from the swaps industry and from other regulators, especially the Federal Reserve. In December 1998, Congress included in the Omnibus Appropriations Act (P.L. 105-277) a provision directing the CFTC not to propose or issue any new regulations affecting swap contracts before March 31, 1999. In November 1999, the President's Working Group on Financial Markets issued a report entitled "Over-the-Counter Derivatives Markets and the Commodity Exchange Act." The report recommended that, to remove uncertainty about the legal and regulatory status of the OTC market, bilateral transactions between sophisticated parties that do not involve physical commodities with finite supplies should be excluded from the Commodity Exchange Act; that is, the CFTC should have no jurisdiction. While the Working Group's report made a distinction between financial commodities and those with finite supplies, and suggested that continuing CEA jurisdiction was appropriate for the latter, the report did *not* recommend that the CFTC should rescind its exemption of OTC energy derivatives. In other words, the Working Group saw no immediate problem with the unregulated status of OTC markets in energy derivatives. In 2000, the 106thCongress considered two bills (H.R. 4541 and S. 2697) that generally followed the Working Group's recommendations. Energy derivatives were exempted—as a matter of statute—from many of the provisions of the CEA, but were not given a blanket exclusion. The treatment of energy derivatives changed in its wording through the various iterations of the legislation, but the substance remained basically the same, from the bills as introduced to the final passage of the Commodity Futures Modernization Act of 2000 (P.L. 106-554, H.R. 5660). That legislation established three classes of commodities. First, financial variables (interest rates, stock indexes, currencies, etc.) are defined as "excluded commodities," and OTC contracts based on these are not subject to the CEA (provided that trading is restricted to "eligible contract participants," that is, not marketed to small investors). Second, derivative contracts based on agricultural commodities cannot be traded except on the futures exchanges; these remain under CFTC jurisdiction. Finally, there is an "all other" category—"exempt commodities"—which includes energy products. Contracts in exempt commodities can be traded in the OTC market without CFTC regulation provided that no small investors participate. However, certain antifraud and anti manipulation provisions of the CEA continue to apply. If an OTC exchange is created—defined in the legislation as one where multiple buyers and sellers may post bids and trade with each other—the CFTC has some over sight jurisdiction and may require disclosure of certain market information.

In summary, the OTC energy derivatives market developed outside CFTC jurisdiction in the late 1980s and early 1990s, despite the CEA's apparent prohibition of such a market. As with financial OTC derivatives, however, the CFTC never challenged the legality of this off-exchange market. As concerns about legal uncertainty mounted, the CFTC in 1993 issued an exemption stating that certain OTC energy transactions did not fall under the CEA. In 2000, Congress essentially codified this exemption, by including energy in the category of "exempt commodities." This removed them from even the possibility of CFTC regulation, except for a limited antifraud and manipulation jurisdiction and some oversight if the present dealer market for OTC contracts should evolve into an exchange-like market. Thus, the 2000 legislation did not deregulate the OTC energy derivatives market; that market had been unregulated since its beginnings Energy derivatives—financial contracts whose value is linked to changes in the price of some energy product—are traded in two kinds of markets in the United States today: the futures exchanges and the off-exchange, or over-the-counter market. The New York Mercantile Exchange (Nymex) offers futures contracts based on prices of crude oil, natural gas, heating oil, and gasoline. (Other futures exchanges offer energy-related contracts, but Nymex is by far the busiest.) Futures exchanges are regulated by the An electronic trading system like Enron Online did not meet this definition, because a single dealer—Enron—was involved in all transactions. Enron Online essentially displayed the prices at which Enron was willing to trade.

Commodity Futures Trading Commission (CFTC) under the Commodity Exchange Act (CEA). The CEA imposes a range of mandates on the exchanges (and on futures industry personnel) regarding record keeping (including an audit trail for all trades), registration requirements, market surveillance, financial standards, sales practices, handling of customer funds, and so on.

The second trading venue for energy derivatives is the off-exchange, or over-the- counter (OTC) market. Unlike the futures market, there is no centralized marketplace for OTC derivatives. Instead, a number of firms act as dealers, offering to enter into contracts with others who wish to manage their risk exposure to energy prices. Derivatives contracts based on energy products are generally exempt from regulation under the CEA, so long as the contracts are offered only to "eligible contract participants," defined as financial institutions, professional traders, institutional investors, governmental units, and businesses or individuals with more than $10 million in assets. The law assumes that sophisticated parties such as these do not need the kind of investor protection that government regulation provides for public customers of the futures exchanges. The CFTC has limited jurisdiction over the OTC market if certain CEA provisions against fraud and price manipulation are violated. In addition, if OTC contracts are traded on an electronic exchange-like facility, where multiple buyers and sellers can post bids and offers and trade with each other, the CFTC can require disclosure of certain transaction price and volume data.

At present, however, the OTC market remains primarily a dealer market, and the dealers do not report to the CFTC. The evolution of the two energy derivatives markets—one regulated, the other largely unregulated.

Derivatives and Hedging Instruments (Risk Management Tools)

- ❑ Forwards
- ❑ Futures
- ❑ Swaps
- ❑ Options
- ❑ Caps and Floors
- ❑ Collars
- ❑ Spread Trades
- ❑ Crack Spreads contract
- ❑ Crack Spread Options
- ❑ Calendar Spreads options
- ❑ Volumetric production payment contract.

Major Derivative Markets

In the energy industry, derivatives can be bought and sold in two main ways: on-exchange and over-the-counter (OTC). On-exchange refers to the futures markets which are found on regulated financial exchanges such the

New York Mercantile Exchange (NYMEX) and\London's International Petroleum Exchange (IPE). The OTC market is specific to the non-standard swaps and OTC options. These are usually traded directly between two companies (principals, players) in the energy markets.

Although the futures markets are important to the energy industry, it relies much more heavily on OTC derivatives. This is because OTC derivatives are customized transactions, whereas their on-exchange counterpart, the 'futures' contract, is a standard contract. In theory, each deal on the OTC market is unique, so it is important to be alert to contract terms, pricing mechanisms and price reference when using OTC derivatives.

Some companies find that the measurement and control of risks can be more difficult with an OTC contract because of the lack of price and liquidity transparency in the OTC market (unlike regulated futures exchanges, which publish public real-time price data) and this can create the possibility of an unexpected loss. There are also sometimes additional legal, credit and operational risks with OTC derivatives compared to on exchange futures contracts. However, the OTC market remains a popular option for price risk management purposes. Many companies find that there are benefits in the flexibility of an OTC derivative because it can be valued against the same price reference as the energy which is being produced or consumed.

As the pie chart in Figure 1.3 shows, energy OTC derivatives markets are far less liquid than most other financial derivatives markets accounting for less than one per cent of the value outstanding on derivatives markets worldwide. This means that those who take part in energy markets whether as market

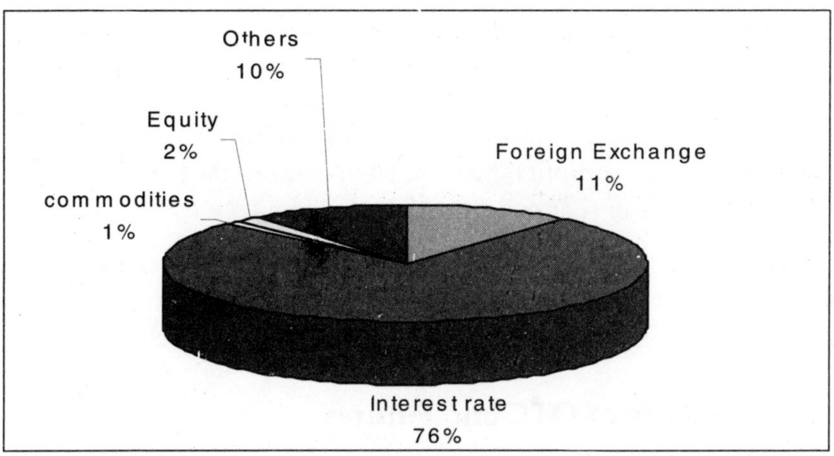

Figure 1.3: OTC Derivative Contracts (Total Amount Outstanding), Dec. 2005

makers, traders or end-users (usually companies with underlying price risk in the energy being hedged either as a producer or consumer), need to have clear policies for derivatives usage, including strong management controls and organizational reporting structures effective before derivatives are employed. They should also provide shareholders with information that will put to rest any unjustified fears associated with their company's use of derivatives. Indeed, as a result of the concerns of regulators and public shareholders around the world, more and more information is now required by international accounting standards.

Futures versus OTC

At one time it was easy to distinguish the futures market from the OTC market and also to establish the pros and cons of using one or the other. As Figure shows, when risk managers or traders used futures contracts they knew that the contract would be traded on an exchange, that they would have an account with their futures broker and that they were operating in a highly regulated market. They could also see the price of the contract on a screen and they could be sure that the security of the contract and its performance would be guaranteed by the clearing house of the exchange. This in turn was guaranteed by 'margins' (good faith payments by everyone with a futures position on that particular exchange), plus, the funding the exchange raised itself and the funds contributed by its clearing broker members.

Margins on a futures exchange can be split into two types: 'initial margins' and 'variation margins'. Initial margins are the good faith deposit that is placed with the clearing house or that a broker finances (at a cost) when a trade is opened, A variation margin is the daily revaluation of a portfolio with the clearing house. If the valuation is negative, you or your broker (if you have a credit line) will have to place a margin to cover that negative variation margin, if the next day the portfolio has a positive variation margin (i.e. it is showing an unrealized profit), because the position has not been traded or closed out yet, some of that margin will be returned.

However when OTC contracts are used there is always the credit risk of the other company in the transaction, as well as a liquidity risk and a lack of price transparency because there is no screen to display a real-time price.

The Convergence of OTC and Futures

The clear distinction between the OTC energy market and the futures

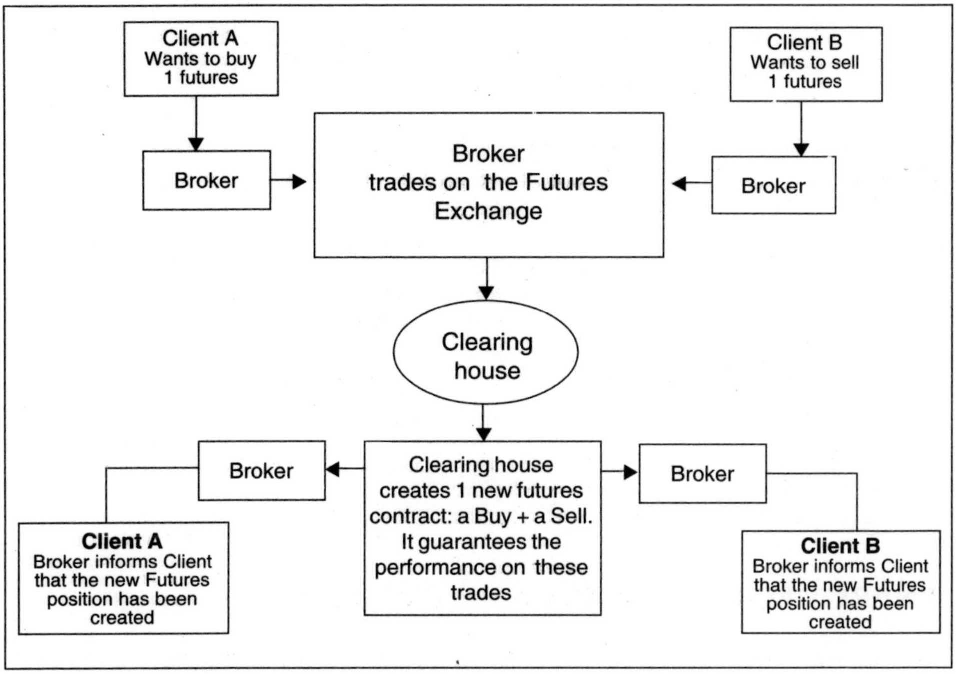

Figure 1.4: Basic Future Trade Transaction Flow

markets is now disappearing as the two markets converge. Basic Future Trade Transaction Flow as shown in Fig. 1.4 explain about Clearing houses around the world have started to accept OTC trades into their guarantee umbrella. This means that after executing bilateral OTC trades with one another, both counterparts can agree to 'give-in' their OTC deal to a clearing house. This process basically makes the clearing house the counterpart to the OTC deal, so that the two OTC counterparts can benefit from the higher credit quality of the clearing house as well as getting other benefits such as more netting opportunities on settlement and offsetting of positions.

The usual market approach for two OTC counterparts to trade an OTC derivative contract with one another directly and to take on one another's credit risk.

Although market share penetration has been slow in the oil sector, we have seen the newer power and gas markets embracing electronic trading platforms in a big way. This has brought about greater price transparency as users can view and trade prices onscreen like futures markets. As a result, power and gas markets have been the quickest to embrace OTC clearing.

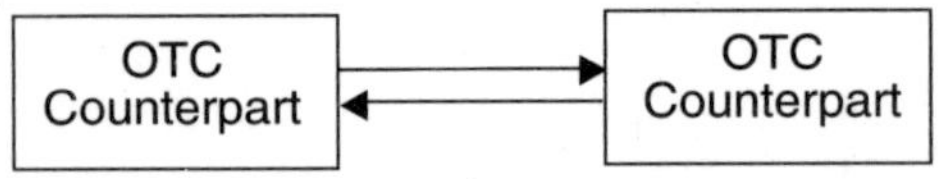

In the new convergence environment we now sometimes have a situation like this:

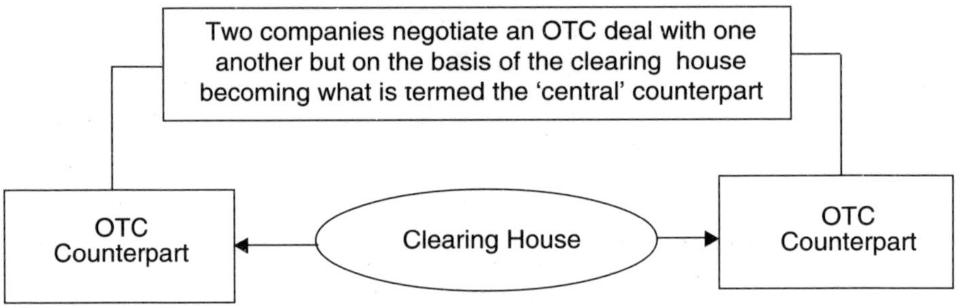

ENERGY FUTURES, PAST AND PRESENT

Energy futures are not nearly as young as you think. In the second half of the 19th century, a Petroleum Exchange flourished in New York. Again in the early 1930s—when market discipline was briefly disrupted by the explosive growth of oil production in Oklahoma and Texas, causing oil prices to fall dramatically—an oil futures market (in West Texas Intermediate) was established in California. It soon collapsed as a formidable alliance of big oil and big government restored discipline to the marketplace. Nearly 40 years of relative price stability ensured, leaving little incentive for the emergence of an oil futures market.

Only with the traumatic price increases accompanying the Arab oil embargo of late 1973 was another attempt made, this time in New York at the cotton Exchange. The contract called for Rotterdam delivery (to avoid the constraints of US price regulations). That attempt was stillborn, however, doomed by continuing US government price controls and a skeptical oil industry.

In the decade that followed, the commercial realities and- equally important – the perceptions of those realities by the international oil industry had gradually changed to the point where oil features could fulfill the industry's need for risk management and provide an outlet for the speculative impulses of investors whose interest in oil had been captured by the commodity's new prominence in daily head-lines and nightly newscasts.

The emergence of oil features markets and their remarkable growth were a natural, indeed inevitable, consequences of three concurrent but only partly interrelated trends in Petroleum, financial and commodity markets. By far the most important determinant was the structural change in oil markets themselves. The nationalization of production by the organization of Petroleum Exporting Countries (OPEC) and non OPEC governments alike, and he subsequent pressure to eliminate large third party crude re-sales, resulted in a disintegration of the oil market that had been highly integrated since the days of J.D. Rockefellet. In the ten years following the 1973 Arab oil embargo, the crude oil available to the major companies fell by nearly 50%, from about 30 million barrels per day (bbl/day) to just more than 15 million bbl/day. Equity oil available to the majors fell even more sharply by some 75%. The net result was a drop in the major's share of internationally traded oil from 62% to 37%.

In addition to the newly created national oil companies a host of oil trading firms and independent refineries entered the picture. The links that had traditionally tied upstream and downstream (vertical integration) were weakened to the breaking point. The reduction of horizontal integration (as large third-party crude sales were curtailed, and joint venture production was nationalized) further eroded the ability of the larger oil companies to exercise control over markets. Simply there were too many actors with divergent commercial and political interests to guarantee market stability. The consequences were not long in coming. After a decade of virtually universal confidence that oil prices would rise, prices began to weaken and fluctuate over an ever-wider range, climaxing in the dramatic events of 1986, when prices fell from nearly $30/bblto less than $10/bbl in a period of only nine months. Although many feel stability returned in 1987, it is interesting to note that prices oscillated between $15 and $22/bbl between September and December of that year alone. The fact is that stability has yet to rear its hoary head in current-day oil markets.

Along with the structural change that was reshaping oil markets during the decade, a second important trend was emerging from the financial; markets. High interest rates (along with high oil prices) at the beginning of the 1980s were making inventory maintenance very expensive. This caused oil company managements to rethink traditional approaches to inventory and risk management. Also hedging of financial risk was increasingly becoming a fact of life in foreign currency and interest rate markets. These trends ensured that oil companies were increasingly respective to the hedging potential of the fledging oil future markets.

Finally the third important factor that set the stage for energy futures' ultimate success was the general growth and diversification of futures contracts in a wide variety of new markets, the growing sophistication with which they were being used and modification offering an ever-wider range of hedging tools. For almost 100 years futures markets (then commonly called commodity markets) were largely confined to the traditional agricultural products (especially grains).

In the past two decades, however there has been a explosion in the variety of products served by these markets. The first waves of expansion brought in new agricultural contracts (especially meats) and precious metals. The second phase starting in the 1970s saw the introduction of financial instruments including currency interest rate and stock index contracts. A third phase brought in oil and a number of other industrial products. The fourth stage saw the introduction and rapid acceptance of options on futures contracts. The fifth stage saw an explosion of trading in over-the-counter (OTC) derivatives often in direct competition with exchange traded instruments.

The introduction and success of oil futures was a product of first three trends. The growing volatility and loss of confidence in the future stability of oil prices demanded the emergence of new market structures and institutions. One obvious sign of the change was the rapid growth of spot markets and the trading companies that thrived on price volatility.

Prior to 1979 less than 5% of internationally traded crude moved at spot prices outside of official term supply contracts arrangement. By the end of 1985, virtually all crude moved at some sort of market-related pricing and experts estimated that oil companies were acquiring anywhere from 30 to 50% of their supplies on a spot, non contract basis. Although the proportion of oil sold on a purely spot basis has subsequently shrunk the price risks remain because term contracts today almost universally call for market related prices.

The trading companies' independents refineries and increasingly the companies developed trading techniques to cope with the growing price volatility of these markets. Their first response was to create informal. "Forward markets". At first they were only 30 days, then 60 days, and more recently 90days out. A second response was an explosive growth in the demand for rapid (often real time) pricing and other market information. Against this backdrop futures became inevitable: a time proven and efficient technique for coping with broad market instability.

Energy futures trading in the 1980s focused on growth of the liquid petroleum markets for crude oil, Natural Gas Liquids (NGL), and the major refined products (gasoline, heating oil, and fuel oil). In the 1990s the boundaries of the energy complex have expanded to include natural gas (in 1990) and electricity (in 1996).

While the breadth of energy markets has expanded, their fundamental purposes remain the same. Futures markets basically spot markets for standardized forward contracts, serve three functions:

Price Discovery—Giving an instantaneous reading of marginal price movements.

Risk management—Allowing companies to hedge their price risks for limited periods of time. However the hedging opportunity rarely extends more than six months forward as a result of a lack of market liquidity in the more distant months.

Speculative opportunity—Attracting additional risk capital to the market from outside the industry. Low margin requirements – lower than in equity markets enhance the attraction of futures as a vehicle for speculation.

These are the necessary conditions for a successful contract – but they are often not sufficient. In reality new futures contracts often fail. The reason is that the criteria for a successful futures contracts are simply too stringent, with too few physical markets that actually meet those criteria.

CRITERIA FOR SUCCESSFUL FUTURES MARKETS

In assessing the suitability of any commodity/market for futures trading the following conditions need to be analyzed:

1. **Price Volatility**: This is perhaps the single most important criterion. It provides the basic economic justification for futures trading which is to provide protection to the hedger against adverse price fluctuation. If a commodity is characterized by a relatively stable—or at least predictable—price there would be little associated risk and there would be no need for a futures market. Price volatility is also necessary to attract risk capital from speculators and essential to ensure sufficient liquidity to maintain the market.

Quantitative Indicators: Variations of plus or minus 20% per annum are assumed to be the minimum necessary to sustain futures trading. In general, the greater the degree of volatility the more likely a futures market will survive.

Uncertain supply and demand are generally the cause of price volatility and therefore are generally present when price volatility is found.

Quantitative indicators: In energy markets which markets, which typically display a rather high inelasticity of price demand variations of plus or minus 10% during a two year period should be sufficient to sustain futures trading.

Sufficient deliverable supplies are the Catch-22 of futures trading. If there are not sufficient deliverable supplies of the commodity meeting the quality specifications of the contract, futures trading will fail. However, there must be some uncertainty about the sufficiently of supplies if the previous conditions are to be met. In the U.S., this dilemma is heightened by the regulatory requirements of the Commodity Futures Trading Commission (CFTC), whose fear of market squeezes at times forces exchanges to overstate deliverable supplies in order to gain government approval.

Quantitative indicators: Storage capacity equal to at least 30 days average demand is highly desirable.

Product homogeneity is another prerequisite. Futures contracts are traded on the premise that product taken on a delivery will meet certain quality specifications. The commodity must therefore have certain key characteristics that are quantifiable, allowing the clear differentiation of the product from other grades. Standardized tests and generally accepted procedures are essential. In oil, for example, the various American Petroleum Institute (API), Deutsche Institut fur Normung (DIM), and ASTM standards generally provide the necessary references. In addition, the existence of generally trusted independent inspection agencies or inspectors to administer these tests is an important aspect. A range of different products (*e.g.*, several types of crude oil) may be suitable for delivery, if the price differences between the various grades are relatively stable, and if the technical characteristics of the various deliverable grades are sufficiently close to one another.

This is often a difficult aspect of contract design, since the price variation between various grades of products fluctuates from time to time. For example, it may be desirable to allow several grades to be deliverable, perhaps with price adjustments for quality, in order to ensure sufficient deliverable supplies. However, if buyers are uncertain of what grades they will receive, and if they place different values on the quality differences among the grades, they may be deterred from trading.

Quantitative indicators: The quality of the product must be capable of being described by objective, quantifiable standards.

2. **Product perishability** can be a deterrent to trading. In general a product should have a shelf life sufficiently long enough to permit storage and delivery as called for under the contract. ill addition, the maintenance of inventories of the commodity will both facilitate deliveries and provide a ready pool of potential hedgers. While perishability is not usually a major concern in oil and natural gas markets, the stability of some oil product blends is an issue. Long storage of gasoline, for example, can result in separation of blended product.

Quantitative indicators: Products should have a minimum shelf or stock life of 6-12 months.

3. **Market Concentration** is a difficult factor to quantify. A successful futures market is a highly competitive market, marked by a large number of buyers and sellers. No one market participant, or plausible combination of market participants, should possess sufficient market power to exert unilateral control either on the supply or the demand for the commodity, either in the short or medium term. ill oil, however, the existence of OPEC has not prevented the emergence of highly successful futures markets. The answer lies in the inability of OPEC to act decisively, and in the availability of alternative sources of supply and stocks that seriously limit OPEC's ability to achieve its stated objectives. However, the concentration of producers and/or consumers can be a serious obstacle in specific regional oil markets. Thus, a U.S. west coast gasoline market would be risky, given the relative concentration of production in the hands of a small number of refiners. Similarly, an east coast residual fuel market might be too much dominated by the demand from a small number of very large utilities to sustain liquid futures trading.

Quantitative indicators: ill general, the market share of the top five firms should be less than 50%, and the top 10 firms should have less than 80%.

4. **Readily available price information** is critical to market success. It should be noted that the opening of a futures market might stimulate a rapid growth of price information services.

However, at the outset, market participants must have a sufficiently broad base of price information to permit evaluation of spot prices and their relationship to futures prices. Convergence between these two prices as the delivery period approaches is essential. A market in which all products are traded on the basis of long- term contracts where prices remain undisclosed would be a very difficult market in which to establish futures trading.

Quantitative indicators: Daily cash market prices should be available from at least two independent sources.

5. **Unique trading opportunity** is another key factor. If an existing market for a commodity has reasonable liquidity and is serving its customers well, it is extremely difficult to launch a copycat contract. Inertia, habit, and personal relationships will tend to keep the traders loyal to the preexisting market. In addition, even if there is no active market at present, recent failures of similar contracts can be a substantial (but not fatal) deterrent.

Quantitative indicators: The ideal candidate would be a commodity that is not currently traded on any futures exchange in the world and has not been the subject of a failed attempt in the previous five years. However, special circumstances may override these concerns.

6. **Market timing** (and blind luck) are often critical to the success or failure of a contract. However, they are often impossible to forecast. Ideally, contracts should be introduced to coincide with periods of high volatility and high levels of cash market activity. For example, a heating oil or natural gas contract would be best introduced in the fall months when physical trading is at its yearly high. Conversely, a gasoline contract would be best introduced in the spring, prior to an anticipated surge of summer driving.

Quantitative indicators: Contracts should be introduced to coincide with high levels of cash market activity to the extent these are predictable. Alternatively, one might just as well consult an astrologer.

FUTURES PRESENT

Since 1974, there have been some 50 attempts to launch energy futures markets. The success rate has averaged about 20% typical of the experience in other commodity markets. In spite of thorough research by the exchanges, often excruciating governmental reviews (particularly in the U.S.), and extensive marketing campaigns, roughly 80% of all future markets opened fail to reach the critical mass needed for takeoff (commonly defined as reaching an average open interest of 5,000 contracts).

Today-after the smoke has settled from various attempts by exchanges in New York, Chicago, London and Singapore there are seven well-established futures contracts (crude, heating oil, unleaded gasoline, natural gas, and electricity in New York; plus crude and gasoil in London). In addition, options contracts have been successful as extensions of those future markets.

When first introduced in late 1978, heating oil futures attracted smaller, independent marketers and refiners who turned to the Merc as an alternative source of supply. Physical deliveries were initially quite high, as these smaller firms sought alternatives in a marketplace dominated by the larger companies. These initial participants were quickly joined by the spot oil traders and by a growing number of pure speculators on and off the trading floor, drawn from other financial and commodity markets. This phase lasted until well into 1983. Then, with the introduction of crude oil futures and the increasing instability of prices, the larger refiners and integrated companies reluctantly entered the market.

By 1984, more than 80% of the 50 largest companies were using futures. Larger end-users, such as airlines and other major energy consumers, also appeared. ill addition, a far wider range of speculators entered the scene, as trading volume and open interest rose high enough to meet the minimum liquidity requirement of the commodity funds.

Finally, another phase, dating from 1986, brought in almost all the remaining holdouts among the larger U.S. companies, more foreign participation, and a new group of traders-the Wall Street Refiners. These were companies such as Morgan Stanley and Bear Steams, which were attracted by the rising volatility of oil prices and the speculative opportunities presented by that price instability, particularly relative to other markets.

As one Bear Steams trader put it, "Plywood was dead, so we looked around for some better action and found it in oil." The low internal cost of capital for margin maintenance and a built-in trading infrastructure made these new entrants formidable competitors for the older oil trading and supply companies.

However, even today, participation by independent producers and smaller end-users remains limited. The former's participation is limited by the lack of liquidity in the more distant months; the latter by ignorance of how the markets operate, the high management cost of setting up a futures trading department, and for a number of domestic as well as international companies, a very real basis-risk problem.

Futures trading has thus survived adolescence and entered a period of youthful maturity. Growth in the coming years will have to come from an expansion of futures trading opportunities in the form of new contracts rather than from bringing in new participants. In other words, to continue to grow, the exchanges will have to offer a bigger and more diverse menu, not just put more seats around the table. The recent success of options would seem to confirm this point of view.

TRADING FUTURES: A PRIMER

Many readers of this book will be thoroughly familiar with the basic mechanisms and concepts of futures trading. This section is not for them. However, for those who are new to any type of futures trading, it is important to understand a few fundamentals about futures markets. Futures markets offer both *hedgers* or *commercials* (*i.e.*, those who use a particular commodity in their business) and speculators the opportunity to buy or sell standardized contracts for a given commodity. In many cases, the same exchanges also offer options contracts on those same commodities. Options contracts as presently traded are options on the futures contract for the same commodity, which is often called the *underlying* futures.

Contract Identification

Both futures and options contracts are identified not only by the particular type of commodity being traded (*e.g.*, heating oil, unleaded gasoline, Brent crude oil), but also by the delivery month called for in the contract. In practice, traders often abbreviate the names of months, so that one should not be surprised to hear references to "Feb Brent" or "Jan gas."

Options contracts are further identified by their strike prices and whether they are options to buy (call) or sell (put). Thus an options trader will talk about "Jan gas 55 puts," meaning options to sell January unleaded gasoline futures contracts at 55¢ *gal.* A buyer of a commodity contract is said to be *long* while he holds that contract. A seller is said to be *short.* The Contracts traded are highly standardized with respect to volume, quality, and delivery terms. The terms of selected contracts are printed for reference in the appendices to this book. Exchanges do, however, change the terms of these contracts from time to time, to keep pace with changes in the physical market. The samples included should therefore not be assumed to be up-to-date. Please check with the appropriate exchange to obtain a copy of the latest contract terms.

Placing Orders

Except in the case of exchange members operating on their own account, all transactions must be conducted through a member of the exchange, who must also be registered to accept customer orders by the Commodity Futures Trading Commission (CFTC) in the U.S. or its counterparts in other countries. Orders can be placed any time a broker is willing to answer the telephone, but exchange trading hours tend to fall between 9:00 A.M. and 5:00 P.M., with the New York exchanges closing earlier and the London exchanges closing later. A buyer normally places an order by telephone to the broker, who may be located anywhere in the world. The broker in turn executes this order by telephone through exchange members on the floor of the appropriate exchange. Buyers can place various conditions on their orders, including price limits or time limits, and they may also simultaneously request a broker to close out the position if losses exceed a certain amount. While brokers will generally accept such conditions on orders, they usually offer no guarantees they can execute the order as given. Only a *market order*, in which the buyer (or seller) agrees to accept the prevailing market price, is virtually guaranteed for execution. Brokers will most often execute orders through the employees of their own firm on the floor. Ill order to camouflage larger orders, execution will sometimes be shared with independent floor brokers, who execute orders on behalf of others. On the exchange floor, all trading must be by *open outcry*, giving all present-at least in theory-an equal opportunity to take the other side of the trade. Assuming a willing seller is found to meet the buyer's order, the trade is posted with the exchange. In practice, exchanges publish price quotations over the various electronic information services to provide an up-to-date record of pricing trends even before the official record of the transaction is entered. The actual trade is usually entered into the exchange's computer within a few minutes of the transaction. The buyer and seller, however, are not matched permanently. At the end of the day, each broker is assigned an appropriate long or short position with the exchange's clearinghouse. Thus, while there must be an equal number of buyers and sellers each day, their respective positions are maintained totally independently. Thus each buyer and seller is free to close his or her position at any time. To do so, the buyer will simply sell his or her contract back into the market, effectively clearing the position from the exchange's books.

Spreads

In addition to straightforward orders to buy or sell a single commodity for a single month, many traders take *spread* positions, which are positions in several different contracts to profit from the relative price movements between those contracts. For example, spreads can be placed between contracts for different delivery months for a single commodity—they can cover different commodities for delivery in the same month-they can cover different commodities and different months. One popular type of spread position in the energy contracts is the *crack spread*, in which a position in crude oil is balanced against positions in both gasoline and heating oil, to approximate the refining process (in which crude oil is transformed by catalytic cracking into refined products). NYMEX has offered option contracts of such spreads since 1994. A newer type of spread trading is the "spark spread" that pairs positions in natural gas with those in electricity to approximate the gross margin of power generation using natural gas.

Margins and Clearinghouses

Exchanges collect margins (or deposits, as they are called in England) from each broker on behalf of his or her customer (and in most cases, the broker in turn collects similar. funds from his or her customer). These margins, which are usually in the range of 5 to 10% of the contract's total face value, are normally designed to be equal to the average daily fluctuation in value of the contract being traded. Exchanges will therefore tend to lower margins in times of low price volatility and raise them in times of high price volatility. Every night, based on the final closing or settlement price, the exchange calculates the effect of that price on each position, and either requests additional margin or pays excess margin to each broker.

The prices go up from one day to the next, a buyer's margin is credited with a gain and a seller's margin is debited. The rules of "margin maintenance" between customers and brokers vary considerably from country to country.

The exchange and its clearinghouse are therefore always in a very strong position to guarantee all outstanding positions. Moreover, the clearinghouse holds its member-brokers-not the ultimate customer-responsible for performing under the contracts. In the unlikely event that a broker is unable to perform as called for under the contract, all the members of the clearinghouse are called upon to guarantee performance. Futures markets therefore offer several levels of financial performance guarantees.

Prices on an exchange are freely determined by the interplay of buyers and sellers. However, exchanges do place certain limits on both the minimum and maximum amounts of fluctuation that can occur in a given time period. The minimum price is referred to as a *tick*, and in the oil contracts is typically equal to 1.00(Z/bbl, 25.00(Z/metric ton (MT), or 0.01(Z/gal in New York. In all cases, there are no limits on the *spot contract*, which is the contract that is next scheduled to go to delivery. All other contracts face limits. In New York, these are typically $1/bbl, $15/MT, or 2.00(Z/gal. In a given day, no trades may take place outside these ranges. However, if a limit is reached on one day, the limits are expanded by 50% for the next day's trading, and so on, up to a maximum of $2/bbl or 4.00!l/gal. In London, the limits don't apply for a full day, but rather trigger cooling off periods before trading is resumed.

Delivery

These markets should always be thought of primarily as financial markets, being used in parallel to physical movement of oil and natural gas. Nevertheless, delivery does take place and serves to ensure that the prices on futures markets remain closely linked to the real world.

The standardization of contracts and their delivery terms are often unnecessarily rigid for the commercial participants, who prefer greater flexibility in their day-to-day operations. As a consequence, delivery typically occurs in only about 2% or less of all futures contracts. In simplest form, all those holding positions in a given contract at the closing bell on the last day of trading for a given contract are automatically required to take or make delivery of the specified commodity. The timing and methods of delivery are clearly spelled out in each contract and in the exchange's rules. The exchanges' staffs match buyers and sellers, and the matched companies are then obligated to meet their respective obligations.

Exchanges have found it useful, however, to permit several variations of this simple process. Prior to the exchange matching process (typically the day after the end of trading), any two market participants may agree to an exchange for physicals (EFP) and transfer title to oil (or natural gas) by mutual agreement in lieu of closing out their position on the exchange. EFPs can also be used to establish future positions by mutual agreement. In fact, in the U.S. crude markets, this mechanism is widely used as a routine means of buying and selling crude, since it has the attraction of the exchange's financial performance guarantees.

Once trading in a given contract has ended and participants are matched, the two matched companies may elect to use an Alternative Delivery Procedure (ADP), which also allows the two to make alternative arrangements. In the case of both EFPs and ADPs, the exchanges are relieved of *any* responsibility for guaranteeing performance. See chapter 7 for a more complete discussion of delivery choices and issues.

Regulation

Exchanges are self-regulating, not-for-profit corporations owned by their members. The degree of governmental oversight and regulation has traditionally been most extensive in the U.S. and least intrusive in the United Kingdom. However, the widespread publicity over the U.S. government's investigation of trading practices in 1989 seems certain to increase government regulations everywhere.

The exchanges maintain active compliance and market surveillance programs to enforce trading rules and to detect any evidence of market manipulation. Traders caught violating rules are typically fined and, in relatively infrequent instances, barred from trading. If evidence of market manipulation is uncovered, exchanges possess a wide range of powers to remedy the situation. These powers include the right to order a given participant to reduce or even eliminate his or her position, to substitute alternative delivery points or additional supplies (*i.e.*, by broadening quality specifications), or even to impose a cash settlement in place of physical delivery (assuming the contract calls for such delivery). These powers are not often used, but their very existence serves as a powerful disincentive to would-be market manipulators.

Perhaps the most controversial aspect of futures trading (particularly in the U.S.) is the permitting of dual trading; *i.e.*, allowing the same individuals to trade for their own account while simultaneously executing orders for customers as a floor broker. Many critics have argued that this practice provides opportunities for floor brokers to jump ahead of large customer orders, profiting from the market movements that those large orders are likely to provoke. While such actions are a clear violation of exchange rules, detection is not always easy. Exchanges counter with the argument that dual trading promotes liquidity and that exchange enforcement activities are sufficient to prevent serious abuses.

As the widespread arrests and prosecutions in both Chicago and New York showed, there will always be temptations. Clearly, exchanges can improve their rules and surveillance. At a minimum, exchanges that want to allow dual trading have an obligation to create dear audit trails so that violations are easier to detect. It seems likely, however, that dual trading will be prohibited in futures trading as it is in securities trading. The exchanges and their floor communities can be expected to resist this development until the bitter end. Chapter 11 discusses the regulatory and legal issues more thoroughly.

That makes it all sound quite simple. All you have to do is figure out whether to go long or short. The following chapters are designed to help you make that decision. If it all seems too simple, just turn to the options chapter and figure out how to do straddles, strangles, fences, and butterfly spreads.

Major Energy Exchanges Across the World

Table 1.4: Comprehensive List

Exchange	*Abbreviation*	*Location*	*Product Types*
Brazilian Mercantile and Futures Exchange	BMF	Brazil	Biofuels, Metals
Bursa Malaysia	MDEX	Malaysia	Biofuels
Central Japan Commodity Exchange		Nagoya	Energy
Chicago Board of Trade	CBOT	Chicago	Biofuels, Metals
Chicago Climate Exchange	CCX	Chicago	Emissions
Chicago Mercantile Exchange	CME	Chicago	Biofuels
Dubai Mercantile Exchange	DME	Dubai	Energy
Dubai Gold and Commodities Exchange	DGCX	Dubai	Precious Metals
European Climate Exchange	ECX	Europe	Emissions
HedgeStreet Exchange		California	Energy
Inter continental Exchange	ICE		Energy, Emissions
London Metal Exchange	LME	London	Industrial Metals
Multi Commodity Exchange	MCX	Mumbai	Energy
National Commodity and Derivatives Exchange	NCDEX	Mumbai	Energy
New York Board of Trade	NYBOT	New York	Biofuels
New York Mercantile Exchange	NYMEX	New York	Energy, Metals
Shanghai Futures Exchange	SFE	Shanghai	Energy
Tokyo Commodity Exchange	TOCOM	Tokyo	Energy, Metals
U.S. Futures Exchange	USFE	Chicago	Energy

Chapter 2

Crude Oil Trading

INTRODUCTION CRUDE OIL TRADING

The word petroleum is derived from the Latin words "Petra" meaning rock and "Oleum" meaning oil. It is also called mineral oil. In some parts of the world, a black, thin sticky liquids seeps out of the ground. This liquid is popularly known as *crude oil* or *petroleum.*

Petroleum is a complex mixture of hydrocarbons. As for the origin, Chinese used petroleum as a fuel as early as 200 BC. They were formed millions of years ago when large area of earth was covered by sea water. Tiny sea creatures called plankton died and sank to the sea bed. They mixed up with mud. The bacteria in mud began to bring about the decay of these tiny creatures. Process of decay took place slowly due to little oxygen dissolved in the depth of sea. The presence on the decaying material increased due to gradual deposition of mud and silt. Bacteria decay at high pressure with little oxygen changed the organic matter into crude oil. Petroleum and natural gas are found together, held in between the layers of non-porous rocks in the ground. These fuels are extracted by drilling a pipe through the rock.

Most geologists view crude oil and natural gas as the product of compression and heating of ancient organic materials over geological time. Oil is formed from the preserved remains of prehistoric zooplankton and algae which have been settled to the sea (or lake) bottom in large quantities under anoxic conditions. Terrestrial plants, on the other hand, tend to form coal. Over geological time this organic matter, mixed with mud, is buried under heavy layers of sediment. The resulting high levels of heat and pressure cause the organic matter to chemically change during diagenesis, first into a waxy material known as kerogen which is found in various oil shales around the world, and then with more heat into liquid and gaseous hydrocarbons in a process known as catagenesis. Because most hydrocarbons are lighter than rock or water, these sometimes migrate upward through adjacent rock layers until they become trapped beneath impermeable rocks, within porous rocks called reservoirs. Concentration of hydrocarbons in a trap forms an oil field, from which the liquid can be extracted by drilling and pumping. Geologists often refer to an "oil window" which is the temperature range that oil forms in—below the minimum temperature oil remains trapped in the form of kerogen, and above the maximum temperature the oil is converted to natural gas through the process of thermal cracking. Though this happens at different depths in different locations around the world, a 'typical' depth for the oil window might be 4–6 km. Note that even if oil is formed at extreme depths, it may be trapped at much shallower depths, even if it is not formed there (the Athabasca Oil Sands is one example). Three conditions must be present for oil reservoirs to form: first, a source rock rich in organic material buried deep enough for subterranean heat to cook it into oil; second, a porous and permeable reservoir rock for it to accumulate in; and last a cap rock (seal) that prevents it from escaping to the surface.

Crude or crude oil is a mixture of hydrocarbons that exists in a liquid phase in natural underground reservoirs. It remains liquid at atmospheric pressure after passing through surface separating facilities. Production volumes reported as crude oil include:

- Liquids technically defined as crude oil;
- Small amounts of hydrocarbons that exist in the gaseous phase in natural underground reservoirs, but which are liquid at atmospheric pressure after being recovered from oil well (casing head) gas in lease separators;
- Small amounts of non-hydrocarbons produced with the oil.

Basics of Crude Oil

1. Crude oils are complex mixtures containing many different hydrocarbon compounds that vary in appearance and composition from one

oil field to another. Crude oils range in consistency from water to tar-like solids, and in color from clear to black. An "average" crude oil contains about 84% carbon, 14% hydrogen, 1%-3% sulfur, and less than 1% each of nitrogen, oxygen, metals, and salts.

Crude oils are generally classified as paraffinic, naphthenic, or aromatic, based on the predominant proportion of similar hydrocarbon molecules. Mixed-base crudes have varying amounts of each type of hydrocarbon. Refinery crude base stocks usually consist of mixtures of two or more different crude oils.

2. Relatively simple crude oil assays are used to classify crude oils as paraffinic, naphthenic, aromatic, or mixed. One assay method (United States Bureau of Mines) is based on distillation, and another method (UOP "K" factor) is based on gravity and boiling points. More comprehensive crude assays determine the value of the crude (i.e., its yield and quality of useful products) and processing parameters. Crude oils are usually grouped according to yield structure.

3. Crude oils are also defined in terms of API (American Petroleum Institute) gravity. The higher the API gravity, the lighter the crude. For example, light crude oils have high API gravities and low specific gravities.

Crude oils with low carbon, high hydrogen, and high API gravity are usually rich in paraffins and tend to yield greater proportions of gasoline and light petroleum products; those with high carbon, low hydrogen, and low API gravities are usually rich in aromatics.

4. Crude oils that contain appreciable quantities of hydrogen sulfide or other reactive sulfur compounds are called "sour." Those with less sulfur are called "sweet." Some exceptions to this rule are West Texas crudes, which are always considered "sour" regardless of their H2S content, and Arabian high sulfur crudes, which are not considered "sour" because their sulfur compounds are not highly reactive.

Crude Oil Types

Crude oil is arguably the world's most important and actively-traded commodity. Oil trades in a world market, and is bought and sold in relation to global prices. Because there are many different varieties and grades of crude oil, buyers and sellers have found it easier to refer to a limited number of reference, or benchmark, crude oils. Other varieties are then priced at a discount or premium, according to how their quality compares to that of the benchmark. The type of crude oil that is used as a benchmark in North America is West Texas Intermediate (WTI) oil, which is a light, sweet (low sulphur) crude. This is the price that is usually quoted in newspaper articles. Light sweet crude oils sell at higher prices than heavy sour (high sulphur) crudes, which are more difficult and expensive to refine and yield less of the more valuable oil products such as gasoline and jet fuel.

Table 2.1: Typical Approximate Characteristics and Properties and Gasoline Potential of various Crudes
(Representative average numbers)

Crude Source	*Paraffins (% vol)*	*Aromatics (% vol)*	*Naphthenes (% vol)*	*Sulfur (% Wt)*	*API gravity (approx.)*	*Napht. yield (% vol)*	*Octane no (typical)*
Nigerian—Light	37	9	54	0.2	36	28	60
Saudi—Light	63	19	18	2	34	22	40
Saudi—Heavy	60	15	25	2.1	28	23	35
Venezuela—Heavy	35	12	53	2.3	30	2	60
Venezuela—Light	52	14	34	1.5	24	18	50
USA—Midcount Sweet	—	—	—	0.4	40	—	—
USA—W. Texas Sour	46	22	32	1.9	32	33	55
North Sea—Brent	50	16	31	0.1	37	31	50

Source: US Deptt. of Labour.

Varieties of Crude Oil

- Abu Bukhoosh
- Aktobe
- Al Shaheen
- Alaska North Slope
- Alba (Equ. Guinea)
- Alba (UK)
- Albian Heavy
- Algerian Condensate
- Al-Jurf
- Amenam Blend
- Ameriven-Hamaca
- Amna
- Antan Blend
- Arab Extra Light
- Arab Heavy
- Arab Light
- Arab Medium
- Arab Super Light
- Ardjuna
- Asgard
- Azeri (BTC)
- Azeri Light

- Bach Ho
- Balder
- Baobab
- Basrah Blend
- Bayu Undan
- BCF-17
- Belanak
- Belayim Blend
- Beryl
- Bintulu Condensate
- Bonga
- Bonny Light
- Boscan
- Bouri
- Bow River
- Brass River
- Brega
- Brent Blend
- Cabinda
- Cano Limon
- Captain
- Ceiba
- Cepu
- Cerro Negro
- Champion
- Chinguetti
- Cinta
- Clair
- Cold Lake
- Cossack
- CPC Blend
- Cusiana
- Dalia
- Daqing
- Dar Blend
- Djeno
- Doba
- Doroud
- Draugen
- Dubai
- DUC
- Dukhan
- Dulang
- Duri
- EA
- Ekofisk
- El Sharara
- Enfield
- Erha
- Es Sider
- Escravos
- Flotta
- Foinaven
- Forcados
- Foroozan Blend
- Forties
- Gippsland
- Girassol
- Grane
- Gullfaks
- Handil
- Harding
- Heavy Louisiana Sweet
- Heidrun
- Hibernia
- Hungo

- Iran Heavy
- Iran Light
- Isthmus
- Karachaganak Cond.
- Kashagan
- Khafji
- Kikeh
- Kirkuk
- Kissanje Blend
- Kole
- Kuito
- Kumkol
- Kutubu
- Kuwait
- Labuan
- Lavan Blend
- Light Louisiana Sweet
- Liuhua
- Liverpool Bay
- Mandji
- Marib
- Marlim
- Mars Blend
- Masila
- Maya
- Medanito
- Mesa-30
- Minas
- Miri
- Murban
- N'Kossa
- Nanhai Light
- Napo
- Nemba
- New Zafiro Blend
- NFC II
- Nile Blend
- Norne
- Northwest Shelf Cond.
- Nowruz/Soroush
- Olmeca
- Oman
- Oriente
- Oseberg
- Oso Condensate
- Palanca Blend
- Panyu
- Peng Lai
- Pennington
- Petrozuata
- Premium Albian
- Qatar Marine
- Qua Iboe
- Rabi Light
- Rang Dong
- Saharan Blend
- Sarir
- Schiehallion
- Senipah
- Seria Light
- Shah Deniz Condensate
- Shengli
- Siberian Light
- Sincor-Zuata
- Siri
- Sirri

- Sirtica
- Sleipner Condensate
- Sokol
- Souedieh
- South Arne
- Southern Green Canyon
- Statfjord
- Su Tu Den
- Suez Blend
- Syncrude Sweet Blend
- Syrian Light
- Tapis
- Terra Nova
- Tia Juana Light
- Triton
- Troll
- Turkmen Blend
- Umm Shaif
- Upper Zakum
- Urals
- Vityaz
- Wafra
- West Seno
- West Texas Intermediate
- West Texas Sour
- Western Canada Select
- White Rose
- Widuri
- Xikomba
- Yoho
- Zakum
- Zarzaitine

Products Derived from Crude

In India, following items are produced from crude oil:

- Light distillates (includes LPG, Mogas, Naphtha, LD i.e. Propylene, C-3, Propane, Hexane, Special Boiling Point Spirit, Benzene, Toluene, Petroleum Hydro Carbon Solvent, Natural Heptane, Methyl Tertiary Butyl Ether, Poly Isobutine, PBFS and MEKFS)
- Middle distillates (includes Kerosene, ATF, RTF, Jet A-1, HSD, LDO, MD i.e. Mineral Turpentine Oil, JP-5, Linear Alkyl Benzene Feed Stock, Aromex, Jute Batching Oil, Solvent 1425, Low Sulphur Heavy fuel HSD, DHCB and Special Kerosene)
- Heavy ends (includes Furnace oil, LSHS, HHS, RFO, Lube oils, Bitumen, Petroleum coke, Paraffin wax, other waxes etc.). There are in fact many products obtained from the processing of crude oil, and other hydrocarbon compounds. These include aviation gasoline, motor gasoline, naphtha, kerosene, jet fuel, distillate fuel oil, residual fuel oil, liquefied petroleum gas, lubricants, paraffin wax, petroleum

coke, asphalt and other products. Following are some of the products:

Gasoline: a mixture of relatively volatile hydrocarbons, with or without small quantities of additives, that have been blended to form a fuel suitable for use in internal combustion engines; includes gasoline used in aviation.

Kerosene: medium hydrocarbon distillates in the 150° to 280°C distillation range, and used as a heating fuel as well as for certain types of internal combustion engine; includes jet fuel, which is a fuel of naphtha, or of kerosene type, suitable for commercial or military purposes in aircraft turbine engines.

Distillates: middle distillate type of hydrocarbons. Included are products similar to number one and number two heating oils and diesel fuels. These products are used for space heating, diesel engine fuel and electrical power generation.

Residual fuel oil: these are fuels obtained as liquid still bottoms from the distillation of crude used alone or in blends with heavy liquids from other refinery process operations. It is used for the generation of electric power, space heating, vessel bunkering and various industrial purposes.

Oil Units

1 Tonne = 7.33 Barrel
= 1.165 Cubic Metres (kilolitres)

1 Barrel = 0.136 Tonnes
= 0.159 Cubic Metres (Kilolitres)

1 Cubic Metre = 0.858 Tonnes
= 6.289 Barrels

1 Million Tonne = 1.111 Billion Cubic Metres Natural Gas
= 39.2 Billion Cubic Feet Natural Gas
= 0.805 Million Tonnes LNG
= 40.4 Trillion British Thermal Units

Over the last fifteen years oil has become the biggest commodity market in the world. During this period, oil trading has evolved from a primarily physical activity into a sophisticated financial market. In the process it has attracted the interest of a wide range of participants who now include banks and fund managers as well as the traditional oil majors, independents and physical oil traders.

As well as being the largest commodity market in the world, oil is also the most complicated. The physical oil market trades many different types of crude oil and refined products, and the relative values of each grade are continually shifting in response to changes in supply and demand on both a global and a local scale. The industry has therefore developed a complex set of interlocking markets not only establish prices across the entire spectrum of crude and products qualities, but also to enable buyers and sellers to accommodate changes in relative prices wherever they might occur.

The initial momentum for the expansion of the oil market came from the changing structure of the oil industry. Prior o 1973, oil trading was a marginal activity for most companies who only used the market to resolve any imbalances and demand that might emerge. Trading volumes were typically small and usually spot, and prices were much less transparent than they are today. And the industry was dominated by large integrated oil companies that have little use of external markets either as a means of obtaining supplies or as a basis for setting prices.

However the structure of the oil industry changed irreversibly in the 1970s with the nationalization of the upstream interest of the major oil companies in the Middle East and elsewhere, and trading become an essential component of any oil company's supply and marketing operations. Having lost access to large volumes of equity oil, the major oil companies were forced to buy at arm's length from their former host governments and the physical base of the international oil market expanded rapidly. With more oil being traded, external markets began to set the price for internal transfers as well as third party sales and companies started to buy and sell oil if better opportunities existed outside their own supply network fuelling the growth of the market.

But the driving force behind the rapid growth I oil trading is the huge variability in the price of oil. Daily price movements of $1/barrel are not uncommon and prices frequently change by up to 50 cents/barrel. Since there is no obvious upper or lower bound to oil prices, the value of a barrel of oil can double within the spaces of a few months. As a result, everyone involved in the industry is exposed to the risk of very large changes in the value of any oil that they are producing transporting, refining or purchasing and range of new markets have evolved in order to provide effective hedging instruments against the elaborate combination of absolute and relative price risks that characterizes the oil business. This has not only generated a very large volume of activity in its own right, but also attracted liquidity from other financial and commodity markets.

Trading Characteristics of Oil

Many of the characteristics features of the oil market are derived from the nature of oil itself. Despite the introduction of highly standardized paper trading instruments, oil remains a physical commodity. Like other primary commodity, the oil market is ultimately concerned with the transportation, processing and storage of an essential raw material as it travels from producer to consumer. However this is slow process, since crude oil may take several months to move from the well head through the refinery to the sales pump. As a result, prices often change because the right oil is not in the right place at the right time. This is very different from the financial markets, where assets can be moved instantaneously from one location to another if required.

Transportation, Processing and Storage

One of the most important characteristics of oil is that it is a liquid. As a liquid it requires specialized handling facilities for transportation, processing and storage. And it is these elements that provide the basic building blocks for the physical oil market.

Transportation

Oil is transported either in ships or pipelines. In the international market, oil moves almost exclusively in ships and it is therefore the size of the ship that forms the basic trading unit. In the case of crude oil, quantities are typically large and usually depend on the capacity of the loading and discharge terminals, the length of the voyage and the relative cost of shipping. In the North Sea, which is the most active waterborne crude market in the world, 500,000 barrel cargoes are the norm. But for longer –haul crudes from West Africa or the Middle East, oil often moves in very large crude carriers (VLCCs) which can take up to 2 million barrels at a time. As a result, the scale of financial exposure associated with crude oil trading can be very large indeed.

Refined products, however, are usually traded in much smaller quantities.

Long distance movements may involve shipments as large as 60,000 tones (about 500,000 barrels, depending on the type of product), but most of the international trade is conducted in smaller vessels holding 20-30,000 tones. And many of the most active product markets deal in much smaller, large sized quantities, of between 1,000 and 5,000 tones. Since products are usually traded ex-refinery and often sold to wholesale distributors who may not have the capacity to receive or store very large quantities, the basic trading units need to be much smaller than in the international crude market.

As well as fixing the size of trading unit the method of transport often determines the terms of trade. Crude oil is usually sold close to the point of production and title is transferred as oil flows from the loading terminal into the ship. Once loaded however, the oil can either be traded on the water or at the point of discharge. As a result, the same cargo of oil may be priced differently depending on the point of sale. Refined products are traded on a variety of terms depending on local circumstances, but it is important to realize that several markets can co –exist for the same product at the same location with prices that reflect different delivery arrangements or parcel sizes.

Oil is also transported and traded via pipelines. The most important pipeline markets are in the US where access is guaranteed in law to those who want to use them. In most cases oil is traded on ratable basis- a specified number of barrels per day over an agreed period such as a fortnight or a month- and the oil is sold free in pipeline (fip) at designated locations. But in the case of West Texas Intermediate, which forms the basis of the Nymex Light Sweet Crude Futures contract, oil is also sold in multiples of 1,000 barrels available from or delivered into storage facilities at Cushing, Oklahoma.

Processing

Oil is a not normally used in its raw state. Crude oil must be processed through a refinery in order to turn it into marketable product such as gasoline, heating oil or fuel oil. The only exception is low sulphur crude oil which is sometimes burnt directly in power stations. Oil is therefore traded twice, first as a refinery feedstock, and secondly as a finished product. Although crude and product markets have rather different characteristics, they are inextricably linked by the technology and economics of refinery processes.

Crude oil markets operate between the producer and the refiner. The characteristics and the behavior of the crude oil market therefore depend on the preferences and needs of the refiner as well as the composition and nature of the supply. Because there are many different types of crude oil, relative value depends on the mix of products that can be obtained from them. In general, crudes that yield a higher proportion of the more valuable light products such as gasoline, naphtha, kerosene and heating oil can command a higher price than those which have a higher price than those which have a high yield of residual fuel oil. But there is no objective method of assessing the price of given crude since every refinery has a different configuration and its market value will depend on who is bidding at the time. And refineries in different regions may have very different views about the price they are prepared to pay.

Products markets operate between the refiner and the blender or wholesaler. They are usually much more localized than crude oil markets, since most refineries are positioned close to the end- user, and their process facilities are tailored to the needs of the local consumer. As a result, refined product prices can differ significantly from one market to another, reflecting the local structure of demand for the various petroleum product quality specifications.

Storage

Oil must also be stored on its journey from the well head to the pump. As oil is a liquid, this requires the construction of specialized storage tanks at every stage in the supply chain. Stocks are necessary in any business that produces, manufactures and markets a physical commodity such as oil, and fluctuations in the level of stocks held at different points along the supply chain play an important role in determining the behavior of prices in the oil market. But holding stocks is also costly since it ties up cash and storage facilities are expensive to rent or build. Oil companies therefore try to keep their stocks as near to the minimum operating level as circumstances allow.

A surprisingly large amount of oil is required simply to fill the supply chain from well-head to customer. In addition, stocks are needed to keep system flowing since deliveries are usually made in discrete quantities and stocks are run down in the intervening period. Also companies need to hold extra stocks as an insurance policy against unexpected interruptions in supply or increases in demand from their customers. And finally companies often build up (or run down) stocks for purely speculative reasons either to profit from an upward price trend or to minimize the losses from downward price trend.

CRUDE OIL SUPPLY CHAIN

The entire oil markets are divided into three phases on the basis of activities as shown in Fig. 2.1 below:

(1) The "**upstream**" comprises exploration and production;

(2) The "**midstream**" are the tankers and pipelines that carry crude oil to refineries, and;

(3) The "**downstream**", includes refining, marketing, and distribution, right down to the corner gasoline station or convenient store.

Any company that includes together significant upstream and downstream activities is said to be "integrated". In detail we can say that,

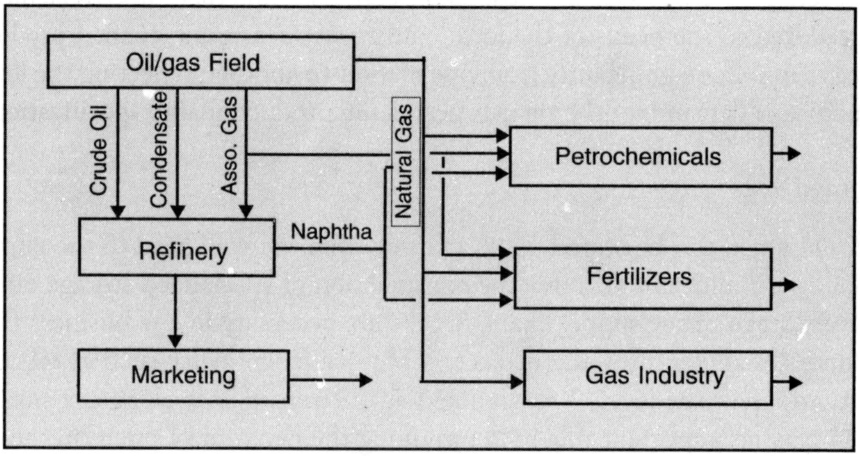

Figure 2.1: Value Chain Block Diagram

Upstream Sector

The upstream sector includes the searching for potential underground or underwater oil and gas fields, drilling of exploratory wells, and subsequently operating the wells that recover and bring the *crude oil* and/or raw *natural gas* to the surface. The upstream activities can be related to following:

PETROLEUM PROSPECTS

A prospect is a potential trap which geologists believe may contain hydrocarbons. A significant amount of geological, structural and seismic investigation is must to drill location from a lead to a prospect.

The five pre-requisites are:

1. A source rock—When organic-rich rock such as oil shale or coal is

subjected to high pressure and temperature over an extended period of time, hydrocarbons form.

2. Migration—The Hydrocarbons are expelled from source rock by three density-related mechanisms: the newly-matured hydrocarbons are less dense than their precursors, which causes overpressure; the hydrocarbons are lighter medium, and so migrate upwards due to buoyancy, and the fluids expand as further burial causes increased heating. Most hydrocarbons migrate to the surface as oil seeps, but some will get trapped.
3. Trap—The hydrocarbons are buoyant and have to be trapped within a structural (e.g. Anticline, fault block) or stratigraphic trap.
4. Seal or cap Rock—The hydrocarbon trap has to be covered by an impermeable rock known as a seal or cap-rock in order to prevent hydrocarbons escaping to the surface.
5. Reservoir—The hydrocarbons are contained in a reservoir rock. This is a porous sandstone or limestone. The oil collects in the pores within the rock. The reservoir must also be permeable so that the hydrocarbons will flow to surface during production.

Terms used Prevalent in Upstream Activities are

- Lead—A structure which may contain hydrocarbons
- Dry Hole—Counter-intuitively, a formation that contains brine instead of oil.
- Flat Spot—An oil-water contact on a seismic section; flat due to gravity.
- Bright Spot—On a seismic section, coda that have high amplitudes due to a formation containing hydrocarbons.
- Prospect—A lead which has been fully evaluated and is ready to drill
- Chance of Success—An estimate of the chance of all the elements (see above) within a prospect working, described as a probability. High risk prospects have a less than 10% chance of working, medium risk prospects 10-20%, low risk prospects over 20%. Typically about 40% of wells recently drilled find commercial hydrocarbons.
- Hydrocarbon in Place—Amount of hydrocarbon likely to be contained in the prospect. This is calculated using the volumetric equation - GRV × N/G × Porosity × Sh × FVF

- GRV—Gross Rock Volume—Amount of rock in the trap above the hydrocarbon water contact
- N/G—Net/Gross Ratio—Percentage of the GRV formed by the reservoir rock (range is 0 to 1)
- Porosity—Percentage of the net reservoir rock occupied by pores (typically 5-35%)
- Sh—Hydrocarbon saturation—Some of the pore space is filled with water - this must be discounted
- FVF—Formation Volume Factor—Oil shrinks and gas expands when brought to the surface. The FVF converts volumes at reservoir conditions (high pressure and high temperature) to storage and sale conditions
- Recoverable Hydrocarbons—Amount of hydrocarbon likely to be recovered during production. This is typically 10-50% in an oil field and 50-80% in a gas field.

Licensing

Petroleum resources are typically owned by the government of the host country. In most nations the government issues licences to explore, develop and produce its oil and gas resources, which are typically administered by the oil ministry. There are several different types of licenses. Typically oil companies operate in joint ventures to spread the risk, one of the companies in the partnership is designated the operator who actually supervises the work.

Tax and Royalty—Companies would pay a royalty on any oil produced, together with a profits tax (which can have expenditure offset against it). In some cases there are also various bonuses and ground rents (license fees) payable to the government—for example a signature bonus payable at the start of the licence. Licences are awarded in competitive bid rounds on the basis of either the size of the work programme (number of wells, seismic etc.) or size of the signature bonus.

Production Sharing Contract (PSA)—A PSA is more complex than a Tax/ Royalty system—The companies bid on the percentage of the production that the host government receives (this may be variable with the oil price), There is often also participation by the Government owned National Oil Company (NOC). There are also various bonuses to be paid. Development expenditure is offset against production revenue.

Service Contract—This is when an oil company acts as a contractor for the host government, being paid to produce the hydrocarbons.

Reserves and Resources

Resources are hydrocarbons which may or may not be produced in the future. A resource number may be assigned to an undrilled prospect or an unappraised discovery. Appraisal by drilling additional delineation wells or acquiring extra seismic data will confirm the size of the field and lead to project sanction.

The three categories of reserves generally used are proven:

1. **Proven reserves**—defined as oil and gas "Reasonably Certain" to be producible using current technology at current prices, with current commercial terms and government consent- also known in the industry as 1P. Some Industry specialists refer to this as P90, i.e having a 90% certainty of being produced.
2. **Probable reserves**—defined as oil and gas "Reasonably Probable" of being produced using current or likely technology at current prices, with current commercial terms and government consent. Some Industry specialists refer to this as P50, i.e. having a 50% certainty of being produced. This is also known in the industry as 2P or Proven plus probable.
3. **Possible reserves**—i.e. "having a chance of being developed under favourable circumstances". Some industry specialists refer to this as P10, i.e having a 10% certainty of being produced. This is also known in the industry as 3P or Proven plus probable plus possible.

Midstream Sector

The midstream sector processes, stores, markets and transports commodities such as crude oil, natural gas and *natural gas liquids* (NGLs) such as *ethane*, *propane* and *butane*.

Marketing and Distribution

The business activities of marketing and distribution segment include purchasing refined oil products from the refining segment and third parities, and wholesale of refined oil products to domestic customers, direct sale and retail of the refined oil products through the retail network owned by this segment and provision of related services.

Downstream Sector

The downstream sector includes *oil refineries*, *petrochemical* plants, petroleum product distribution, retail outlets and natural gas distribution companies. The downstream industry touches consumers through thousands of products such as gasoline, diesel, jet fuel, *heating oil*, asphalt, *lubricants*, *synthetic rubber*, *plastics*, *fertilizers*, *antifreeze*, *pesticides*, *pharmaceuticals*, natural gas and propane.

The Refining Process

As mentioned previously, a barrel of crude oil has a mixture of all sorts of hydrocarbons in it. Oil refining separates everything into useful substances. Chemists use the following steps:

The oldest and most common way to separate things into various components (called fractions), is to do it using the differences in boiling

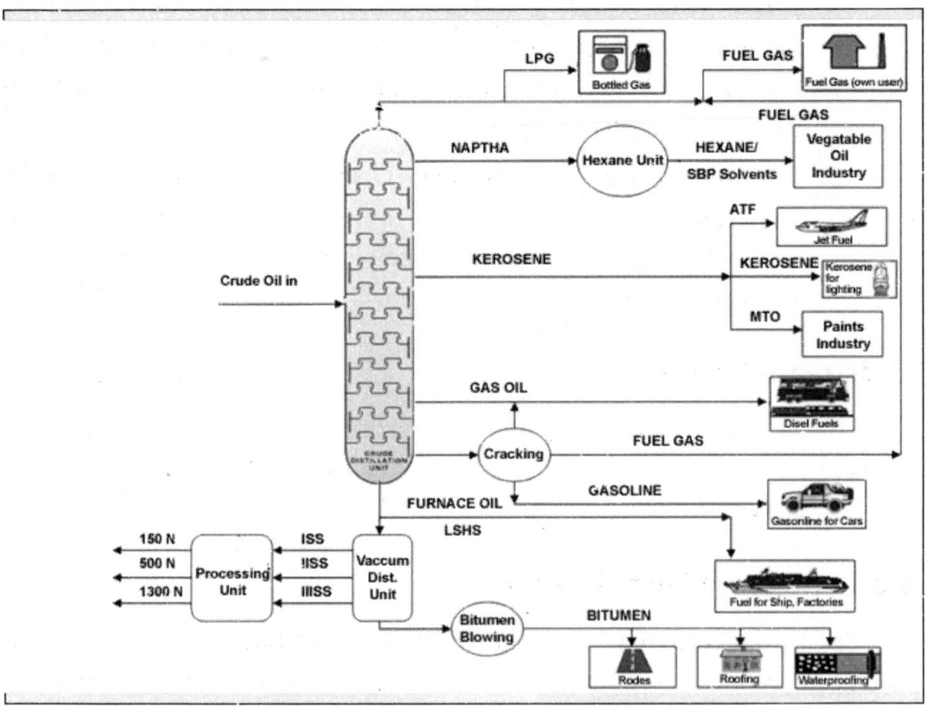

Figure 2.2: Refining Processes

temperature. This process is called fractional distillation. You basically heat crude oil up, let it vaporize and then condense the vapor.

Newer techniques use Chemical processing on some of the fractions to make others, in a process called conversion. Chemical processing, for example, can break longer chains into shorter ones. This allows a refinery to turn diesel fuel into gasoline depending on the demand for gasoline.

Refineries must treat the fractions to remove impurities.

Refineries combine the various fractions (processed, unprocessed) into mixtures to make desired products. For example, different mixtures of chains can create gasoline with different octane ratings.

However, midstream operations are usually simply included in the downstream category.

OIL ECONOMICS: DEMAND, SUPPLY AND STOCKS

The price of oil has traditionally been determined by how closely supply and demand match each other. When there is more supply than consumers want, they can shop around for the best price leading to lower prices. If demand is higher than the amount available, consumers will compete with each other, bidding for the supplies they need driving prices up.

However, it is not only the current supply/demand balance that determines market prices. Buyers and sellers also factor in what they expect will happen to prices in the future. If buyers think that supply might be lower in a few weeks or months and the price could go up, they will want to stockpile some oil now and might even be willing to pay a premium today to protect against a higher price in the future. Similarly, if buyers think that the supply of oil will increase in the future or that the price can be expected to decline soon, they will delay their purchases as long as possible or demand a discount on the price.

The behavior of prices in any primary commodity market is strongly influenced by the fundamental forces of demand and supply. Although prices frequently change for other more ephemeral reasons, especially now that trading screens and on-line news services play such an important role of fundamentals in shaping the course of prices should not be forgotten.

Demand

The demand for oil, like other primary commodities, depends on mainly on the state of the global economy. Despite improvements in energy efficiency as a result of the price increase of the 1970s and early 1980s, oil demands remains closely linked to the growth in economic activity.

Recently, oil demand has been growing fastest in the newly industrializing countries of the Asia-Pacific Rim where the economies are expanding very rapidly indeed. By contrast oil demands in industrialized countries are only just emerging from recession. And oil demand in the former Soviet Union has continued to fall as the economy contracts and the old, energy –intensive industries are no longer viable. However, the OECD countries still consume more than half the world's oil and it is in these countries that the oil markets are most developed and least constrained by government controls.

Oil demand is also highly seasonal. Peak demand for heating fuels such as kerosene, gas oil and residual fuel oil obviously comes in the winter, while peak demand for transport fuels such as gasoline and diesel comes in the summer. In addition, other products such as bitumen, which is used for road building, also display a clear seasonal pattern that can also affect oil price behavior at certain times of the year. Although the steady shift towards a greater share of transport fuels in the global demand barrel has reduced the annual variation in world oil consumption, there is still a difference of 3 to 4 million b/d between the winter peak and the summer trough in demand.

Prices play an ambivalent in determining the oil demand. In short term, they appear to have very little impact on the level of oil consumption except in those markets such as electricity generation where there is direct competition with other fuels. In most markets, oil consumers cannot easily react to price increases because this requires investment, either in a new car or new boiler. As a result, the impact of higher prices may take years to filter through. But in the longer-term, there is no doubt that the prices have a significant impact on the level of oil consumption.

The effect of prices on demand is clearly demonstrated by comparing the impact of consumer government taxes on the amount of oil consumed per head of the population in countries with similar levels of economic development. For example the US which still imposes very low taxes on oil products, consumes nearly twice as much oil per capita as the UK and France, which impose much higher taxes. And the fact oil products are either not taxed, or even subsidized, in many developing countries helps to explain the very high rates growth of oil demand achieved in recent years.

We can list factors that affect the demand of crude oil in the international market as:

1. *Economic Factors*

As the funds, cost and revenue all comprise of the economic factors. The major constituents of economic factors are:

(a) Production & consumption levels
(b) Storage availability and costs
(c) Insurance costs
(d) Interest rates
(e) Transportation costs
(f) Currency rates
(g) Other related markets

2. *Geographical Factors*

Since crude oil is energy source driving the needs of the whole globe, geographical factors do play a mentionable role:

(a) Pipeline/shipping availability
(b) Localized weather report
(c) Seasonality
(d) Locality

3. *Comparative Factors*

When different alternatives are available to fulfill the energy needs a comparison do arises like:

(a) Preference shift
(b) Transaction costs
(c) Alternative commodities
(d) Product yields
(e) Relative quality

4. *Political Factors*

Major all producing countries experiences political instability and the political state of the region thus affected by:

(a) Cartels/trade agreements
(b) Global events-war, embargoes etc.
(c) Taxation/trade tariffs
(d) Regulation/legislation
(e) Environmental pressure

Supply

Matching oil supply to demand has become much more difficult since the oil industry ceased to be properly integrated. Most oil producers simply maximize their output, subject to the technical constraints of the field, in order to get a quick return on the very large amounts of money they have invested in developing the oil field in the first place. And because their operating costs are typically much lower than the sunken capital costs, they will continue to produce until oil prices reach very low levels.

In the North-Sea, for example, most of the fields have operating costs of less than $5/barrel and are unlikely to be shut in unless prices fall below this level. As a result, the responsibility for restraining production below capacity lies with the twelve remaining members of the Organizations of Petroleum Exporting Countries (OPEC), who are committed to maintaining prices above their marginal cost of production in order to extract what they regard as a fair economic rent for oil. So far, they have succeeded, although competition for market share between OPEC members has frequently forced prices down until falling revenues have eventually restored a sense of discipline to the Organization. OPEC was particularly successful during the first half of the 1080s when Saudi Arabia was prepared to play the role of swing producer alone, but it has become more difficult to balance the market since the Saudis refused to continue cutting production at the end of 1985.

Two factors have made OPEC's self-appointed task more difficult. First there is the continued expansion of oil production outside OPEC. Although lower oil prices were initially expected to slow down the development of non-OPEC. Oil fields, this has not proved to be the case. By encouraging technological developments and forcing companies to cut costs, lower oil prices have actually made it easier to develop new oil fields outside the OPEC. Countries. As a result the call on OPEC crude continues to grow more slowly than OPEC would like to see despite rising oil consumption.

Secondly, there is the inherent seasonality of oil demand. As the residual supplier to the world oil market, OPEC potentially faces large fluctuation in the level of production required by refiners at different times of the year. This not only makes it difficult to keep track of the underlying level of demand, but is also difficult to administer since OPEC. Members normally find it very hard to agree on how to allocate production between themselves. Recently, the problem has been solved by setting (and almost sticking to) a fixed production quota over a much longer period of time, thus leaving the market to handle the seasonal variation in the demand for crude.

Stocks

The level of stocks held by the world oil industry has fallen since the early 1980s. The reduction in partly due to the transfer of responsibility for strategic stocks from the oil companies to their governments, partly due to changes in the structure of oil demand, and partly due to improvements in the efficiency of company operations. And with renewed demand growth in recent years, the forward cover provided by OECD industry stocks has been sharply reduced/ since the end of 1991, the seasonally adjusted level of OECD industry stocks has not increased while demand has grown by more than 2 million b/d. As a result the forward cover provided by total OECD industry stocks had fallen to only 64 days at the end of June 1995 compared with more than 80 days in the early 1980s, and dropped to only 59 days at the end of 1995 after supply disruptions and unexpectedly cold weather left companies holding very low stocks. However there is still some way to go before companies reach their historical minimum operating stock level of 55 days.

A detailed study of the US oil industry published by Exxon showed that the US held a total of 89 days of oil stocks at the start of 1981 measured in terms of forward consumption. Out of this total, 7 days' worth was held by the government in the Strategic Petroleum Reserve (SPR), and 82 days' worth was held by companies. According to Exxon 58 of the 82 days' worth of company stocks were minimum operating stocks. More than a third of the minimum operating stocks (20 days' worth) occupied the pipelines and tankers that transport the oil filled the refineries that process it, and provided the "tank bottoms "for the storage facilities. The remaining 38days' worth of stocks represented the oil in transit through the system, of which a quarter (10 days' worth) was in the form of crude oil and three quarters (28 days' worth) was in the form of refined products.

Companies need to hold more stocks in the form of products than crude for two reasons. First the different types of refined product need to be kept separate from each other and move along their own distribution channels, which simply increases the amount of oil tied up in the supply chain once it has passed through the refinery. And secondly, refineries are not sufficiently flexible to vary their products yields in line with the seasonal variation in demand. For this reason, refiners are obliged to accumulate unwanted stocks of heating oil and residual fuel oil when they increase runs to meet peak gasoline demand during the summer, while the reverse occurs during the winter. It is this involuntary stock builds by refiners that create the characteristics seasonal pattern in the level of stocks held by the oil industry and influences the behavior of prices in the forward and futures markets.

WORLD OIL MARKETS

Market Players

Oil Producers

There is a great deal of concentration in the world oil industry: just ten companies control 68 percent of the world's proven oil reserves. Nine of the ten biggest oil reserve holders are state-owned National Oil Companies (NOCs). Many of these were formerly private sector companies that were nationalized in the 1970s. Eight of the ten largest oil producers in the world are NOCs. The others are large integrated private sector energy companies.

World's Top 10 Crude Oil Producers

Since 1960 the world oil market has been significantly influenced by the Organization of Petroleum Exporting Countries (OPEC). The goal of OPEC is to stabilize oil prices by adjusting their production levels and influencing the world's oil supply and demand balance. There are currently eleven members of OPEC, most of which are located in the Middle East and Africa. OPEC countries control close to 70 percent of the world's proven oil reserves and in 2005 accounted for about 41 percent of the world's supply of oil.

Canada holds the second largest oil reserves in the world, with over 178 billion barrels of oil. Over the next decade, Canada's importance as a leading oil producer is expected to increase, as oil sands production is projected to triple. Other key non-OPEC producers include: Russia, the United States, Mexico, China and Norway. Refer Figure 2.3.

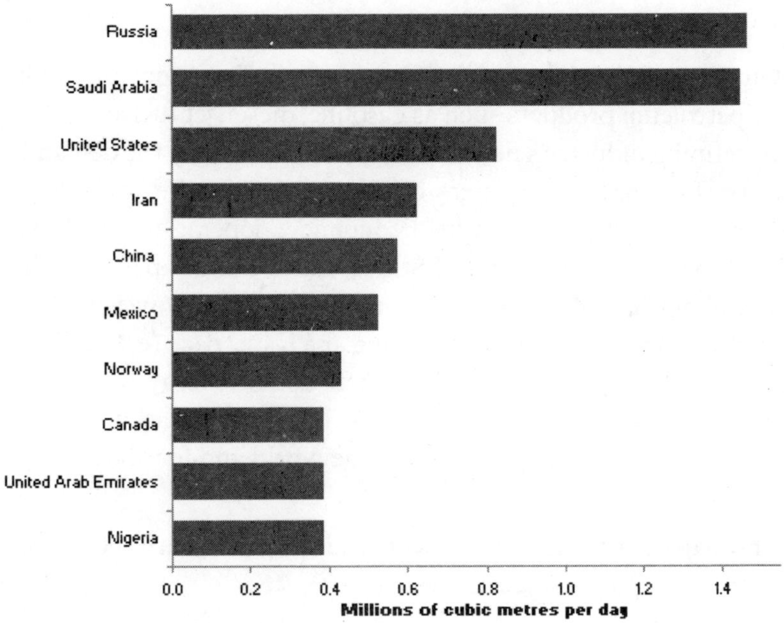

Source: *Oil and Gas Journal*, 2006

Figure 2.3

World's Top 10 Crude Oil Reserve Holders

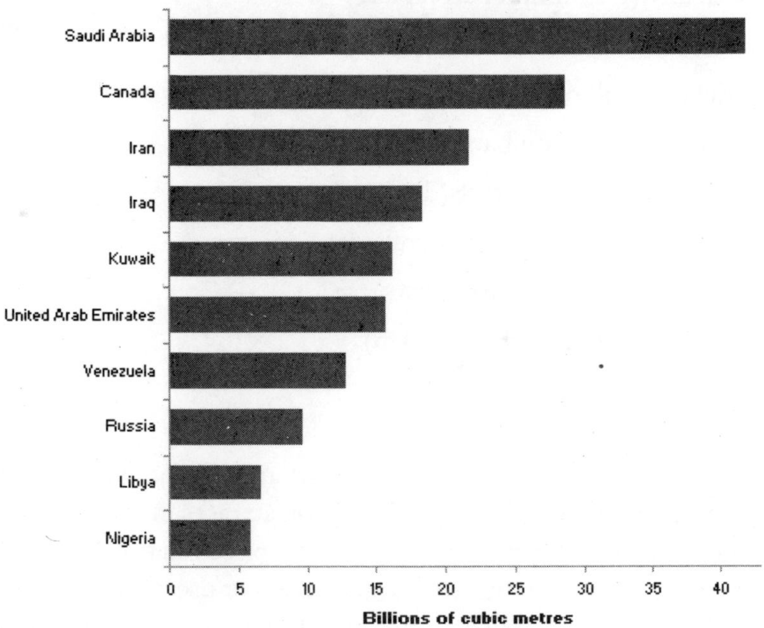

Source: *Oil and Gas Journal*, 2006

Figure 2.4

Oil Consumers

Oil refineries are the primary users of oil. They convert crude oil into useable petroleum products such as gasoline, diesel, jet fuel and home heating oil. The refining industry's need for crude oil is driven by the demand for these products. The main consumers of oil continue to be the industrialized countries of the Organization for Economic Cooperation and Development (OECD), particularly the United States, Europe and Japan, which together consume about half of the world's annual oil output. However, consumption in emerging market regions is expanding at a faster pace (especially in China) as these markets grow rapidly and their use of energy in transportation, industry and residential sectors expands. The transportation sector accounts for about two-thirds of the oil used in the world and for about half of the oil consumed in the United States.

The major consumer countries of crude oil along with their consumption figures pertaining to the year 2004 are:

- United States of America (20.7 million barrels/day)
- China (6.5 million barrels/day)
- Japan (5.4 million barrels/day)
- Germany (2.6 million barrels/day)
- Russia (2.6 million barrels/day)
- India (2.3 million barrels/day)
- Canada (2.3 million barrels/day)
- Brazil (2.2 million barrels/day)
- South Korea (2.1 million barrels/day)
- France (2.0 million barrels/day)
- Mexico (2.0 million barrels/day)

Oil Traders

Oil is a commodity that is widely traded around the world. Similar to other commodities, like coffee and soybeans, oil attracts investors who see an opportunity to make money by speculating on its price volatility. These traders are not generally involved in the actual production or use of oil—they buy and sell paper contracts, not actual oil—but can often have a significant influence on market prices.

The major crude oil exporting countries with their exporting figures pertaining to the year 2004 are:

- Saudi Arabia* (8.73 million barrels per day)
- Russia (6.67 million barrels per day)
- Norway (2.91 million barrels per day)
- Iran* (2.55 million barrels per day)
- Venezuela* (2.36 million barrels per day)
- United Arab Emirates* (2.33 million barrels per day)
- Kuwait* (2.20 million barrels per day)
- Nigeria* (2.19 million barrels per day)
- Mexico (1.80 million barrels per day)

The following is list of the countries with their net import figures that are the major importers of crude oil in the world pertaining to the year 2004 are:

- United States of America (12.1 million barrels per day)
- Japan (5.3 million barrels per day)
- China (2.9 million barrels per day)
- Germany (2.4 million barrels per day)
- South Korea (2.2 million barrels per day)
- France (1.9 million barrels per day)
- Italy (1.7 million barrels per day)
- Spain (1.6 million barrels per day)
- India (1.5 million barrels per day)
- Taiwan (1.0 million barrels per day)

The countries from which India imports crude oil are:

- Venezuela
- Nigeria
- Sudan
- Iran
- Kuwait

Major Oil Markets

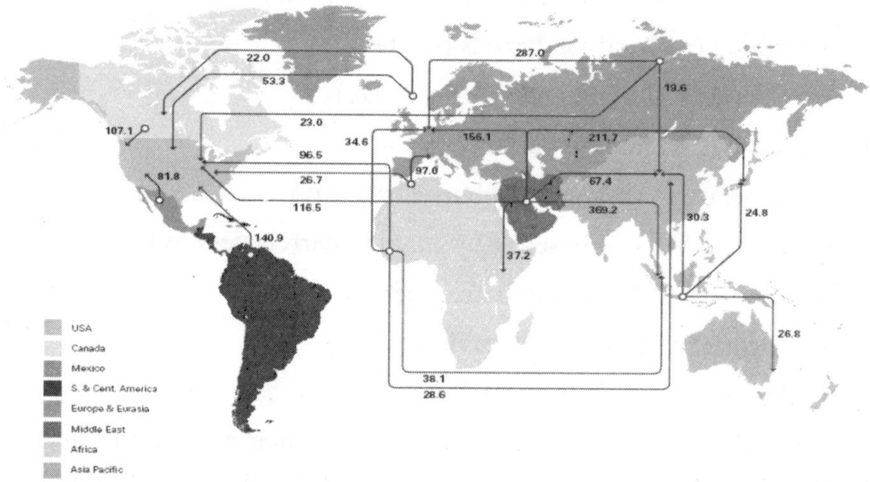

Figure 2.5: Major Trade Movements: Trade Flow Worldwide (million tonnes)

Broadly the markets wherein the oil flows internationally has been classified as the:

- North sea
- Mediterranean
- Far east
- West Africa
- United states
- Middle East Gulf

On elaborating on these markets we see that:

1. North Sea

Market comprises of United Kingdom, Norway, Denmark and Netherland. Market witnesses physical trade of the commodity Brent. For the purpose forward paper of 15-day Brent at the IPE. Brent is also traded through swap contracts and also through Brent CFD's i.e. Contract for Differences.

United Kingdom

With its significant North Sea reserves, the United Kingdom is a major European oil and natural gas producer. The United Kingdom (UK) is an important political and economic power in Europe and the world. It has the second-largest economy in the European Union (EU) with a nominal 2005 gross domestic product (GDP) of $2.2 trillion. The UK is the largest producer of oil and natural gas in the EU. However, after years of being a net exporter of both fuels, the UK became a net importer of natural gas in 2004. Government estimates also predict that the country will become a net importer of oil by the end of the decade. Due to decline in the production of oil by the reason of mismatching of discovery and maturity of oil fields, UK government is aiming at exploiting marginal fields.

Norway

Norway is a major non-OPEC source of oil. It is a major world supplier of oil and natural gas, especially to the European Union. Norway's economy is highly dependent on its offshore oil and natural gas sector, which provides the government with its largest single source of revenue and the largest contribution to GDP. In recent years, high oil prices have made for government budget and current account surpluses, and rising disposable income. Norway's dependence upon oil and gas revenues present long-term challenges for the country, especially because many industry analysts believe that North Sea oil and gas production has already reached or passed its peak. Norway's dependence upon oil and gas revenues present long-term challenges for the country, especially because many industry analysts believe that North Sea oil and gas production has already reached or passed its peak.

2. *Mediterranean*

Mediterranean markets mainly comprises of Algeria, Libya, Egypt, Syria, Tunisia and Russia. Crude mainly flows from former Soviet Union and Iran on FOB basis via Sidi Kerir. Also the oil is shipped via Black Sea port of Novorossiysk and Ukrainian.

Syria

Syria is the only significant oil producer in the Eastern Mediterranean, with crude oil production of an estimated 365,000 barrels per day (bbl/d) and total liquids production of 416,000 bbl/d in 2005. Israel and the Palestinian Authority, Jordan, and Lebanon import almost all of their petroleum requirements. After the initiative enacted by the Cypriot government to proceed in handing out research and drilling rights for expected oil reserves deep under the sea, estimated to be worth some 450 billion USD at current prices.

Egypt

Egypt is a significant oil producer and a rapidly growing natural gas producer. The country's first Liquefied Natural Gas (LNG) export terminal began operation in January 2005. The Suez Canal and Sumed Pipeline are strategic routes for Persian Gulf oil shipments, making Egypt an important transit corridor. Though Egypt's net exports of crude oil and petroleum products have declined in recent years, higher prices on world markets have pushed Egypt's oil revenues upward. Additionally, Egypt's economy is continuing its gradual recovery from the declining growth rates it experienced in 2001 and 2002, but with a growth rate still far below what was achieved in the 1990s.

Russia

Russia holds the world's largest natural gas reserves, the second largest coal reseı ves, and the eighth largest oil reserves. Russia is also the world's largest exporter of natural gas, the second largest oil exporter and the third largest energy consumer. Russia's economic growth over the past seven years has been driven primarily by energy exports, given the increase in Russian oil production and relatively high world oil prices during the period. The share of energy use from coal and nuclear has stayed constant, while energy use from oil has decreased from ?7 percent to around 19 percent. Russia's economy is heavily dependent on oil and natural gas exports, making it vulnerable to fluctuations in world oil prices. According to an International Monetary Fund (IMF) a $1 per barrel increase in Urals blend oil prices for a year is estimated to raise federal budget revenues by 0.35 percent of GDP, or $3.4 billion. In order to manage windfall oil receipts, the government established a stabilization fund in 2004 worth. Raw materials, such as oil, natural gas, and metals, dominate merchandise exports and account for over two-thirds of all Russian export revenues.

3. *West Africa*

Angola, Nigeria, Gabon, Congo, Cameroon are the countries that formed the crude basket of west Africa. Out of these Nigeria and Gabon are members of the OPEC and yield sweet crude for the European and American markets needs.

Angola

Angola, a significant Sub-Saharan Africa oil producer, joined the

Organization of Petroleum Exporting Countries (OPEC) in January 2007. On January 1, 2007, Angola became the 12th member of the Organization of Petroleum Exporting Countries (OPEC). As an OPEC member, Angola will have to pay $2 million per year in membership fees and might be restricted by OPEC quotas on oil production. Angola is the second largest oil producer in Sub-Saharan Africa behind Nigeria. Angola is set to experience oil production increases over the next five year period as new offshore projects come online. Angola exports crude oil primarily to China, the United States, Europe and Latin America. The majority of natural gas produced in Angola is either flared or used in oil recovery. To help reduce flaring, Chevron and Sonangol are planning to build a five-million-ton liquefied natural gas (LNG) plant, which could be operational in 2010.

Nigeria

Nigeria is rich in mineral wealth, with petroleum and natural gas being the country's major mineral products. Nigeria's economic growth primarily comes from the country's oil sector. On April 21, 2007, Nigeria held presidential elections, first time in Nigeria's history that the country passed control from one civilian government to another. During the 16 months preceding the election, militant activity in the Niger Delta (especially near Warri and Port Harcourt) has severely impacted Nigeria's oil production potential by shutting-in an estimated 20 percent of total production. The Nigerian economy is heavily dependent on the oil sector, which accounts for 95 percent of the country's total export revenues.

Gabon

Gabon's economic growth is highly dependent on oil production. As a result, Gabon is seeking to simultaneously increase investment in oil and boost non-oil sector growth for future stability. Gabon's economy is highly dependent on oil production, with the country's oil exports accounting for 51 percent of GDP and 63 percent of government revenues. Gabon hopes to increase growth in non-oil sectors as it is currently facing significant declines in both oil production and reserves. The country's other main exports are timber, uranium and manganese but oil still represents 70 percent of the total exports. In recent years, Gabon has taken steps to market itself as a high end ecotourism destination. Nonetheless, the country is expected to continue relying on oil production in the near future. Gabon has been in a dispute with Equatorial Guinea over three islands in the Corsico Bay that could potentially contain oil deposits. Gabon is also a signatory to the Extractive Industries Transparency Initiative that supports governance and revenue transparency from the oil, gas and mining sectors. In 1996, Gabon retracted its membership in the Organization of Petroleum Exporting Counties (OPEC), citing the organization's high annual dues as the reason.

Algeria

Algeria's hydrocarbon sector accounts for 98 percent of export revenues. Oil and natural gas exports, which made up 98 percent of Algerian exports (by value) in 2006, are the main driver of Algerian economic growth. With continuing investments being made in Algerian oil and gas development, both sectors have potential for increasing production capacity over the next few years.

The Economic Community of West African States (ECOWAS) was formed to promote economic and development growth in West Africa. Major exports from the region include energy products, minerals and agricultural products. The Gambia, Ghana, Guinea, Guinea-Bissau, Liberia, Mali, Niger, Nigeria, Senegal, Sierra Leone, and Togo. The leaders established ECOWAS to promote regional integration and economic growth in West Africa, as well as to create a monetary union in the region. However, ECOWAS has encountered problems in the process of regional integration including: political instability and lack of good governance that has plagued many member countries, the insufficient diversification of national economies, the absence of reliable infrastructure, and the multiplicity of organizations for regional integration with the same objectives

4. *United States*

United States of America has oil reserves but suffers from economic inviability of exploiting those resources. The market comprises of East coast, Gulf Coast and Mid- Continent. East cost is dependent on crude imports from North Sea, West Africa, Middle east and Latin America on FOB basis. Gulf coast is the biggest refining centre in the US. Key domestic crude in the US are WTI, Light Louisiana Sweet (LLS), Heavy Louisana Sweet (HLS),West Texas Sour (WTS),Alaskan North Slope (ANS). Active Spot markets for domestic and imported Crude, which in turn have supported the growth of very large forward, future and Derivative markets.

CANADA

Canada is a net exporter of oil, natural gas, coal, and electricity. It is one of the most important sources for U.S. energy imports. Canada has considerable natural resources and is one of the world's largest producers and exporters of energy. In 2004, Canada produced 18.6 quadrillion British Thermal Units (Btu) of total energy, the fifth-largest amount in the world. Canada is consistently among the top sources for U.S. oil imports, and it is the largest source of U.S. natural gas and electricity imports. In total for 2006, Canada exported to the United States 2.3 million barrels per day (bbl/d) of oil and petroleum products (11 percent of U.S. supply), 3.6 trillion cubic feet of natural gas (16 percent of U.S. supply), and 41.2 billion kilowatt hours of electricity (1 percent of U.S. supply).

MEXICO

Mexico is a major non-OPEC oil producer, with one of the world's largest oil companies, Pemex.

In 2006, Mexico was the sixth-largest oil producer in the world, and the second largest in the Western Hemisphere (behind the United States). State-owned Petroleos Mexicanos (Pemex) holds a monopoly on oil production in the country and is one of the largest oil companies in the world. However, oil production in the country has begun to decrease, as production at the giant Cantarell field declines. The oil sector is a crucial component of Mexico's economy: while its relative importance to the general Mexican economy has declined, the oil sector still generates over 10 percent of the country's export earnings. More importantly, the government relies upon earnings from the oil industry (including taxes and direct payments from Pemex) for one-third of total government revenues. Therefore, any decline in production at Pemex has a direct effect upon the country's overall fiscal balance.

VENENZUELA

Venenzuela contains some of the largest oil and natural gas reserves in the world. It consistently ranks as one the top suppliers of U.S. oil imports and is among the top ten crude oil producers in the world. Venezuela is one of the world's largest exporters of crude oil and the largest in the Western Hemisphere. In 2006, the country was the sixth-largest net oil exporter in the world. The oil sector is of central importance to the Venezuelan economy: it accounts for more than three-quarters of total Venezuelan export revenues, about half of total government revenues, and around one-third of total Gross Domestic Product (GDP). Venezuela was a founding member of the Organization of the Petroleum Exporting Countries (OPEC).

Central America

Although Central America has limited energy resources, it is important to world energy markets as a transit center for oil via the Panama Canal and as a potential energy transit center between North and South America. With hardly any domestic hydrocarbon reserves, Central American countries rely heavily on imported oil for their energy needs. The countries of Central America, including Belize, Costa Rica, El Salvador, Guatemala, Honduras, Nicaragua, and Panama, have traditionally been dependent upon agricultural exports for a large portion of their economic activity. The countries have been especially affected by high world oil prices in recent years. Partially offsetting this, many have been able to secure preferential pricing for oil from Venezuela and Mexico. Despite the lack of sizable oil reserves, Central America remains an important transit center for oil via the Panama Canal and as a potential energy transit center between North and South America.

5. *Middle East Gulf*

Middle East Gulf basket of crude oil basket is the richest in all other markets. It comprises of Saudi Arabia, Iran, Iraq, Kuwait, Oman, Qatar, UAE and Yemen. Other then Oman all is OPEC members. Most Gulf crude is sold on a term basis, partly because of the time required to ship oil to refineries in the US, Europe, Far East and partly because major OPEC Producers such as Saudi Arabia and Kuwait are reluctant to see their Crude being traded on the spot market and term contracts usually prohibit the secondary trading of Gulf Crudes.

Iran

Iran, one of OPEC's founding members, holds the world's third-largest proven oil reserves, and the world's second-largest natural gas reserves and ranks amongst the world's top three holders of proven oil and natural gas reserves. Iran is OPEC's second-largest exporter after Saudi Arabia, and is the fourth-largest exporter of crude oil globally after Saudi Arabia, Russia, and Norway. Natural gas accounts for half of Iran's total domestic energy consumption, while the remaining half is predominately oil consumption. The continued exploration and production of the offshore South Pars natural gas field in the Persian Gulf is a key part of in Iran's energy sector development plan.

Iraq

Security issues continue to hold back rehabilitation of Iraq's energy sector. Iraq has the world's third largest proven petroleum reserves and some of the lowest extraction costs, although just a fraction of its known fields are in development. In 2006, crude oil export revenues represented around 60 percent of GDP and 89 percent of government revenues. Iraq was the world's 15th biggest oil producer and Iraq meets approximately 94 percent of its energy needs with petroleum. Iraq's use of abundant natural gas resources and hydropower is limited. The stabilization of Iraq is highly correlated with Iraq's economic success or failure, which in the medium-term is highly dependent on its hydrocarbons industry.

Kuwait

Kuwait contains 101.5 billion barrels of proven oil reserves (including its share of the Neutral Zone), or roughly 8 percent of the world's total oil reserves. Kuwait's economy is heavily dependent on oil export revenues. Current high oil prices are producing a surge in oil export revenues for Kuwait, with 2005 the best year for oil export revenues in the past decade. Non-oil sectors of the Kuwaiti economy, particularly services, have also experienced strong growth fueled by the inflow of oil revenues. Kuwait would like to diversify its economy away from near-complete dependence on oil revenues. Currently, the country relies on oil revenues for around 90-95 percent of total export earnings and around two-fifths of GDP. Kuwait channels around 10 percent of its oil revenues into the "Future Generations Fund" for the day when oil income runs out. The bulk of this reserve is invested in the United States, Germany, the United Kingdom, France, Japan, and Southeast Asia. In order of importance, foreign assets are believed to be invested in stocks and bonds, fixed yield instruments (mostly short-term), and real estate. Kuwait follows a generally conservative investment policy.

Oman

Oman is a significant non-OPEC oil exporter, although production has declined in recent years. Oman's economy is heavily reliant on oil revenues, which account for about 75 percent of the country's export earnings and 40 percent of its gross domestic product (GDP). The slowdown in economic growth occurred largely as a result of declining oil production in Oman. To help offset these declines, the government has devoted considerable resources to new exploration and production activities, enhanced oil recovery projects, and introduced policies aimed at diversifying the country's economy away from the oil sector. The development of natural gas reserves in Oman is a central part of this effort, and natural gas production is likely to expand considerably during the next several years.

All of Oman's domestic energy consumption is supplied by natural gas and oil, reflecting the country's relative abundance of oil and natural gas reserves.

Qatar

Qatar holds the world's third largest natural gas reserves and is the single largest supplier of liquefied natural gas. Qatar is also a member of OPEC and exports considerable amounts of oil. Qatar is a member of the Organization of the Oil Exporting Countries (OPEC) and is a significant oil producer. Domestically, the vast majority of Qatar's total energy consumption comes from natural gas (79 percent), while the balance is supplied by oil.

Saudi Arabia

Saudi Arabia is the biggest oil producer in the Organization of the Petroleum Exporting Countries (OPEC). With one-fifth of the world's proven oil reserves, some of the lowest production costs, and an aggressive energy sector investment initiative, Saudi Arabia is likely to remain the world's largest net oil exporter. From January-November 2006, Saudi Arabia supplied the United States with 1.4 million barrels per day of crude oil, or approximately 14 percent, of U.S. crude oil imports. Between mid-2003 and mid-2006, Saudi Arabia showed strong economic performance due to high oil prices, increasing oil production and export earnings, paired with structural reforms, economic diversification, and stable macroeconomic policymaking. Saudi Arabia remains heavily dependent on oil and petroleum-related industries, including petrochemicals and petroleum refining. Saudi Arabia is increasing its oil production capacity to 12 million barrels per day (bbl/d), by 2009.

6. Far-East

The markets includes no major oil producer. Australia, Brunei, China,

Indonesia, Malaysia, Papua New Guinea, Vietnam constitutes this markets. Majority of Far East Crude are traded on the basis of the Weekly Asian Petroleum Price Index (APPI).

MALAYSIA

Malaysia is a net exporter of oil and natural gas. Malaysia is a significant Southeast Asian producer of oil and natural gas, although proven oil reserves have declined in recent years. Malaysia's western coast runs alongside the Strait of Malacca, an important route for seaborne energy trade that links the Indian and Pacific Oceans.

AUSTRALIA

Australia is rich in energy resources and leads the world in total coal exports. However, in 2006, severe drought, increasing inflation, and high oil prices all contributed to a deceleration of economic growth. Australia is rich in natural resources with significant petroleum, natural gas and coal reserves. Petroleum accounts for a large share of energy consumption, but due to declining output, Australia is facing a growing dependence on petroleum imports. Australia is one of the few countries belonging to the Organization for Economic Cooperation and Development (OECD) that is a significant net energy exporter.

CHINA

The People's Republic of China (China) is the world's most populous country and the second largest energy consumer behind the United States. Rising oil demand and imports have made China a significant factor in world oil markets. Together with strong economic growth, China's demand for energy is surging rapidly. EIA forecasts that China's oil consumption will increase by almost half a million barrels per day in 2006, or 38 percent of the total growth in world oil demand. China is the world's third-largest net importer of oil behind the United States and Japan, an important factor in world oil markets.

INDIA

India boasts a growing economy, and is increasingly a significant consumer of oil and natural gas. Together with the country's impressive growth, India has also become a significant consumer of energy resources.

According to EIA estimates, India was the fifth largest consumer of oil in the world during 2006.

HISTORY OF CRUDE OIL PRICES

Crude oil prices behave much as any other commodity with wide price swings in times of shortage or oversupply. The crude oil price cycle may extend over several years responding to changes in demand as well as OPEC and non-OPEC supply.

The U.S. petroleum industry's price has been heavily regulated through production or price controls throughout much of the twentieth century. In the post World War II era U.S. oil prices at the wellhead averaged $24.20 per barrel adjusted for inflation to 2006 dollars. In the absence of price controls the U.S. price would have tracked the world price averaging $26.16. Over the same post war period the median for the domestic and the adjusted world price of crude oil was $18.53 in 2006 prices. That means that only fifty percent of the time from 1947 to 2006 have oil prices exceeded $18.53 per barrel. (See note in box on right.)

Until the March 28, 2000 adoption of the $22-$28 price band for the OPEC basket of crude, oil prices only exceeded $24.00 per barrel in response to war or conflict in the Middle East. With limited spare production capacity OPEC abandoned its price band in 2005 and was powerless to stem a surge in oil prices which was reminiscent of the late 1970s.

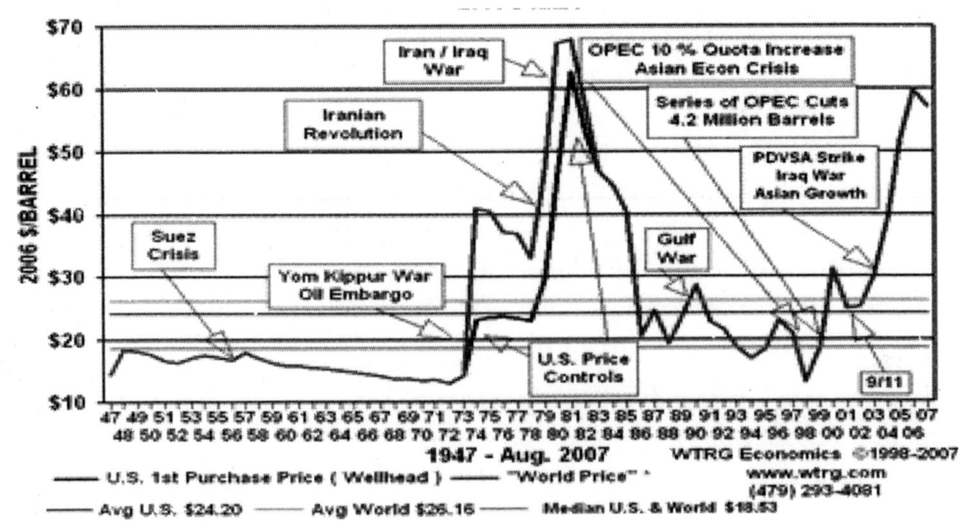

Figure 2.6: Crude Oil Prices 1947-2007 (Dollars)

*World Price—The only very long-term price series that exists is the U.S. average wellhead or first purchase price of crude. When discussing long-term price behavior this presents a problem since the U.S. imposed price controls on domestic production from late 1973 to January 1981. In order to present a consistent series and also reflect the difference between international prices and U.S. prices we created a world oil price series that was consistent with the U.S. wellhead price adjusting the wellhead price by adding the difference between the refiners acquisition price of imported crude and the refiners average acquisition price of domestic crude.

Post-World War II

Pre-Embargo Period

Crude Oil prices ranged between $2.50 and $3.00 from 1948 through the end of the 1960s. The price oil rose from $2.50 in 1948 to about $3.00 in 1957. When viewed in 2006 dollars an entirely different story emerges with crude oil prices fluctuating between $17-$18 during the same period. The apparent 20% price increase just kept up with inflation.

From 1958 to 1970 prices were stable at about $3.00 per barrel, but in real terms the price of crude oil declined from above $17 to below $14 per barrel. The decline in the price of crude when adjusted for inflation was amplified for the international producer in 1971 and 1972 by the weakness of the US dollar.

OPEC was formed in 1960 with five founding members Iran, Iraq, Kuwait, Saudi Arabia and Venezuela. Two of the representatives at the initial meetings had studied the Texas Railroad Commission's methods of influencing price through limitations on production. By the end of 1971 six other nations had joined the group: Qatar, Indonesia, Libya, United Arab Emirates, Algeria and Nigeria. From the foundation of the Organization of Petroleum Exporting Countries through 1972 member countries experienced steady decline in the purchasing power of a barrel of oil.

Throughout the post war period exporting countries found increasing demand for their crude oil but a 40% decline in the purchasing power of a barrel of oil. In March 1971, the balance of power shifted. That month the Texas Railroad Commission set proration at 100 percent for the first time. This meant that Texas producers were no longer limited in the amount of oil that they could produce. More importantly, it meant that the power to control crude oil prices shifted from the United States (Texas, Oklahoma and Louisiana) to OPEC. Another way to say it is that there was no more spare capacity and therefore no tool to put an upper limit on prices. A little over two years later OPEC would, through the unintended consequence of war, get a glimpse at the extent of its power to influence prices.

Crises in Iran and Iraq

Events in Iran and Iraq led to another round of crude oil price increases in 1979 and 1980. The Iranian revolution resulted in the loss of 2 to 2.5 million barrels per day of oil production between November 1978 and June 1979. At one point production almost halted.

While the Iranian revolution was the proximate cause of what would be the highest prices in post-WWII history, its impact on prices would have been limited and of relatively short duration had it not been for subsequent events. Shortly after the revolution production was up to 4 million barrels per day.

Iran weakened by the revolution was invaded by Iraq in September 1980. By November the combined production of both countries was only a million barrels per day and 6.5 million barrels per day less than a year before. As a consequence worldwide crude oil production was 10 percent lower than in 1979.

The combination of the Iranian revolution and the Iraq-Iran War cause crude oil prices to more than double increasing from $14 in 1978 to $35 per barrel in 1981.

Twenty-six years later Iran's production is only two-thirds of the level reached under the government of Reza Pahlavi, the former Shah of Iran.

Iraq's production remains about 1.5 million barrels below its peak before the Iraq-Iran War.

US Oil Price Controls—Bad Policy?

The rapid increase in crude prices from 1973 to 1981 would have been much less were it not for United States energy policy during the post Embargo period. The US imposed price controls on domestically produced oil in an attempt to lessen the impact of the 1973-74, price increase. The obvious result of the price controls was that U.S. consumers of crude oil paid about 50 percent more for imports than domestic production and U.S. producers received less than world market price. In effect, the domestic petroleum industry was subsidizing the U.S. consumer.

Did the policy achieve its goal? In the short term, the recession induced by the 1973-74 crude oil price rise was less because U.S. consumers faced lower prices than the rest of the world. However, it had other effects as well.

In the absence of price controls U.S. exploration and production would certainly have been significantly greater. Higher petroleum prices faced by consumers would have resulted in lower rates of consumption: automobiles would have had higher miles per gallon sooner, homes and commercial buildings would have been better insulated and improvements in industrial energy efficiency would have been greater than they were during this period. As a consequence, the United States would have been less dependent on imports in 1979-80 and the price increase in response to Iranian and Iraqi supply interruptions would have been significantly less.

OPEC's Failure to Control Crude Oil Prices

OPEC has seldom been effective at controlling prices. While often referred to as a cartel, OPEC does not satisfy the definition. One of the primary requirements is a mechanism to enforce member quotas. The old joke went something like this. What is the difference between OPEC and the Texas Railroad Commission? OPEC doesn't have any Texas Rangers! The only enforcement mechanism that has ever existed in OPEC was Saudi spare capacity.

With enough spare capacity at times to be able to increase production sufficiently to offset the impact of lower prices on its own revenue, Saudi Arabia could enforce discipline by threatening to increase production enough to crash prices. In reality even this was not an OPEC enforcement mechanism unless OPEC's goals coincided with those of Saudi Arabia.

During the 1979-80 period of rapidly increasing prices, Saudi Arabia's oil minister Ahmed Yamani repeatedly warned other members of OPEC that high prices would lead to a reduction in demand. His warnings fell on deaf ears.

Surging prices caused several reactions among consumers: better insulation in new homes, increased insulation in many older homes, more energy efficiency in industrial processes, and automobiles with higher efficiency. These factors along with a global recession caused a reduction in demand which led to falling crude prices. Unfortunately for OPEC only the global recession was temporary. Nobody rushed to remove insulation from their homes or to replace energy efficient plants and equipment—much of the reaction to the oil price increase of the end of the decade was permanent and would never respond to lower prices with increased consumption of oil.

Higher prices also resulted in increased exploration and production outside of OPEC. From 1980 to 1986 non-OPEC production increased 10 million barrels per day. OPEC was faced with lower demand and higher supply from outside the organization.

From 1982 to 1985, OPEC attempted to set production quotas low enough to stabilize prices. These attempts met with repeated failure as various members of OPEC produced beyond their quotas. During most of this period Saudi Arabia acted as the swing producer cutting its production in an attempt to stem the free fall in prices. In August of 1985, the Saudis tired of this role. They linked their oil price to the spot market for crude and by early 1986, increased production from 2 MMBPD to 5 MMBPD. Crude oil prices plummeted below $10 per barrel by mid-1986. Despite the fall in prices Saudi revenue remained about the same with higher volumes compensating for lower prices.

A December 1986 OPEC price accord set to target $18 per barrel bit it was already breaking down by January of 1987and prices remained weak.

The price of crude oil spiked in 1990 with the lower production and uncertainty associated with the Iraqi invasion of Kuwait and the ensuing Gulf War. The world and particularly the Middle East had a much harsher view of Saddam Hussein invading Arab Kuwait than they did Persian Iran. The proximity to the world's largest oil producer helped to shape the reaction.

Following what became known as the Gulf War to liberate Kuwait crude oil prices entered a period of steady decline until in 1994 inflation adjusted prices attained their lowest level since 1973.

The price cycle then turned up. The United States economy was strong and the Asian Pacific region was booming. From 1990 to 1997 world oil consumption increased 6.2 million barrels per day. Asian consumption accounted for all but 300,000 barrels per day of that gain and contributed to a price recovery that extended into 1997. Declining Russian production contributed to the price recovery. Between 1990 and 1996 Russian production declined over 5 million barrels per day.

OPEC continued to have mixed success in controlling prices. There were mistakes in timing of quota changes as well as the usual problems in maintaining production discipline among its member countries.

The price increases came to a rapid end in 1997 and 1998 when the impact of the economic crisis in Asia was either ignored or severely underestimated by OPEC. In December 1997 OPEC increased its quota by 2.5 million barrels per day (10 percent) to 27.5 MMBPD effective January 1, 1998. The rapid growth in Asian economies had come to a halt. In 1998 Asian Pacific oil consumption declined for the first time since 1982. The combination of lower consumption and higher OPEC production sent prices into a downward spiral. In response, OPEC cut quotas by 1.25 million b/d in April and another 1.335 million in July. Price continued down through December 1998.

Prices began to recover in early 1999 and OPEC reduced production another 1.719 million barrels in April. As usual not all of the quotas were observed but between early 1998 and the middle of 1999 OPEC production dropped by about 3 million barrels per day and was sufficient to move prices above $25 per barrel.

With minimal Y2K problems and growing US and world economies the price continued to rise throughout 2000 to a post 1981 high. Between April and October, 2000 three successive OPEC quota increases totaling 3.2 million barrels per day were not able to stem the price increases. Prices finally started down following another quota increase of 500,000 effective November 1, 2000.

GEOPOLITICAL FACTORS

'Geopolitics traditionally indicates the links and causal relationships between political power and geographic space. It is often seen as a body of thought assaying specific strategic prescriptions based on the relative importance of land power and sea power in world history. The geopolitical tradition had some consistent concerns, like the geopolitical correlates of power in world politics, the identification of international core areas, and the relationships between naval and terrestrial capabilities'.—*Oyvind Osterud*.

Energy is the vital ingredient in the world economy. While we are working hard on energy efficiency and investing to develop new energy technologies, oil and natural gas will remain critical for many years to come. Economic development around the world means global demand for oil and gas will continue growing in the near term. Most significantly, China's rapid growth and increase in overall energy demand continue to affect energy markets. Some analysts estimate that China could account for as much as one-third of the world's marginal increase in oil demand in the coming years.

As a result, the world must find and develop more reliable supplies of oil and gas at prices that permit sustained economic growth. Unfortunately, it is almost an axiom in the petroleum business that oil and gas are most often found in countries with challenging political regimes or difficult physical geography.

Several realities shape our thinking about energy security and how we should build reliability into our energy supplies:

- Two-thirds of the world's known oil reserves are in the Middle East.
- Imports supply roughly half of the oil and 15 percent of natural gas consumed by the United States, and an even greater share of the needs of some of the United State's most important allies and economic partners.
- Oil-supply shocks in any region of the world will have an impact on the U.S. economy through the instantaneous operation of international oil markets.

Reliability Through Diversification

Energy investments are costly and risky, requiring long-term commitments. Recognizing this reality, U.S. energy policy seeks to encourage expansion and diversification of energy supplies. A number of regions are attracting increasing interest from energy companies in the United States and elsewhere. We see interesting prospects for expanded oil and gas production in the Caspian region, Russia, West Africa, and North and South America, as well as the promise of increased oil and gas production in the Middle East. In each of these regions, our policy aims to support private sector-led development of energy resources by reducing the political uncertainty that otherwise might hinder needed investment.

Russia and the Caspian Basin

Russia already is an energy superpower. To achieve its full potential, Russia needs to strengthen corporate governance and the legal/regulatory framework for business, improve its foreign investment climate, allow competition in the transportation system, open the gas and oil companies Gazprom and Transneft up to reform and competition, improve its technological capabilities, and move domestic energy prices to world levels.

The Caspian Basin has tremendous potential, offering the possibility of production increases from 1.6 million barrels/day (b/d) in 2001 to 5.0 million b/d in 2010. The key issues in Caspian energy development at the moment are to: (1) complete the second pillar of the East-West Energy Corridor by developing the South Caucasus natural gas pipeline; (2) improve the investment climate throughout the region; and (3) bring Kazakhstani oil into the East-West corridor.

Multiple pipelines that economically bring Caspian resources to the world market strengthen the sovereignty and economic viability of the new nation states in the region. U.S. efforts in the Caspian are intended to complement ¾ not detract from ¾ U.S. support for Russia's efforts to develop its energy export potential.

Africa

Africa is playing an increasingly important role as an energy supplier to U.S. and global markets. In 2003, both Nigeria and Angola were among the top 10 suppliers of oil to the United States. Oil production generates substantial revenue in countries such as Nigeria, Angola, Gabon, Equatorial Guinea, Republic of Congo, Chad, and Cameroon. Sao Tome and Mauritania also may become oil suppliers in the coming years. Foreign direct investment is needed to develop African energy resources as most new fields are in deepwater offshore environments that require advanced capital-intensive facilities for development. Growing oil and gas production could be a powerful engine for national economic development in these countries. However, the Niger Delta experience of 2002, in which protesters stormed oil facilities and caused their temporary shutdown, shows that oil can also be a disruptive force if a country's oil revenues are not managed in a fair and transparent manner. Nigeria has learned from its experience in the Niger Delta and is setting an example on transparency and economic reform enabled by oil revenues that the United States hopes other countries in Africa will follow.

North America

The most important and reliable sources of energy for the United States are its neighbors and we are strengthening our energy cooperation with Canada and Mexico. Senior energy experts from Canada, Mexico, and the United States recently released a North American Energy Picture report that, for the first time, jointly measures energy stocks, trading balances, and energy flows. What often goes unrecognized is that North American energy trade is a two-way street. Mexico is becoming an important source of U.S. oil imports. At the same time, the United States is a net natural gas exporter to Mexico, and U.S. refineries supply over 15 percent of Mexico's refined petroleum products.

The reliability of North American energy trade is enhanced by geographic proximity. More important than geography, however, are the rule of law and predictable investment conditions created by the North American Free Trade Agreement, integrated pipeline networks, and long-term reliable supply relationships. We are continually working to enhance this framework of rule of law and predictable investment conditions in North America even as we seek to build similar frameworks in other regions.

Venezuela

Venezuela and the United States have enjoyed strong historical energy ties. Venezuelan oil policy, until recently, has been built upon a reputation of reliability. Unfortunately, actions and statements by parties from all sides over the last 18 months have called into question the priority Venezuelans place on their reputation as a reliable supplier. The United States will continue to work to help Venezuelans resolve their political differences. But until a constitutional, democratic, peaceful, and electoral solution is achieved, and the level of rhetoric lowered, world energy markets simply cannot view Venezuela with the same certainty that they once did. When the Venezuelan parties show a commitment to reconciliation, they will find a willing and ready partner in the United States.

Saudi Arabia and the Gulf Producers

The Middle East holds some two-thirds of proven world oil reserves. The size of its reserves, combined with its low production cost, guarantees that the Middle East will continue to play a pivotal role in the world energy market. Saudi Arabia plays a key role in global oil markets as the world's largest oil exporter. Moreover, Saudi Arabia supports international energy security by maintaining considerable excess production capacity that can be brought on line quickly in the event of a serious supply disruption anywhere in the world.

Diversifying global oil supplies should not be interpreted as diversifying "away" from Saudi Arabia or other Gulf producers. Gulf producers will continue to have an indispensable role in the world market, and the United

States encourages them to increase foreign investment and steadily expand supplies. What we seek is better balance and a more flexible, resilient oil market that responds to price signals.

In this regard, Gulf producers could reap greater benefits by opening their economies to more private investment so that oil and gas capacity could grow and energy supplies could respond more fully to shifts in demand. Investment in natural gas is one sector where this process is beginning. Once only for local or regional use or wasted through harmful flaring, natural gas in the form of Liquefied Natural Gas (LNG) has become an increasingly globally traded energy source for key markets. Qatar is working with major international energy companies to become a leading LNG exporter.

In the United Arab Emirates, the successful Taweelah power and water privatization project is another example of the dynamic role foreign investment can play in the energy sector. The United States supports these positive private investment initiatives because they expand and diversify its energy sources, provide opportunities for U.S. companies, and foster economic growth in energy-producing nations.

Promoting Transparency and a Good Investment Climate

Promoting transparency and good governance is a key part of the U.S. strategy of encouraging diversification. Oil and gas projects are controversial in many developing countries because revenue flows are hidden, or diverted, and average citizens feel they receive no benefit from their country's natural wealth. The United States wants oil-producing countries to invest energy revenue in solid and sustainable economic development for their populations, not only because it is the right thing to do, but also because it builds political support for the further development of energy projects. Democratic processes and the development of responsive governing institutions promote political and economic stability, the use of mineral wealth for poverty reduction and economic development, and the reduction of oil-related conflicts in energy-producing countries around the world.

A comprehensive approach to transparency is particularly important. At the June 2003 Group of Eight (G-8) Summit, President Bush and the other leaders endorsed a comprehensive action plan on Fighting Corruption and Improving Transparency. The core of this approach is forging a partnership to give willing host countries technical and political support to strengthen domestic institutions and enhance transparency and accountability. We want to focus specifically on budget, procurement, and concession-letting transparency, including G-8 support for technical needs identified by experts.

In addition to support for developing country action plans in these areas, the G-8 leaders committed to:

1. Denying safe haven to corrupt leaders and their assets by, among other things, denying visas to corrupt officials.
2. Pushing for accelerated implementation of the Organization for Economic Cooperation and Development's Anti-Bribery Convention.
3. Encouraging the World Bank and other international financial institutions to insist on greater transparency in the use of funds by borrowing countries.
4. G-8 countries are supporting voluntary compacts among governments, the companies operating in those countries, and civil society to improve transparency in public financial management and accountability. These compacts outline both the political commitment of the G-8 and host governments to achieve specific mutually agreed transparency objectives, with assistance from the G-8 and international financial institutions, and a specific concrete action plan to achieve those goals.

In the long-run we need new technologies such as hydrogen and carbon sequestration that can fuel our economy while increasing energy security and minimizing the environmental impact of energy use. In the interim, our international energy policy must address the familiar challenges posed by a hydrocarbon-based economy where oil reserves are concentrated in various challenging regions of the world. Transparency and good governance are increasingly important to sustaining international investments in energy development in regions of opportunity for energy production. The United States will continue to engage intensively with energy partners all over the world to diversify supplies, improve investment opportunities, and assure that market forces work as transparently and efficiently as possible.

Strategic Petroleum Reserves (SPR)

US Perspective

The Strategic Petroleum Reserve (SPR) is an emergency petroleum store maintained by the United States Department of Energy. The US SPR is the largest emergency supply in the world with the current capacity to hold up to 727 million barrels (116 million m^3) of crude oil. The second largest emergency supply of petroleum is Japan's with a 2003 reported capacity of 579 million barrels.

The current inventory is displayed on the SPR's website. As of January 2, 2008, the current inventory was 697.5 million barrels. At current market prices ($100 a barrel) the SPR holds almost $70 billion worth of petroleum.

The United States started the petroleum reserve in 1975 after oil supplies were cut off during the 1973-74 oil embargo, to mitigate future temporary supply disruptions. According to the World Fact book, the United States imports a net 12 million barrels of oil a day (MMbd), so the SPR holds about a 57-day supply. However, the maximum total withdrawal capability from the SPR is only 4.4 MMbd.

Access to the reserve is determined by the conditions written into the 1975 Energy Policy and Conservation Act (EPCA), primarily to counter a severe supply interruption. The maximum removal rate, by physical constraints, is 4.4 million barrels per day (8 m^3/s). Oil could begin entering the marketplace 13 days after a Presidential order. The Dept. of Energy says that it has about 59 days of import protection in the SPR. This, combined with private sector inventory protection, is estimated to equal 115 days of imports.

The SPR was created following the 1973 energy crisis. The EPCA of December 22, 1975, made it policy for the U.S. to establish a reserve up to one billion barrels (159 million m^3) of petroleum. A number of existing storage sites were acquired in 1977. Construction of the first surface facilities began in June 1977. On July 21, 1977, the first oil—approximately 412,000 barrels (66,000 m^3) of Saudi Arabian light crude—was delivered to the SPR. Fill was suspended in FY 1995 to devote budget resources to refurbishing the SPR equipment and extending the life of the complex. The current SPR sites are expected to be usable until around 2025. Fill was resumed in 1999.

Establishment of the SPR

From the mid-1970s until 2006, world markets have had to absorb roughly five significant spikes in the price of crude oil and petroleum products. Whether driven by disruptions in the physical supply of crude or refined fuels, or by uncertainties owing to international conflicts and instabilities, these price increases can have consequences for the United States balance of trade and, owing to the relative inelasticity of demand for gasoline at prices up to $3.00 per gallon, siphon away disposable income that might be spent to support other economic activity or savings.

The origin of the U.S. Strategic Petroleum Reserve (SPR) stems from the 1973 Arab-Israeli War. In response to the United States' support for Israel, the Organization of Arab Exporting Countries (OAPEC) imposed an oil embargo on the United States, the Netherlands, and Canada, and reduced production. While some Arab crude did reach the United States, the price of imported crude oil rose from roughly $4/barrel (bbl) during the last quarter of 1973 to an average price of $12.50/bbl in 1974. While no amount of strategic stocks can insulate any oil consuming nation from paying the market price for oil in a supply emergency, the availability of strategic stocks can help blunt the magnitude of the market's reaction to a crisis. More importantly, one of the original perceptions of the value of a strategic stockpile was that its very existence would discourage the use of oil as a political weapon. The embargo imposed by the Arab producers was a stark, politically motivated event intended to create a very discernible physical disruption. This probably explains, in part, why the genesis of the SPR was focused especially on deliberate and dramatic physical disruptions of oil flow.

In response to the experience of the embargo, Congress authorized the Strategic Petroleum Reserve (SPR) in the Energy Policy and Conservation Act (EPCA, P.L. 94-163) to help prevent a repetition of the economic dislocation caused by the Arab oil embargo. The program is managed by the Department of Energy (DOE). Physically, the SPR comprises five underground storage facilities, hollowed out from naturally occurring salt domes, located in Texas and Louisiana. The caverns were finished by injecting water and removing the brine. Similarly, oil is removed by displacing it with water injection. For this reason, crude stored in the SPR remains undisturbed, except in the event of a sale or exchange. Multiple injections of water, over time, will compromise the structural integrity of the caverns. By 2005, the capacity of the SPR reached 727 million barrels. It held virtually 700 million barrels before Hurricanes Katrina and Rita in 2005. Following the storms, some crude was loaned or sold, leaving the Reserve with 685 million barrels in mid-March 2006. As already noted, it was hoped that the creation of a significant operational reserve of crude oil would discourage the use of oil as a weapon. In the event of an interruption, introduction into the market of oil from the Reserve was expected to help calm markets, mitigate sharp price spikes, and reduce the economic dislocation that had accompanied the 1973 disruption. In so doing, the Reserve would also buy time—time for the crisis to sort itself out or for diplomacy to seek some resolution before a potentially severe oil shortage escalated the crisis beyond diplomacy. The SPR was to contain enough crude oil to replace imports for 90 days, with a goal initially of 500 million barrels in storage. In May 1978, plans for a 750-million barrel Reserve were implemented.

SPR oil is sold by competitive sale. A Notice of Sale is issued, including the volume, characteristics, and location of the petroleum for sale; delivery dates and procedures for submitting offers; as well as measures for assuring performance and financial responsibility. Bids are reviewed by DOE and awards offered. The Department of Energy estimates that oil could enter the market roughly two weeks after the appearance of a notice of sale.

The Arab oil embargo also fostered the establishment of the International Energy Agency (IEA) to develop plans and measures for emergency responses to energy crises. Strategic stocks are one of the policies included in the agency International Energy Program (IEP). Signatories to the IEA5 are committed to maintaining emergency reserves, developing programs for demand restraint in the event of emergencies, and agreeing to participate in allocation of oil deliveries among the signatory nations to balance the shortage among IEA members.

While the U.S. SPR holds government held crude oil stocks, some IEA nations require a level of stocks to be held by the private sector or by both the public and private sectors. Including the U.S. SPR, roughly two-thirds of IEA stocks are held by the oil industry, whereas one-third is held by governments and supervisory agencies.

Emergency Sales and Loans

Oil has been released and sold in the open market under emergency conditions just twice, in 1991 and 2005. However, oil has also been temporarily loaned out or exchanged to private oil companies on several occasions, then returned to the reserve after the specified loan period including "premium barrels". These oil exchanges include an ARCO pipeline disruption in April 1996; an exchange of 11 million barrels (1,800,000 m^3) of Maya crude oil for 8.5 million barrels (1,400,000 m^3) of higher value crude oil in 1998; a dry dock collapse in June 2000 just north of the Intracoastal Waterway near Lake Charles, Louisiana used by CITGO and ConocoPhillips refineries; and temporary loans in response to supply disruptions following Hurricane Lili in 2002, Hurricane Ivan in 2004, and Hurricane Katrina in 2005.

On August 31, 2005, President George W. Bush authorized the SPR to loan oil to help refineries whose operations had been affected by Hurricane Katrina. In addition, the President announced the sale of 30 million barrels of oil as part of a coordinated, international sale of 60 million barrels to maintain supplies and calm markets. Katrina had shut down an estimated 95% of crude production and 88% of natural gas output in the Gulf of Mexico. This amounted to a quarter of total U.S. output. About 735 oil and natural gas rigs and platforms had been evacuated due to the hurricane.

On April 25, 2006, George W. Bush announced a temporary halt to petroleum deposits to the SPR as part of a four point program to alleviate high fuel prices.

Emergency Sales to Israel

According to the 1975 Second Sinai withdrawal document signed by the United States and Israel, in an emergency the U.S. is obligated to make oil available for sale to Israel for up to 5 years.

The SPR and Hurricanes Ivan, Katrina, and Rita (2004-05)

Crude oil prices exceeded $50/barrel during October 2004, accompanied by declines in crude and product inventories. A major factor was Hurricane Ivan, which rampaged through the Gulf Coast in mid-September and temporarily interrupted more than 70% of offshore crude production, affecting crude oil deliveries to refineries. On September 23, 2004, the Administration agreed to a request placed to the Department of Energy from a couple of refineries seeking to borrow crude oil from the SPR, to be replaced within a short period of time. Subsequent requests raised the amount of borrowed crude to roughly 5.4 million barrels. The volume of oil returned was greater than the volume borrowed, in keeping with the mechanics of a "swap" of oil conducted in 2002 under comparable circumstances.

Critics claimed that it was a belated and insufficient use of the SPR, and that it even backfired in terms of calming the market. However, because the swap was limited and sharply focused, and represented such a tiny volume of oil, it may have been a misinterpretation to see it as intended to do anything more than it did—which was to provide supply to refiners to whom deliveries of crude were temporarily affected by Hurricane Ivan. As there is provision in law for limited uses of the SPR to mitigate the effects of domestic interruptions in supply, the Administration argued that the decision to loan oil to these refineries was consistent with its overall SPR policy not to suspend fill or to authorize a broader drawdown for the purpose of reducing high prices. The swap was not characterized as a broader market-calming measure. The fact that the price of oil rose even after the announcement was a reflection of much stronger factors and uncertainties then prevailing in world markets than could be offset by such a limited swap.

Hurricanes Katrina and Rita in 2005 shut down oil and gas production from the Outer Continental Shelf in the Gulf of Mexico, the source for 25% of U.S. crude oil production and 20% of natural gas output. Katrina, which made landfall on August 29, 2005, resulted in the shutdown of most crude oil and natural gas production in the Gulf of Mexico, as well as a great deal of refining capacity in Louisiana and Alabama. Offshore oil and gas production was resuming when Hurricane Rita made landfall on September 24 and an additional 4.8 million barrels per day (mbd) of refining capacity in Texas and nearby Louisiana was closed.

Combining the effects of both storms, 1.3 mbd of refining—about 8% of national capability—was shut down, reducing the supply of domestically refined fuels commensurately. Much of the refined product shortfall was made up by imports of refined products, some of which were made available by strategic supplies released by International Energy Agency (IEA) member nations on September 2. As part of the IEA drawdown, 30 million barrels of crude oil were made available from the SPR, which holds only crude. Only 11 million barrels was sold from the SPR, in part because limited refinery capacity reduced the call on crude.

Stocks of heating oil proved more than adequate during the winter of 2005-06. There were no calls for use of the SPR during that winter. More attention was focused on providing economic relief through the Low Income Home Energy Assistance Program to low-income heating oil consumers.

A Change in the Market Dynamics (2005-06)

As the history of the SPR lays bare, there are differences of opinion over what should be termed a "severe energy supply interruption." A spike in crude and product prices often stirs calls for use of the SPR. However, as already noted, the SPR is intended by statute to ameliorate discernible physical shortages of crude oil. The price of gasoline and other petroleum products rose sharply following Hurricanes Katrina and Rita. However, these price increases were not a response to any shortage of crude, but to shortages of products owing to the shutdown of major refining capacity in the United States and to an interruption of product transportation systems. Demand growth that has strapped refinery capacity even before (as well as after) the hurricanes, has significantly altered the traditional correlation between crude and product prices. During 2005 and 2006, owing to pressure on product supplies and continued international tensions, the price of products has been divorced, in part, from its traditional correlation with crude supply and price. Depending upon future events, this new dynamic may complicate reconciling developments in markets with possible use of the SPR.

Limitations

The Strategic Petroleum Reserve is exclusively a crude oil reserve, not a stockpile of refined petrochemical products, such as gasoline, diesel and kerosene. Although there are small-scale (2 million barrels) heating oil reserves in Connecticut, Rhode Island and New Jersey under the aegis of the Department of Energy (DOE), the Federal government maintains no gasoline reserves on anything like the scale of the SPR. Consequently, while the US enjoys some protection from disruptions in oil supplies, it would have to depend on other stockpiling members of the International Energy Agency for relief from any major disruption to refinery operations. Since no new refineries have been constructed in the US for thirty years, there is little reserve capacity. This was illustrated during Hurricane Katrina, when many of the Gulf coast oil refining complexes were disrupted for some time.

There have been suggestions that the DOE should stockpile both gasoline and jet fuel, to rectify this weakness. However, since gasoline has a short shelf-life, a gasoline reserve would require regular refreshment of stocks, which would make it vulnerable to inappropriate draw downs. However, a jet fuel reserve may be a possibility since other countries have strategic reserves of jet fuel. The Secretary of Energy, Samuel Bodman, has said the Department will consider refined products as part of the expansion between 1 billion and 1.5 billion barrels.

Indian Perspective

India will begin construction of strategic crude oil storages this year as insurance against disruptions during wars and other emergencies.

Of the three sites selected to hold 5 million tonnes a year of crude oil reserves, equivalent to country's 15 days requirement, Visakhapatnam in Andhra Pradesh would be the first site with Hindustan Construction Co emerging as the lowest bidder, official sources said.

The contract is likely to be awarded this week. Visakhapatnam will have underground caverns to hold 1.33 million tonnes of crude oil that will be managed by Indian Strategic Petroleum Reserves Ltd, a subsidiary of Oil Industry Development Board. Two other sites identified for the construction of crude storage facilities are Mangalore (1.5 million tonnes) and Podur (2.5 million tonnes), some 40-km from Mangalore.

India has said it eventually wants to double the overall strategic reserve capacity to 73.3 million barrels, twice the 15 days cover planned currently, but his is yet to be approved by the central cabinet. Sources said Vizag site has already secured environment clearance and land acquisition is almost complete.

The Vizag project envisages storage of high sulphur and low sulphur crude oil in the ratio of 70% and 30% respectively in two caverns.

The government set up Indian Strategic Petroleum Reserves Ltd in 2006, to build and operate the storage facilities. A total investment of Rs 112, 67 crores for the strategic reserves project had been approved with an annual operating cost of $ 20 million.

The 5-million tonne strategic reserves would be in addition to stocks already held by refineries to meet their own crude needs. At present, refiners maintain oil reserves representing three weeks of consumption, but the country has no strategic stockpiles.

The government has been planning since the mid-1990s to build and maintain strategic crude reserves but funding and who would own the reserves have hampered the plans.

The strategic reserve at Mangalore and Visakhapatnam will be funded collected through levy of Rs 2,500 per tonne cess on domestically produced crude oil, they said.

THE ROLE OF OPEC IN THE 21ST CENTURY

When the Organization of Petroleum Exporting Countries (OPEC) was established on September 14, 1960, it consisted of just five developing countries. Who would have expected this small organization to soar to prominence on the world stage little more than a decade later, and to retain a high profile into the new millennium?

This article seeks to explain why it was possible for a small group of developing countries, with all the odds stacked against them in a world dominated by the established industrial powers, to achieve this success.

OPEC's Role

The answer clearly lies in OPEC's role in the international oil market. This role is as valid today as it was four decades ago. Further, it appears likely that this will remain the case for decades to come. We will now examine this role more closely and then address the issue as to whether OPEC should seek to revise it for the new millennium.

The founding members of the Organization of the Oil Exporting Countries are Iran, Iraq, Kuwait, Saudi Arabia and Venezuela. OPEC's six other members are Qatar (which joined in 1961), Indonesia (joined in 1962), Libya (joined in 1962), the United Arab Emirates (which took over the membership of Abu Dhabi in 1974), Algeria (joined in 1969) and Nigeria (joined in 1971).

This membership provides a geographical spread from Latin America in the west to Southeast Asia in the east, with Africa and the Middle East in between. The total population of the OPEC members is nearly half a billion, and there is a rich diversity of cultures, religions and languages. However, the eleven members are united by their common status as oil-producing developing countries.

OPEC's objectives are spelled out in the OPEC Statute, which dates from the earliest days of the organization: "OPEC's principal aims are the coordination and unification of the petroleum policies of Member Countries and the determination of the best means for safeguarding their interest, individually and collectively. The Organization shall devise ways and means of ensuring the stabilization of prices in international oil markets, with a view of eliminating harmful and unnecessary fluctuations. Due regard shall be given at all times to the interest of the producing nations and to the necessity of securing a steady income to the producing countries, an efficient, economic and regular supply of petroleum to consuming nations and a fair return on their capital to those investing in the petroleum industry."

In addition to this, OPEC issued a Declaratory Statement of Petroleum

Policy in Member Countries in 1968. This referred to the inalienable right, as expressed by the United Nations, of all countries to exercise permanent sovereignty over their natural resources in the interest of their national development. Accordingly, it claimed that the exploitation of OPEC's indigenous, exhaustible resources should be aimed at securing the greatest possible benefit for its Member Countries.

Put together, the Statute and Declaratory Statement meant that OPEC should focus its activities on ensuring order and stability in the international oil market, with reasonable prices, secure supply and fair returns to investors, and that oil producers themselves should have the right to determine the destiny of their indigenous crude oil reserves.

Early OPEC Activities

These documents were adopted in the 1960s, when the world oil industry, outside the former centrally planned economies, was dominated by the "The Seven Sisters" multinational oil companies. In such an environment, oil prices were at extremely low levels, with minimal returns for those countries within whose borders the crude reserves lay.

OPEC asserted its role in the 1970s, supporting its member countries as they took control of their domestic oil industries and acquired a major say in the pricing of oil on world markets. While the situation has moved on since then, with a broadening of the power base in a more integrated and consensual global industry, OPEC is nevertheless envisaged today as a major player in the world oil market.

There is one other important early document of relevance to OPEC's role—the "Solemn Declaration" adopted by a conference of OPEC sovereigns and heads of state in Algiers in 1975. This declaration carried a proposal for a "New International Economic Order" aimed at promoting a more equitable global economic system, with particular emphasis on alleviating poverty and other injustices affecting developing countries by encouraging greater interdependence among nations from the north and south.

The proposal for a new international economic order led to the establishment of the OPEC Fund for International Development, which is a multilateral development finance institution seeking to promote cooperation between OPEC members and other developing countries. Over the years, the OPEC Fund has distributed loans and grants to 104 countries located in Africa, Asia, Latin America, the Caribbean and Europe. Including grants and contributions to other institutions, the Fund's total approved commitments, as of the end of September 1999, stood at $5.4 billion (U.S.), with disbursements reaching $3.7 billion.

A New Summit

The 1975 Conference in Algiers is commonly referred to as the "OPEC Summit." The second such meeting is due to take place this year, as a landmark event commemorating OPEC's 40th anniversary.

The second summit will concern itself with the present condition of the oil industry (which is very different from that of 1975), the outlook for the new century and the challenges that are likely to present themselves. The heads of state will examine OPEC's objectives to see whether they require amendment in the light of today's market realities. The idea is to start OPEC off on a fresh new footing in the new millennium.

Although the agenda had not been finalized at the time of writing this article, it is likely to include topics that have aroused much interest in OPEC circles in recent years. Possible topics include pricing and production agreements, cooperation with non-OPEC producers, a dialogue with consumers, the provision of adequate future production capacity, the role of natural gas as a "sister export" to crude oil, the impact of the technology and communications revolutions, the not-too-distant depletion of crude oil reserves for some member countries, intensified diversification, the drive for a cleaner and safer environment and, finally, the ongoing negotiations under the umbrella of the United Nations Framework Convention on Climate Change (UNFCCC).

Two of these items—pricing and production agreements and climate change—warrant special attention in this article because of their topicality and because they relate directly to OPEC's ability to shift its oil on world markets both now and in the future. However, this is not to diminish the importance of the other items.

Pricing and Production Agreements

Let us first look at OPEC's pricing and production agreements. The events of the final two years of the 20th century have reminded us once again how inherently fragile the oil price structure is, how market psychology can grossly exaggerate initial impulses, and how disorder can prevail until collective action reverses the trend and returns the market to an orderly state.

Within the space of 20 months, from December 1997 to July 1999, crude oil prices fell heavily, remained for an apparent eternity at critically low levels, and then recovered to more or less their starting point, principally as a result of the responsible collective action of OPEC and some leading non-OPEC producers.

In figures, the average price of OPEC's spot reference basket in 1998 was $12.27 (U.S.) per barrel, which compared with an average of well over $18/b across the previous eight years of the decade, 1990-97. The average fell below $10/b for December 1998 and was just over $11/b for the first quarter of 1999.

In order to tackle this disturbing situation, a decision was taken by our member countries at the OPEC conference in March 1999 to join forces with four front-line non-OPEC producers—Mexico, Norway, Oman and Russia—in reducing output by a total of 2.104 million barrels a day, to go into effect on April 1, 1999.

This quickly had the desired effect. By the end of April, the first month of the agreement, the weekly average basket price had reached almost $16/b. As OPEC's producers demonstrated a high level of compliance with the voluntary agreement during the summer, the price continued to rise, averaging well over $18/b for July, to complete the 20-month period to which I referred earlier.

Maintaining the upward trend, the basket price pushed past the $20/b mark in the middle of August. By then, prices had reached levels considered by many market analysts and operators as being consistent with long-term equilibrium in the market. Such prices allow sufficient returns for producers to obtain a reasonable economic return from their finite resources, as well as assure a secure supply for the future.

The Need for Cooperation

This all demonstrates the importance of broad-based cooperation in the international oil market, reinforced by the agreements reached at the meetings of the OPEC conference. The market will not look after itself. If OPEC acts alone, it can only do so with a limited degree of success. Although OPEC is responsible for nearly 60 percent of the world's crude oil exports, it is obviously preferable that we receive the support and commitment of other major producers to ensure that market-stabilizing measures succeed.

It is up to all of us to see that the market functions effectively in the new millennium. OPEC has been greatly heartened by the new spirit of cooperation in the market and this gives something for all of us to build upon for the future.

But the achievement of an orderly market must be sustainable. What we have witnessed over the past two years is reaction to a crisis. What the market requires is "pro-action." Damaging situations should not be allowed to arise in the first place. If one does arise, then there should be a means available at all times of nipping it in the bud. This is an issue that requires examination in re-appraising OPEC's role for the future.

Climate Change

This leads me onto the second item that warrants special attention in this article—the climate change negotiations. This is a phenomenon that could greatly dominate the future performance of the international oil market. The negotiations, which have been pursued relentlessly since the early 1990s, may eventually result in response measures to the supposed threat of global warming that will do enormous damage to the vulnerable economies of oil-producing countries.

Our calculations show losses in annual oil export revenue of tens of billions of U.S. dollars for OPEC's member countries, compared with reference-case levels, if OECD countries impose carbon taxes of sufficient levels to achieve their emissions targets by 2010, as set out be the Kyoto Protocol of December 1997.

While OPEC and its member countries already are presenting the oil producers' case in the negotiations and seeking to defend their legitimate interests, it is, at the same time, clear that any reassessment of OPEC's role in the 21st century should be able to accommodate all the likely outcomes of the negotiations, so as to prevent the feared occurrence of dramatic revenue losses.

Whether all of this may require revision to the OPEC Statute is difficult to ascertain at the present time. As was implied earlier, the OPEC Statute so succinctly captures the spirit of our organization's raison d'être that it is probably already compatible with the emerging realities of the 21st century international oil market. The important thing is to ensure that OPEC moves with the times, and the organization already has a proven record of doing this in the international oil market during its 40-year history.

Pricing Differences Among Various Types of Crude Oil

According to The International Crude Oil Market Handbook, 2001-02 published by the Energy Intelligence Group, there are about 161 different internationally traded crude oils. They vary in terms of characteristics, quality, and market penetration.

Two crude oils which are either traded themselves or whose prices are reflected in other types of crude oil include West Texas Intermediate and Brent. Comparing these two crude oils with EIA's Imported Refiner Acquisition Cost (IRAC), the OPEC Basket, and NYMEX futures is important to understand the differences among the various types of crude oil that are often referred to in the press and by analysts. Generally, differences in the prices of these various crude oils are related to quality differences, but other factors can also influence the price relationships between each other.

West Texas Intermediate

West Texas Intermediate (WTI) crude oil is of very high quality and is excellent for refining a larger portion of gasoline. Its API gravity is 39.6 degrees (making it a "light" crude oil), and it contains only about 0.24 percent of sulfur (making a "sweet" crude oil). This combination of characteristics, combined with its location, makes it an ideal crude oil to be refined in the United States, the largest gasoline consuming country in the world. Most WTI crude oil gets refined in the Midwest region of the country, with some more refined within the Gulf Coast region. Although the production of WTI crude oil is on the decline, it still is the major benchmark of crude oil in the Americas. WTI is generally priced at about a $2-per-barrel premium to the OPEC Basket price and about $1-per-barrel premium to Brent; although on a daily basis the pricing relationships between these can vary greatly.

Brent

Brent Blend is actually a combination of crude oil from 15 different oil fields in the Brent and Ninian systems located in the North Sea. Its API gravity is 38.3 degrees (making it a "light" crude oil, but not quite as "light" as WTI), while it contains about 0.37 percent of sulfur (making it a "sweet" crude oil, but again slightly less "sweet" than WTI). Brent blend is ideal for making gasoline and middle distillates, both of which are consumed in large quantities in Northwest Europe, where Brent blend crude oil is typically refined.

However, if the arbitrage between Brent and other crude oils, including WTI, is favorable for export, Brent has been known to be refined in the United States (typically the East Coast or the Gulf Coast) or the Mediterranean region.

Brent blend, like WTI, production is also on the decline, but it remains the major benchmark for other crude oils in Europe or Africa. For example, prices for other crude oils in these two continents are often priced as a differential to Brent, i.e., Brent minus $0.50. Brent blend is generally priced at about a $1-per-barrel premium to the OPEC Basket price or about a $1-per-barrel discount to WTI; although on a daily basis the pricing relationships can vary greatly.

NYMEX Futures

The NYMEX futures price for crude oil, which is reported in almost every major newspaper in the United States, represents (on a per-barrel basis) the market determined value of a futures contract to either buy or sell 1,000 barrels of WTI or some other light, sweet crude oil at a specified time. Relatively few NYMEX crude oil contracts are actually executed for physical delivery. The NYMEX market, however, provides important price information to buyers and sellers of crude oil in the United States (and around the world), making WTI the benchmark for many different crude oils, especially in the Americas. Typically, the NYMEX futures prices tracks within pennies of the WTI spot price described above, although since the NYMEX futures contract for a given month expires 3 days before WTI spot trading for the same month ceases, there may be a few days in which the difference between the NYMEX futures price and the WTI spot price widens noticeably.

OPEC Basket Price

For a discussion of crude oil pricing in general, and of the OPEC Basket price in particular, see EIA's OPEC Fact Sheet. OPEC collects pricing data on a "basket" of seven crude oils, including: Algeria's Saharan Blend, Indonesia's Minas, Nigeria's Bonny Light, Saudi Arabia's Arab Light, Dubai's Fateh, Venezuela's Tia Juana Light, and Mexico's Isthmus (a non-OPEC crude oil). OPEC uses the price of this basket to monitor world oil market conditions. As mentioned above, because WTI crude oil is a very light, sweet (low sulfur content) crude, it is generally more expensive than the OPEC basket, which is an average of light sweet crude oils such as Algeria's Saharan Blend and heavier sour crude oils (with high sulfur content) such as Dubai's Fateh. Brent is also lighter, sweeter, and more expensive than the OPEC basket, although less so than WTI. Since OPEC has (at least informally) tied its production management activity to the goal of maintaining the OPEC Basket price between $22 and $28 per barrel, market watchers now pay close attention to this oil price indicator.

Imported Refiner Acquisition Cost

The Imported Refiner Acquisition Cost (IRAC) is a volume-weighted average price of all crude oils imported into the United States over a specified period. Because the United States imports more types of crude oil than any other country, it may represent the truest "world oil price" among all published crude oil prices. The IRAC is also usually similar to the OPEC Basket price, so it too is typically about $2 per barrel less than the WTI spot price and about $1 per barrel less than the Brent price. However, because the IRAC is not reported by EIA until nearly 2 months after the end of the month in question, i.e., the August IRAC average price would be reported sometime in late October, the IRAC is not a particularly timely measure of a "world oil price". Although EIA is generally the only organization that uses the IRAC, it is used by EIA as the "world oil price" in all of its forecast publications, including the Short-Term Energy Outlook, released monthly, as well as the Annual Energy Outlook and International Energy Outlook, both of which are released annually and provide an annual forecast looking out approximately 20 years in the future.

CRUDE OIL FUTURES

Crude oil traded futures and options have several economic benefits like managing the price risk of market positions. These are open markets where large number of buyers and sellers compete for the best prices. Companies discover and establish competitive prices on futures markets. A large amount of risk capital is involved in futures markets and they are among the most liquid of all global financial markets as they have low transaction costs and ease of entry and exit. Today, futures markets have clearing house guarantees and exchange self-regulation along with other institutional arrangements.

Facts and Features of Futures Markets

1. A futures contract is a legally binding agreement to buy or sell a specific quantity and grade of oil, gas or any other specified commodity or

financial instrument sometime in the future at a price agreed upon at the time of the trade.

2. The expiry of the contract provides either for delivery of the underlying physical energy product or a final cash payment (cash settlement).

3. The contracts are traded on regulated exchanges, mostly electronically via a computerized network. However, in some specified trading areas called pits or rings they are still traded by open outcry.

4. In a futures contract, all open positions are marked-to-market daily at the settlement price and the resulting daily gains and losses are passed to the gaining or losing futures accounts held by brokers for their customers.

5. In case of delivery, the tenderable goods must meet the contract specifications. In addition, these goods must be certified for quantity and quality by an approved surveyor.

6. Because futures contracts are standardized, sellers and buys can exchange one contract for another and "offset" their obligation to take or give delivery of a commodity or instrument underlying the futures contract. Offset in the futures market means taking another futures position opposite or equal to one's initial futures transaction. For e.g. if a trader bought one December MCX Brent Crude Oil contract, he must sell one December MCX Brent Crude Oil contract before the contracts call for delivery. This will offset his position.

7. Majority of futures contracts are terminated by offset or a final cash payment rather than by physical delivery (only about 2%).

Mechanics of a Futures Trading

Buyers and sellers deposit initial margin (a sort of good faith deposit) with a brokerage firm who would be a clearing member of the exchange where the futures contract is being traded. This initial margin amount is around 5-10 percent of the total notional contract value.

Table 2.2: Margins in Futures Trading

Position	*Price of Underlying*	*Profit/Loss*	*Amount*
Buy a futures contract	Price goes up	Profit	Price Increase × Contract Size
Buy a futures contract	Price goes down	Loss	Price Decrease × Contract Size
Sell a futures contract	Price goes up	Loss	Price Increase × Contract Size
Sell a futures contract	Price goes down	Profit	Price Decrease × Contract Size

These profits and losses are paid daily via the variation futures margin which a clearing broker must deposit with the clearing house every day on behalf of its customers. The broker either finances this for its customer or calls its customer for collateral against unrealized losses.

Commercial Applications of the Exchange's Energy Futures and Options Contracts

The Exchange provides buyers and sellers with price insurance and arbitrage opportunities that can be integrated into cash market operations. Trading Exchange contracts can improve the credit worthiness and add to the borrowing capacity of natural resource companies, thus augmenting the companies' financial management and performance capabilities.

Cash vs. Futures Price Relationships

Cash prices are the prices for which the commodity is sold at the various market locations. The futures price represents the current market opinion of what the commodity will be worth at some time in the future. Under normal circumstances of adequate supply, the price of the physical commodity for future delivery will be approximately equal to the present cash price, plus the amount it costs to carry or store the commodity from the present to the month of delivery. These costs, known as carrying charges, determine the normal premium of futures over cash.

As a result, one would ordinarily expect to see an upward trend to the prices of distant contract months. Such a market condition is known as *contango* and is typical of many futures markets. In most physical markets, the crucial determinant of the price differential between two contract months is the cost of storing the commodity over that particular length of time. As a result, markets which compensate an individual fully for carry charges interest rates, insurance, and storage—are known as full contango markets, or full carrying charge markets.

Under normal market conditions, when supplies are adequate, the price of a commodity for future delivery should be equal to the present spot price plus carrying charges. The contango structure of the futures market is kept intact by the ability of dealers and financial institutions to bring carrying charges back into line through arbitrage.

Futures markets are typically contango markets, although seasonal factors in energy markets play an important role in market relationships. For example, during the summer, heating oil futures are often in contango as the industry begins to build inventory for the approaching cold weather. On any given day, prices in the forward contract months are progressively higher through the fall, reflecting the costs of storage, interest rates, and the assumption of increased demand.

The opposite of contango is *backwardation*, a market condition where the nearby month trades at a higher price relative to the outer months. Such a price relationship usually indicates a tightness of supply; a market can also be in backwardation when seasonal factors predominate.

Convergence of Futures and Cash Markets

As a futures contract approaches its last day of trading, there is little difference between it and the cash price. The futures and cash prices will get closer and closer, a process known as convergence, as any premium the futures have had has disappeared over time. A futures contract nearing expiration becomes, in effect, a spot contract.

Hedging in Futures Markets

We use various hedging strategies with the purpose of avoiding the risk of losses due to adverse market moves. However, there is no 'Perfect Hedge' because the physical cash markets and the futures markets do not always have a perfect price correlation. Hence, almost always there is a profit or loss in hedging.

In futures markets, we take a futures position opposite to that of a cash market position for the purpose of hedging. That is, an energy producer or consumer might want to buy or sell energy futures against their price risk exposure in anticipation of a market price increase/decrease.

Basis

As noted earlier, futures contracts are standardized instruments that stipulate the quantity, quality, and delivery points for a wide cross section of the underlying industry. Basis is the differential that exists between the cash price of a given commodity and the price of the nearest futures contract for the same, or a related commodity.

The predictability and size of the basis can involve three price relationships:

1. The difference between the futures contract and the spot price of the underlying commodity.
2. The difference between the price at the futures contract delivery point and the price at a different location.
3. The price at the future's contract delivery point and the price of a similar, but not identical, quality commodity at the same location.

The cash/futures basis can be effectively minimized if delivery is made or accepted at the same time that the trading of a futures contract nears expiration. Because of price convergence, a futures contract nearing expiration becomes, in effect, a spot contract.

Locational basis is a consideration for firms that desire to hedge but do not make deliveries at the futures contract location. In theory, the price relationship between two different markets will be based on the cost of transportation between them. Sudden local shifts in supply or demand, however, can distort this price relationship.

The extent to which these changes in relative market conditions are predictable will determine the hedged firms' exposure to locational basis risk.

The product basis concerns those firms that desire to hedge the purchase or sale of a specific commodity not offered as a liquid futures contract. Firms base their hedge on the historical relationship of the commodity underlying the contract to the commodity to be hedged.

For example, the NYMEX Division heating oil futures contract is widely used as a hedging proxy for jet fuel, as the products are chemically similar and often trade within a narrow price range in relation to each other.

The NYMEX Division light, sweet crude oil futures contract, likewise, is used to hedge crudes not specified for delivery by the contract, but which nevertheless trade at a high correlation to the futures contract.

For the futures trader, the critical period for assessing basis is between the time that the futures transaction is entered into and the time it is closed, or liquidated.

If a short hedger (a seller of futures) experiences a widening in the basis during the time the hedge is held, a basis loss may result. This narrowing implies means that the cash prices have declined relative to futures prices. That is, they have fallen more or risen less than futures prices.

The short hedger's cash loss in a declining market would exceed the gain on the short futures transaction. Or, conversely, the cash gain in a rising market would be exceeded by the loss on the futures transaction.

On the other hand, a basis gain would occur in the case of a long hedge and a widening basis because the futures price would rise relative to the cash price.

Thus, a narrowing basis yields gains for the short hedger and losses for the long hedger.

Table 2.3: Potential Basis Changes

	Rising Market		*Falling Market*	
Cash/Futures Position	*Cash Rises Less than Futures*	*Cash Rises More than Futures*	*Cash Falls Less than Futures*	*Cash Falls More than Futures*
Bought the cash/Sold the futures	Loss	Gain	Gain	Loss
Sold the cash /bought the futures	Gain	Loss	Loss	Gain

Exchange of Futures for Physicals (EFP) and Deliveries via Futures Markets

It is estimated that more than 95% of all energy futures contracts do not directly result in physical delivery. Nevertheless, significant volumes of crude oil, heating gasoline, natural gas, coal, and propane are delivered, and companies using energy futures for delivery have several options. They can choose standard delivery as per the specifications of the futures contracts; attempt to arrange an Alternative Delivery Procedure (ADP) or effect an Exchange of Futures for Physicals (EFPs). Alternate Delivery Procedure means two parties that are stuck with a position decide to cash settle by negotiating with each other. ADP also includes a case when a party wishes to deliver some energy commodity which is not as per the specifications of the futures contract. Such an energy commodity that does not meet futures contract specifications cannot be delivered through the exchange or clearing house. In ADP transactions, the exchange and the clearing brokers do not have any liability related to the delivery negotiated between parties. Traders and hedgers can also execute an Exchange of Futures for Physicals (EFP).

In order to engage in an EFP, it is not necessary for both sides to be in the futures market when the EFP is initiated except during EFP-only sessions. A futures market long, for example, might effect an EFP with a cash market long. The net result of the transaction would be delivery of a commodity to the futures hedger and the assumption by the physical market participant of the hedger's futures market contracts (next Example)

Why Companies go for EFP?

1. Companies that use energy futures contracts for hedging purposes are mostly not interested in making or taking delivery at the specified locations.
2. They also do not prefer being matched to a trading partner by the futures exchange.
3. Mostly, it is more economical for a hedger using futures to make or take delivery of physical energy at a location as per his need and logistics rather than taking delivery at a location specified in the futures contract.
4. An EFP provides the mechanism for such transactions and is usually the preferred method of delivery because it allows flexibility in choosing the delivery location, the trading counterpart, time of delivery and the grade of the commodity.
5. EFP mechanism also allows the two parties to negotiate price for their physical energy market transaction.

Note: The major concern of the futures exchanges is to ensure that the quantity of the cash commodity involved in an EFP must be approximately equal to the quantity specified by the number of futures contracts involved in the EFP.

Practical Mechanics of an EFP Transaction

To understand the mechanics of an EFP transaction lets consider the following example:

A party having long position in crude oil in the futures market would take delivery of the crude oil from a party which has a short position in crude oil in the futures market. In this transaction both party's' hedge is liquidated and actual transfer of crude oil takes place between the parties but not through the exchange.

Companies looking for some counterpart to an EFP transaction usually contact the futures brokers first, as futures brokers are the ones among whom EFP market is normally quoted.

Exchange of Futures for Swaps (EFS)

Exchange of Futures for Swaps (EFS) is also an extremely useful trading instrument. The mechanics of the transaction are similar to that of the EFP. EFS permits the substitution of a futures position for an over-the counter cash-settled position, letting market participants avoid having to liquidate a physical delivery contract. It also gives market participants the ability to liquidate a swaps position in a market which may have limited liquidity. Two parties are allowed to privately negotiate the execution of an integrated over-the-counter swaps and related futures transaction on pricing terms agreed upon by the involved parties. The transaction must involve approximately equal but opposite side-of-market quantities of futures and swap exposures in the same or related commodities and are be permitted until two hours after trading terminates in the underlying futures contract. EFS transactions are permitted to liquidate, initiate, and transfer futures market positions between the two parties involved in the transaction.

OTC Energy Derivative Markets

There are two broad groups of the derivative contracts: Over-the-counter (OTC) Derivatives and Exchange-traded Derivatives. They are different in the way they are traded in the market.

Over-the-counter (OTC) Derivatives are contracts that are traded (and privately negotiated) directly between two parties, without going through an exchange or other intermediary. The counterparts negotiate the key terms of the contracts like pricing reference, the payment terms and the volume. It is beneficial for the organizations with unique price risk to use OTC derivatives for hedging. Today, there is a fair amount of standardized OTC contracts in oil, gas and electricity markets. Standardized here means they have a standard floating price reference and the minimum traded volume.

OTC Derivatives market has now become a well established and liquid market. It is the main reason why the futures exchanges are not launching new energy futures contracts as the needs of the market are increasingly being met by the OTC Derivatives market. This is evident from the example of Asian market. Asia is now second only to US in energy consumption but still Asia does not have a well established and liquid energy futures exchange The reason behind this is that Singapore, the hub of a well established Asian OTC market, serves the needs of energy derivatives contracts in Asia.

Tokyo Commodity Exchange (TOCOM) with its Middle East crude

futures contract and product futures is the only major energy futures exchange in Asia but it is still far from achieving the kind of liquidity and range of market participants that is there on New York Mercantile Exchange (NYMEX) or Intercontinental Exchange (ICE).

In an attempt to strengthen the core functions of futures markets – to hedge risk and achieve price discovery, Singapore Exchange Limited (SGX) and the Tokyo Commodity Exchange (TOCOM) signed an agreement in 2002, to launch the Middle Eastern Crude Oil (MECO) futures on SGX. The MECO futures contract on SGX follows similar contract specifications as the very successful TOCOM MECO futures contract, except that it is denominated in USD/barrel instead of JPY/kilolitre. The contract's final settlement is based on the Monthly Average of the Daily Dubai and Oman crude oil prices assessed by Platts, a unit of McGraw-Hill Companies, Inc. The aim was to bring together the liquidity in TOCOM's oil derivatives contracts and the participation of international oil refiners and traders based in Singapore and the Asia-Pacific region. However, the contract was not a big success on SGX as it was on TOCOM. Traders on SGX had to deal with the already present oil price volatility in the market and the additional risk of volatility in the exchange rates of Japanese Yen (JPY) and United States Dollar (USD).

Pricing of OTC Oil Derivatives Market

Platt's, which is a division of McGraw-Hill, publishes a daily price assessment of any given crude oil or oil product in any given location, according to Platt's own specifications. It also publishes an assessment of the forward curve. This is an industry recognized publication and is used for pricing the majority of physical transactions and OTC swaps. These daily value assessments are based on the aggregated bids and offers from many brokers and dealers around the world during a specified time window for each geographic region (Usually towards the end of each business day in each major time zone: Asia (Singapore), Europe (London), USA (New York, and then the West Coast).

For pricing of swaps the monthly average of these Platt's assessments is used. The difference between the traded fixed price and the calculated average floating price from the Platt's assessments is found and multiplied by the monthly quantity of the contract. The amount hence found is the monthly financial payment that is paid and there is no exchange of physical energy.

Following are the main Global Oil Trading/Pricing hubs:

1. Asia—Singapore is the main pricing hub.
2. Europe—Mediterranean and Arab Gulf Prices, North West Europe and Amsterdam-Rotterdam-Antwerp (ARA) are the main pricing hubs.
3. USA—New York Harbor, US Gulf Coast, US West Coast are the main pricing hubs.

Futures versus OTC

Following are the features of a Futures Contract:

1. Contract is traded on an exchange.
2. Highly regulated market.
3. Price of the contract can be seen on a screen.
4. Clearing house of the exchange guarantees the security and performance of the contract.
5. Margins are deposited by everyone with a futures position on that particular exchange. Margins are of two types—**Initial Margins** are the deposits that are placed with the clearing house when a trade is opened. The clearing house does a daily revaluation of the portfolio. A **Variation Margin** is the payment made by clearing members to their respective clearing houses based upon adverse price movements of the futures contracts that these members hold. It is paid by clearing members on a daily or intraday basis in order to reduce the exposure created by carrying highly risky positions. By demanding variation margin from its members, clearing organizations are able to maintain a suitable level of risk and cushions against significant devaluations.

Following are the features of the OTC market:

1. No guarantor is involved.
2. There is credit risk of the counterpart to the contract.
3. Liquidity risk is there.
4. Lack of price transparency as there is no screen to display the real-time price.

Convergence of OTC Markets and Futures

The OTC market and the Futures Market are now stating to converge despite of the distinction between them. This has been made possible because more and more clearing houses are accepting to act as guarantor in the OTC trades. A clearing house decouples the risk involved in a trade for counterparty A, from the risk involved in the trade for counterparty B. As the whole function of credit risk and collateral is centralized, it makes a more level playing field for all parties. The clearing house is responsible for defining the rules, and setting the margin rates, based on an assessment of risks.

Futures Contracts Settlement on Expiry

Both parties of a "futures contract" must fulfill the contract on the settlement date. The seller delivers the commodity to the buyer, or, if it is a cash-settled future, then cash is transferred from the futures trader who sustained a loss to the one who made a profit. To exit the commitment prior to the settlement date, the holder of a futures position has to offset his position by either selling a long position or buying back a short position, effectively closing out the futures position and its contract obligations. However, only about 2% of the total outstanding contracts on a Futures exchange are settled by physical delivery. The majority of trades on these markets are for hedging and or speculative purposes, with consumers or producers of energy preferring to make delivery via the normal physical markets rather than through the futures markets.

Contracts Study

Commodity Markets

Commodity markets are markets where raw or primary products are exchanged. These raw commodities are traded on regulated commodities exchanges, in which they are bought and sold in standardized Contracts.

Commodity Exchanges

A commodities exchange is an exchange where various commodities and derivatives products are traded. There are many commodity markets across the world that trade energy products and contracts based on them. These contracts can include spot prices, forwards, futures and options on futures.

Commodities exchanges, usually trade futures contracts on commodities. Such as trading contracts to receive something, say gasoline, in a certain month. A refiner can sell a future contract on his gasoline, which will not be produced for several months, and guarantee the price he will be paid when he delivers; a large gasoline consuming company buys the contract now and guarantees the price will not go up when it is delivered. This protects the refiner (seller) from price drops and the consuming company (buyer) from price rises.

Following are the main Global Energy Futures Exchanges:

1. NYMEX (New York Mercantile Exchange), New York http://www.nymex.com
2. ICE (Intercontinental Exchange), London http://www.theice.com
3. TOCOM, (Tokyo Commodity Exchange),Tokyo http://www.tocom.or.jp
4. SGX (Singapore Exchange), Singapore http://www.sgx.com
5. SFE (Sydney Futures Exchange), Sydney

Following are the main Indian Energy Futures Exchanges:

1. MCX (Multi Commodity Exchange), Mumbai
2. NCDEX (National Commodity Exchange), Mumbai

Energy Futures Contracts

Energy futures contracts, or simply energy futures, are exchange traded energy derivatives. A futures contract gives the holder the obligation to buy or sell. Both parties of a "futures contract" must fulfill the contract on the settlement date. The seller delivers the energy commodity to the buyer, or, if it is a cash-settled future, then cash is transferred from the futures trader who sustained a loss to the one who made a profit. To exit the commitment prior to the settlement date, the holder of a futures position has to offset his position by either selling a long position or buying back a short position, effectively closing out the futures position and its contract obligations.

Following are the major specifications of a Futures Contract:

(1) *Trading Period/Trading Session:* It signifies the days and hours during which the trading at a particular exchange takes place.

(2) *Unit of Trading:* It signifies the lot size.

(3) *Grade and Quality Specifications:* It signifies the quality specifications of the commodity that is deliverable under a particular contract.

(4) *Quotation:* It tells us the base value of commodity in which it is traded on the exchange.

(5) *Tick Size:* It is the Minimum Price Fluctuation that is allowed in a

contract. It gives the minimum amount by which the price of the contract is allowed to increase or decrease.

(6) *Maximum Daily Price Fluctuation:* It is the maximum amount by which the price of a contract is allowed to increase or decrease in a day.

(7) *Initial Margin:* Parties have to deposit margins with the exchange's clearing house in order to initiate positions in Futures.

(8) *Special Margin:* Parties may have to deposit an special margin, in an amount deemed fit the exchange's clearing house, in case of additional volatility in the price of futures contract.

(9) *Position Limits:* It is the maximum number of contracts of a commodity, a client or a clearing member can hold at a time.

(10) *Settlement/Delivery Terms and Procedure:* It spells out the terms and conditions on the basis of which a futures contract is settled (either by cash or physical delivery) on expiry.

Futures Contracts

I. Brent Crude Oil

Exchange: MCX

Commodity: Brent Crude Oil

Settlement: Both cash as well as physical delivery

Duration of Contract: 3 months

Trading Unit: 100 bbl

Price Quotation: Rs. per bbl

Minimum Price Movement: Rs. 1 per bbl

Maximum Daily Price Fluctuation: 4%

Maximum Allowable Open Position:

(i) For individual clients: 150,000 barrels

(ii) For a member collectively for all clients: 600,000 bbl or 20% of open interest, whichever is higher

Margins: Margins are required to initiate a position on the exchange.

1. *Initial Margin:* Buyers and Sellers have to submit a 5% initial margin to initiate a position on the Exchange.
2. *Special Margin:* In case of additional volatility, a special margin at such

percentage, as deemed fit, will be imposed immediately on both buy and sale side in respect of all outstanding position, which will remain in force for next 2 days, after which the special margin will be relaxed.

3. *Delivery Period Margin:* A Delivery Period Margin of 25% will be imposed during tender and delivery period on both buyers and sellers on matched quantity.

Working:

1. On the contract expiry day by 6.00 p.m. sellers and buyers will submit Notices of Intention to Deliver and Notices of Intention to Accept, respectively with the exchange.

2. Sellers will also submit copies of relevant documents as a proof of holding stock at the time of giving Notice of Intention to Deliver.

3. On the basis of Notices of Intentions to Deliver and Accept the Exchange will match the total quantity offered by the buyers and sellers and with respect to the matched quantity, the allocation of delivery between the buyers and sellers will be done.

4. *Penalty:* After receipt of intentions from the buyer and seller to take or give delivery, if any of the party fails to honor his obligations, a penalty of 1% of the DDR will be imposed on him, out of which 90% will be passed on to the other party and 10% will be retained by the Exchange.

5. Cash Settlement:

(i) All positions that are offset before the expiry of the contract are cash settled.

(ii) All outstanding positions on the expiry of contract where Notice of Intention to Deliver or Accept has not been received and such positions where Notices of Intention have been received but have not found the counter party for honoring the intentions, shall be closed out at due date rate and respective pay-in and pay-out of funds of such close out positions shall be take place on the following day of contract expiry day by 11.00 a.m.

6. *Physical Delivery:* Physical Delivery takes place for the open positions after the expiry date where the Exchange is able to match the Notices of Intention to Deliver and Accept.

Note: This contract is mainly used for hedging/speculation purposes by players in the market. Also, trading participants are still not doing physical trading on exchanges in India. They go for OTC market for physical trade as there they know and can choose the counter party and can negotiate the terms of contract. Hence, all the contracts are cash settled even though there is a provision for physical settlement. Another reason for absence of physical delivery is that there is no supply of Brent Crude Oil in India. Moreover, the contract size is also too small to attract traders to go for physical delivery.

Due Date Rate: Due date rate of Brent Crude Oil will be calculated by taking Bloomberg fixings i.e., international spot price of Brent Crude Oil as reported by Bloomberg. The Bloomberg price will pertain to the last trading day (expiry date) of the MCX Brent Crude Oil contract and it would be multiplied by Rupee – US Dollar rate as notified by the Reserve Bank of India on that particular day.

Delivery Center: Port installation at Mumbai/JNPT port .

Delivery Grades: Brent Blend confirming to the following quality specification is deliverable:

(i) API Gravity: Between 38 degree – 39 degree

(ii) Sulfur: 0.4% by weight or less

The buyer has no option to select a particular grade and the delivery offered by the seller and allocation by the Exchange shall be binding on buyer.

Delivery and Payment: The seller has to make the delivery by 11:00 a.m. on the 3rd day from the day of expiry of contract. The buyer submits the payment with the clearing house by 11:00 a.m. on the 2nd working day from the day of expiry of the contract. The clearing house will release this amount to the seller by 11:00 a.m. on the 3rd working day from the day of expiry of contract.

Extension of Delivery Period: As per the Exchange decision due to a force majeure or otherwise.

Endorsement of Delivery Order: The buyer member can endorse delivery order to a client or any third party with full disclosure given to MCX. Responsibility for contractual liability would be with the original assignee.

II. Exchange: NCDEX

Commodity: Brent Crude Oil
Settlement: Both cash as well as physical delivery.
Duration of Contract: 3 months
Trading Unit: 100 bbl
Price Quotation: Rs. per bbl
Minimum Price Movement: Rs. 0.50 per bbl

Maximum Daily Price Fluctuation: The daily price limit will be 6% and will be raised to 9% after a 15-minute cooling period if the price limit of 6% is reached. If the price limit reaches 9%, trading will continue within the 9% limit.

Maximum Allowable Open Position:

(i) For individual clients: 150,000 barrels
(ii) For a member collectively for all clients: 600,000 bbl or 20% of open interest, whichever is higher

Margins: Margins are required to initiate a position on the exchange.

1. *Initial Margin:* NCDEX will use Value at Risk (VaR) based margin calculated at 99% confidence interval for one day time horizon.
2. *Special Margin:* 5% of the value of the contract will be applied whenever the rise or fall in price from the first day's closing price is 20%.This is payable by buyer or seller depending on whether prices rise or fall respectively. The margins shall stay in force so long as price stays beyond the 20% limit and will be withdrawn as soon as the price is within the 20% band.
3. *Delivery Period Margin:* Buyers who have been matched by the exchange to receive deliveries would have to deposit with the exchange the whole value of the delivery on the day after the expiry of the contract. The seller matched by the exchange to give deliveries would have to deposit a delivery margin as determined by the exchange from time to time. This margin will have to be given on the day after the expiry of the contract. Open unmatched positions would not attract any delivery margins.

Working:

1. NCDEX has a delivery request window that covers the three trading days prior to expiry of the contract (including the date of expiry). The buyers and seller shall give intentions of delivery/receipt during this time window.

2. NCDEX would thereafter complete the matching process based on the factor(s) that the Exchange deems appropriate for completion of the matching process, on the last trading day.

3. The buyers/sellers who have to receive/give delivery would be notified by the Exchange on the last day of trading after the close of trading hours.

4. Cash Settlement:

(i) All positions that are offset before the expiry of the contract are cash settled.

(ii) All open positions for which delivery intentions have not been received or for which delivery intentions have been rendered but remain unmatched for want of counterparty to settle delivery, will be cash settled at Final settlement Price on the expiry of the contract.

5. *Physical Delivery:* Physical Delivery takes place for the open positions after the expiry date where the Exchange is able to match the delivery requests submitted by buyers and sellers during the delivery request window.

Note: This contract is mainly used for hedging/speculation purposes by players in the market. Also, trading participants are still not doing physical trading on exchanges in India. They go for OTC market for physical trade as there they know and can choose the counter party and can negotiate the terms of contract. Hence, all the contracts are cash settled even though there is a provision for physical settlement. Another reason for absence of physical delivery is that there is no supply of Brent Crude Oil in India. Moreover, the contract size is also too small to attract traders to go for physical delivery.

Final Settlement Prices: The Final Settlement Price (FSP) in Indian Rupees (INR) will be determined by the Exchange on maturity of the contract. The FSP will be the value of Brent Index published by International Petroleum Exchange (IPE), London for a similar corresponding contract expiring on IPE. The exchange rate to be used as the conversion factor shall be the RBI reference spot exchange rate on that day.

Taxes, Duties, Cess, Levies, Insurance and Freight charges: The seller shall be responsible to bring the Cargo to Mumbai Port/JNPT Area. The Buyer will be responsible for the freight cost, insurance, import duty and all other taxes & levies on actual basis. Freight and insurance will be paid on actual basis on production of satisfactory documentary evidence by the seller.

Delivery Center: Mumbai Port / JNPT

Delivery Grades:

Crude Type	*API Gravity*	*Sulphur Content*
Brent	38.5 degrees	0.36%
Also Deliverable		
Crude Type	*API Gravity*	*Sulphur Content*
Forties	41.5-42.5 degrees	0.25-0.3%
Osberg	35.9degrees	0.32%

Note: No premium or discount on the basis of quality specifications will be applicable for NCDEX IPE Brent Crude Oil.

Actual Delivery

1. The seller would have to deliver the product to storage facility at Mumbai Port/JNPT Area.

2. This will be tested for quality and quantity by an NCDEX appointed assayer. Based on the satisfactory report by the assayer the credit of this crude oil would be transferred into the sellers account in the electronic form.

3. When crude oil is sold for delivery in a specified month, the seller must have requisite electronic credit of such crude oil holding in his Clearing Member's Pool Account before the scheduled date of pay in.

4. On settlement, the buyer's Clearing Member Pool Account would be credited with the said delivery quantity after pay out. The clearing member is expected to transfer the same to the buyer's depository account. However, the buyer must take actual physical delivery of Crude oil within thirty days after the expiry of the contract.

Electronic Transfer

1. Any buyer or seller receiving and or effecting NCDEX IPE Brent Crude Oil would have to open a depository account with an NCDEX Depository Participant (DP) to hold the NCDEX IPE Brent Crude Oil in electronic form.

2. On settlement, the buyer's account with the DP would be credited with the quantity of NCDEX IPE Brent Crude Oil received and the corresponding seller's account would be debited.

3. The Buyer wanting to take physical delivery of the NCDEX IPE Brent Crude Oil holding has to make a request to his DP with whom depository account has been opened.

4. The DP would route the request to the warehouse for issue of the physical commodity i.e. NCDEX IPE Brent Crude Oil to the buyer and debit his account, thus reducing the electronic balance to the extent of NCDEX IPE Brent Crude Oil so rematerialized.

III. Exchange: NYMEX

Commodity: Brent Crude Oil

Settlement: Financial

Duration of Contract: 12 months

Trading Unit: 1,000 bbl

Price Quotation: US dollars and cents per barrel

Minimum Price Movement: One cent ($0.01) per barrel

Maximum Daily Price Fluctuation: There shall be no maximum price fluctuation.

Maximum Allowable Open Position: 20,000 net futures contracts (1 contract = 1,000 bbl), but not to exceed 3,000 contracts in the last three days of trading in the spot month.

Termination of Trading: Trading shall cease one business day prior to the termination date of the Brent Crude Oil (ICE) Futures Contract for the delivery month.

Working

1. *Cash Settlement:* Delivery under the contract shall be by cash settlement. Final settlement, following termination of trading for a contract month, will be based on the Floating Price.
2. *Physical Delivery:* Physical settlement is only possible when a futures position holder gets into an EFP agreement with a party holding a position in the physical market.

Final Settlement Price: The final settlement price will be based on the ICE Brent Crude Oil (Physical Contract) Futures first nearby contract settlement price on the penultimate trading day for the delivery month.

Delivery Center: No Physical Delivery.

Exchange of Futures for Physical (EFP)

1. The commercial buyer or seller may exchange a futures position for a physical position of equal quantity by submitting a notice to the Exchange. EFPs may be used to either initiate or liquidate a futures position.

2. At the time such EFP transactions are effected, the buyer of the futures

contract must be the seller of the physical product (for EFP) and the seller of the futures contract must be the buyer of the physical product (for EFP).

3. Each EFP transaction shall be posted, immediately when relevant cash terms are determined, but it should not be later than the next business day or the end of the permissible posting period for EFPs following the expiration of the underlying futures contract.

4. Each buyer and seller must satisfy the Exchange, at its request, that the transaction is a legitimate EFP transaction.

Exchange of Futures for Swap (EFS)

1. An exchange of futures for, or in connection with, a swap (EFS) consists of two discrete, but related, transactions; a swap transaction and a futures transaction.

2. At the time such transaction is effected, the buyer and seller of the futures must be, respectively, the seller and the buyer of the swap.

3. The swap component shall involve the commodity underlying the futures contract.

4. The quantity covered by the swap must be approximately equivalent to the quantity covered by the futures contracts.

5. A report of EFS transactions shall be submitted to the Exchange by each Clearing Member representing the buyer and/or seller.

IV. Exchange: ICE

Commodity: Brent Crude Oil

Settlement: Both cash as well as physical delivery (EFP)

Duration of Contract: 12 consecutive months

Trading Unit: 1,000 bbl

Price Quotation: US dollars and cents per barrel

Minimum Price Movement: One cent ($0.01) per barrel

Maximum Daily Price Fluctuation: No limit.

Maximum Allowable Open Position: No limit.

Working: The ICE Brent Crude futures contract is a deliverable contract based on EFP delivery with an option to cash settle, i.e. the IPE Brent Index price for the day following the last trading day of the futures contract.

1. *Physical Delivery:* The Seller and Buyer shall, in respect of Contracts remaining open at cessation of trading on the last trading day for the contract month, enter into an EFP and make and take delivery of oil.

2. *Cash Settlement:* (i) The contract is cash settled when the players offset their positions before the expiry of the contract.

(ii) The contract also has the provision for the parties to give notice in accordance with Clearing House procedures up to one hour after the relevant time of cessation of trading that the Contract shall be subject to the cash settlement procedure.

Settlement Price: The Exchange shall publish a cash settlement price on the next Trading Day following the last day of trading for the contract month. The Brent Crude futures settlement price is established daily by calculating the trade weighted average price of ICE Brent crude futures executed for the relevant contract month between 19:27:00 and 19:29:59, London local time (settlement period). It can be traded up to the end of the calculation period.

Delivery Center: As per EFP arrangement between participants.

Deliverable Grade: Current pipeline export quality Brent blend for delivery at storage and terminal installations at Sullom Voe.

Sr.No.	*Characteristics*	*Specifications*
1	API Gravity	38%
2	Sulfur Content	0.45%

Payment: In respect of every lot comprised in the Contract, the following payments shall be made:

Where the cash settlement price

1. exceeds the contract price, payment by the Seller to the Clearing House,
2. exceeds the contract price, payment by the Clearing House to the Buyer,
3. is less than the contract price, payment by the Clearing House to the Seller,
4. is less than the contract price, payment by the Buyer to the Clearing House, of an amount calculated by multiplying the difference between the cash settlement price and the contract price by 1000 (because the size of 1 contract is 1000 bbl).

These payments shall be made no later than the business day following the date of publication of the cash settlement price.

Exchange of Futures for Physical (EFP)

1. The EFP facility allows Members to register Futures trades linked to physical and forward transactions. This allows more effective hedging opportunities for market participants with over-the-counter positions.

2. Reporting of EFP trades may take place at any time during trading hours and for 30 minutes after the close of the relevant individual Contract.

3. On an expiry day, EFP in respect of the expiring contract date may be reported up to one hour after the expiry of the contract date.

4. The Exchange may require Members to supply evidence of the underlying physical transaction either prior to or following registration of the trade and may refuse registration in its sole and final discretion.

5. In the case of EFP transactions, the underlying OTC contract must be properly documented and available for production to the ICE Futures compliance department on demand in order to validate its legitimacy.

6. The registration of the EFP should be at the current market price or within plus/minus $0.30 per lot limit (the Exchange may amend the limit at any time as necessary), otherwise the exchange must be satisfied that the transaction is a legitimate use of facility and not for money laundering or any other purpose other than as a consequence of normal commercial activity, before EFP's registration can take place.

V. Exchange: DME

Commodity: Brent-Oman Financial Spread

Settlement: Financial

Duration of Contract: 12 months

Trading Unit: 1,000 bbl

Price Quotation: US dollars and cents per barrel

Minimum Price Movement: One cent ($0.01) per barrel

Maximum Daily Price Fluctuation: There shall be no maximum price fluctuation limit.

Working: Contract is based on the spread between Brent Crude Oil and Oman Crude Oil. Performance under the contract shall be by cash settlement. Final settlement shall take place following termination of trading for a Contract Month and will be based on the Floating Price.

Final Settlement Price: The Exchange shall publish the Final Settlement Price on the last Trading Day in that Contract Month.

The Exchange shall determine a Settlement Price for each Trading Day of a Contract Month of the Brent-Oman Financial Spread Contract. The Settlement Price for each Trading Day of a Contract Month (including the final Trading Day of a Contract Month) shall be determined as at 14.30 (New York time) on a Trading Day using:

1. the DME Daily Post Close Price determined in respect of:

(i) the same Trading Day; and

(ii) the corresponding Contract Month in the DME Oman Crude Oil **Futures Contract**

(the **Relevant DME Oman Price**); and

2. the NYMEX Brent Financial Crude Oil Daily Settlement Price determined in respect of:

(i) the same day; and

(ii) the corresponding contract month on NYMEX, Inc. in the Brent **Financial Crude Oil Contract**

(the **Relevant NYMEX Brent Price**).

The daily Settlement Price for each Trading Day of a Contract Month (including the final Trading Day of a Contract Month) shall be the Relevant NYMEX Brent Price minus the Relevant DME Oman Price.

Delivery Center: No Physical Delivery.

Note: **Corresponding NYMEX Brent Financial Crude Oil Daily Settlement Price** means, in relation to the DME Daily Post Close Price published on the last Trading Day of a Contract Month, the NYMEX Brent Financial Contract (Code BB) first nearby month daily settlement price published in respect of trading up to the same time on the same day as such DME Daily Post Close Price is published in respect thereto.

Challenges before India's Energy Futures Market

(1) There is no structured spot market in India. Thus, lack of transparent spot price availability makes it difficult to calculate Due Date Rate of futures contracts.

(2) MCX has taken the initiative to open National Spot Market to facilitate spot trading in the country as well as benefit the futures market but it is mostly for agricultural products.

(3) Currently cash settlement of outstanding contracts at maturity is not allowed by the Forward Contracts (Regulation) Act (FCRA). This means that at maturity a party can ask for delivery. To avoid this, traders square-off their positions before maturity, which is practically equivalent to cash settlement. Options' trading is also not allowed in commodities on Indian futures exchanges. The parliamentary committee's report recommending options trading in commodities is lying with the government but it has not taken any step to implement it so far.

(4) With the growing refining business in the country, it is the demand of time to have crack spread contracts to be introduced in country's futures exchanges.

(5) The PSUs are still reluctant to trade on MCX and NCDEX because of the following reasons:

- Absence of refined product futures like Aviation Turbine Fuel, Naphtha etc. These products can be used for crack spread hedging. Refiners find it very useful to lock their margins.
- MCX and NCDEX have limited trading hours. They have trading hours from 10:00 a.m. to 11:30 p.m. which is not the ideal way to go when one is trading in commodities that are truly global.

- Moreover, the contract size at these exchanges is also too small to be good enough for physical delivery.

(6) As the PSUs are not interested in trading on Indian futures exchanges, there is practically no physical delivery in futures contracts of energy commodities on these exchanges.

(7) Lack of an appropriate marker for Asia:

Pricing of crude oil is done through the use of marker crudes. Some of the major marker crudes are:

- West Texas Intermediate (USA)
- Brent (Europe and Africa)
- Dubai and Oman (Asia)
- Tapis (Australia)

The main criteria for a marker crude is for it to be sold in sufficient volumes to provide liquidity (many buyers and sellers) in the physical market as well as having similar physical qualities of alternative crudes. In addition, the marker crude should provide pricing information. WTI does this through its use on the New York Metals Exchange (NYMEX) as the basis of a futures contract. Brent offers pricing information based more on the physical trading of oil through spot trading.

In Asia there is no futures exchange where crude oil is traded and which would provide pricing information to the same extent as WTI and Brent. Because of this the prices of Light Sweet crude for the Asian market have been higher than those for U.S./European markets. The prices for supplies to Europe are linked to the average spot price of North Sea Brent crude and that for U.S. supplies to WTI crude. Prices for supplies to Asia are linked to a 30-day spot average of Oman and Dubai crude during the month of delivery.

Major reason for this is the absence of strong trading markets in Asia. Also, today the production of Dubai crude has declined substantially to less than four cargoes per month (less than 100,000 bpd). It is difficult to determine the price of Dubai crude on spot trading at present because of the decline in its production.

India should join other Asian countries to use their bargaining power for a better price marker for Asia as the markers have been decided by OPEC on the basis of consumption and buying power. The fact that Asian nations led by India and China has led the global oil demand growth in recent years makes the case even more strong.

(8) Despite the size and importance of Asian market, price of oil in the continent is dependent on less effective crudes like, Tapis, Minas and Dubai crude. India should work with other Asian nations to develop stronger markets in the region. This will help in real price discovery.

(9) For the success of trading in India, it is a must that government deregulates the markets. In India, we still have government controlling the prices of important petroleum products like, petrol, diesel and LPG.

CHAPTER 3

Natural Gas Trading

INTRODUCTION NATURAL GAS TRADING

Natural gas is a gaseous fossil fuel consisting primarily of methane but including significant quantities of ethane, propane, butane, and pentane—heavy hydrocarbons removed later on as condensate—as well as carbon dioxide, nitrogen, helium and hydrogen sulfide. It is found in oil fields (associated) either dissolved or isolated in natural gas fields (non associated), and in coal beds (as coalbed methane). When methane-rich gases are produced by the anaerobic decay of non-fossil organic material, these are referred to as biogas. Sources of biogas include swamps, marshes, and landfills (see landfill gas), as well as sewage sludge and manure by way of anaerobic digesters, in addition to enteric fermentation particularly in cattle.

Since natural gas is not a pure product, when non associated gas is extracted from a field under supercritical (pressure/temperature) conditions, it may partially condense upon isothermal depressurizing—an effect called retrograde condensation. The liquids thus formed may get trapped by depositing in the pores of the gas reservoir. One method to deal with this problem is to re-inject dried gas free of condensate to maintain the underground pressure and to allow re-evaporation and extraction of condensates.

Natural gas is often informally referred to as simply gas, especially when compared to other energy sources such as electricity. Before natural gas can be used as a fuel, it must undergo extensive processing to remove almost all materials other than methane. The by-products of that processing include ethane, propane, butanes, pentanes and higher molecular weight hydrocarbons, elemental sulfur, and sometimes helium and nitrogen.

The practice of locating natural gas and petroleum deposits has been transformed dramatically in the last 15 years with the advent of extremely advanced, ingenious technology. In the early days of the industry, the only way of locating underground petroleum and natural gas deposits was to search for surface evidence of these underground formations.

Those searching for natural gas deposits were forced to scour the earth, looking for seepages of oil or gas emitted from underground before they had any clue that there were deposits underneath. However, because such a low proportion of petroleum and natural gas deposits actually seep to the surface, this made for a very inefficient and difficult exploration process. As the demand for fossil fuel energy has increased dramatically over the past years, so has the necessity for more accurate methods of locating these deposits.

Exploration

The exploration for natural gas typically begins with geologists examining the surface structure of the earth, and determining areas where it is geologically likely that petroleum or gas deposits might exist. It was discovered in the mid 1800's that anticlinal slopes had a particularly increased chance of containing petroleum or gas deposits. These anticlinal slopes are areas where the earth has folded up on itself, forming the dome shape that is characteristic of a great number of reservoirs.

By surveying and mapping the surface and sub-surface characteristics of a certain area, the geologist can extrapolate which areas are most likely to contain a petroleum or natural gas reservoir. The geologist has many tools at his disposal to do so, from the outcroppings of rocks on the surface or in valleys and gorges, to the geologic information attained from the rock cuttings and samples obtained from the digging of irrigation ditches, water wells, and other oil and gas wells. This information is all combined to allow the geologist to make inferences as to the fluid content, porosity, permeability, age, and formation sequence of the rocks underneath the surface of a particular area.

Extraction

Once a potential natural gas deposit has been located by a team of exploration geologists and geophysicists, it is up to a team of drilling experts to actually dig down to where the natural gas is thought to exist

The decision of whether or not to drill a well depends on a variety of factors, not the least of which are the economic characteristics of the potential natural gas reservoir. It costs a great deal of money for exploration and production companies to search and drill for natural gas, and there is always the inherent risk that no natural gas will be found

Production

Once a well has been drilled, and the presence of commercially viable quantities of petroleum has been verified, the next step is actually lifting the natural gas or oil out of the ground and processing it for transportation.

Natural gas, as it exists underground, is not exactly the same as the natural gas that comes through the pipelines to our homes and businesses. Natural gas, as we use it, is almost entirely methane. Natural gas as we find it underground, however, can come associated with a variety of other compounds and gases, as well as oil and water, which must be removed. Natural gas transported through pipelines must meet purity specifications to be allowed in, so most natural gas processing occurs near the well.

Transportation

The efficient and effective movement of natural gas from producing regions to consumption regions requires an extensive and elaborate transportation system. In many instances, natural gas produced from a particular well will have to travel a great distance to reach its point of use. The transportation system for natural gas consists of a complex network of pipelines, designed to quickly and efficiently transport natural gas from its origin, to areas of high natural gas demand. Transportation of natural gas is closely linked to its storage, as well; should the natural gas being transported not be required at that time, it can be put into storage facilities for when it is needed.

NATURAL GAS MARKETS

In the IEO2007 reference case, natural gas consumption in the non-OECD countries grows more than twice as fast as in the OECD countries. Production increases in the non-OECD region account for more than 90 percent of the growth in world production from 2004 to 2030.

Consumption of natural gas worldwide increases from 100 trillion cubic feet in 2004 to 163 trillion cubic feet in 2030 in the *IEO 2007* reference case (Figure 3.1). By energy source, the projected increase in natural gas consumption is second only to coal. Natural gas remains a key fuel in the electric power and industrial sectors. In the power sector, natural gas is an attractive choice for new generating plants because of its relative fuel efficiency. Natural gas also burns more cleanly than coal or petroleum products, and as more governments begin implementing national or regional plans to reduce carbon dioxide emissions, they may encourage the use of natural gas to displace liquids and coal.

Much of the world's natural gas use is for industrial sector processes. The industrial sector accounted for 44 percent of world natural gas consumption in 2004 and is projected to account for 43 percent in 2030. With world oil prices expected to remain high relative to historical levels throughout the

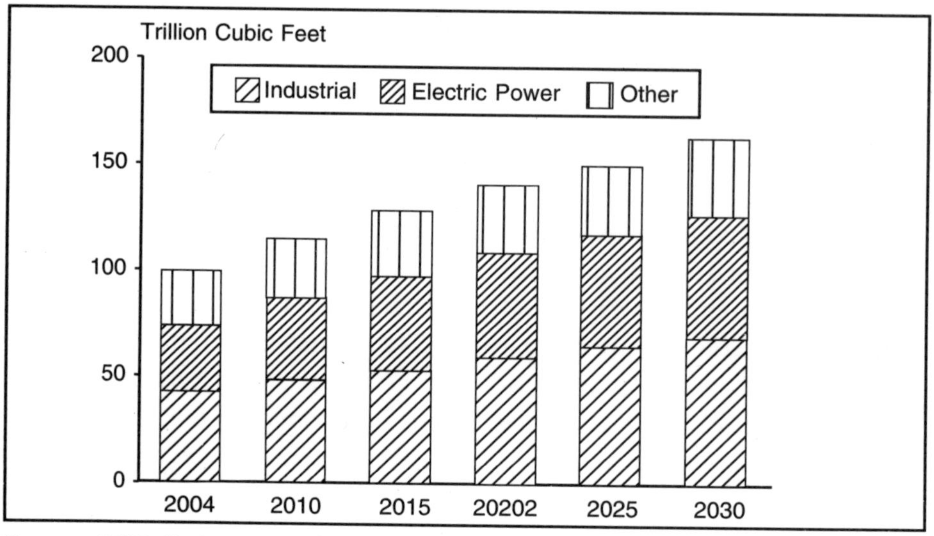

Sources: **2004:** Derived from Energy Information Administration (EIA*), International Energy Annual 2004* (May-July 2006), Website www.eia.doe.gov/iea. **Projections:** EIA, system for the Analysis of Global Energy Markets (2007).

Figure 3.1: World Natural Gas Consumption by End-Use Sector, 2004-30

projection period, natural gas is projected to displace liquids in the industrial sector to some extent. Industrial use of natural gas is projected to increase at an average annual rate of 1.9 percent from 2004 to 2030, as compared with an average increase of 1.1 percent per year for liquids consumption in the industrial sector.

Much of the world's natural gas use is for industrial sector processes. The industrial sector accounted for 44 percent of world natural gas consumption in 2004 and is projected to account for 43 percent in 2030. With world oil prices expected to remain high relative to historical levels throughout the projection period, natural gas is projected to displace liquids in the industrial sector to some extent. Industrial use of natural gas is projected to increase at an average annual rate of 1.9 percent from 2004 to 2030, as compared with an average increase of 1.1 percent per year for liquids consumption in the industrial sector.

Reserves and Resources

As of January 1, 2007, proved world natural gas reserves, as reported by *Oil & Gas Journal*, were estimated at 6,183 trillion cubic feet—71 trillion cubic feet (about 1 percent) higher than the estimate for 2006.

The largest revisions to natural gas reserve estimates were reported for

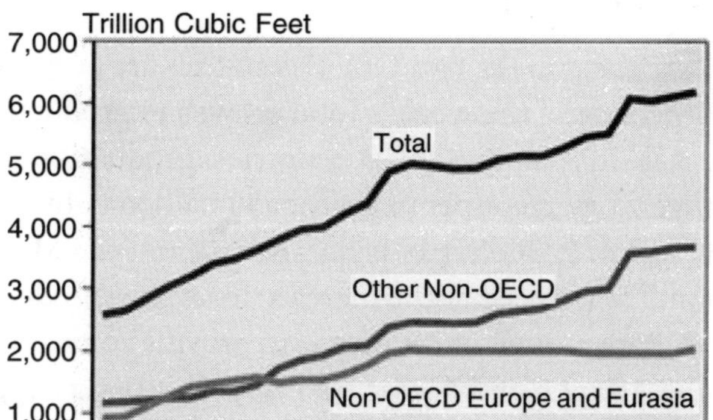

Sources: **1980-1993:** "Worldwide Oil and Gas at a Glance", *International Petroleum Encycloedia* (Tulsa, OK: PennWell Publishing,various issues). **1994-2007:** *Oil & Gas Journal* (various issues).

Figure 3.2: World Natural Gas Reserves by Region, 1980-2007

Kazakhstan, Turkmenistan, and China. Kazakhstan added an estimated 35 trillion cubic feet (a 54-percent increase over 2006 proved reserves), Turkmenistan 29 trillion cubic feet (41 percent), and China 27 trillion cubic feet (50 percent). The United States also reported an increase of 12 trillion cubic feet over its 2006 reserves—a 6 percent increase and the largest increment in U.S. annual reserves since 1970. Declines in natural gas reserves were reported for the Netherlands (a decrease of 12 trillion cubic feet), Trinidad and Tobago (7 trillion cubic feet), Argentina (3 trillion cubic feet), Nigeria (3 trillion cubic feet), and Italy, Norway, the United Kingdom, and Saudi Arabia (about 2 trillion cubic feet each).

Almost three-quarters of the world's natural gas reserves are located in the Middle East and Eurasia. Russia, Iran, and Qatar combined accounted for about 58 percent of the world's natural gas reserves as of January 1, 2007. Reserves in the rest of the world are fairly evenly distributed on a regional basis.

Despite high rates of increase in natural gas consumption, particularly over the past decade, most regional reserves-to-production ratios are substantial. Worldwide, the reserves-to-production ratio is estimated at 65 years. Central and South America has a reserves-to-production ratio of about 52 years, Russia 80 years, and Africa 88 years. The Middle East's reserves-to-production ratio exceeds 100 years.

World Natural Gas Supply

Production increases in the non-OECD countries are projected to account for more than 90 percent of the world's total growth in production from 2004 to 2030 (Figure 3.3). In the non-OECD countries, production is projected to grow by an average 2.6 percent per year, from 59 trillion cubic feet in 2004 to 119 trillion cubic feet in 2030. In particular, Russia and the Middle East each account for around 20 percent of the increase in annual production over the projection period. Both regions are expected to provide connections to natural gas markets in the Atlantic and Pacific basins, with Russia exporting mainly by pipeline and most Middle East exports being shipped as LNG.

Russia has an extensive pipeline network reaching into Europe and has proposed the construction of pipelines to China and South Korea. In addition, Russia is beginning to enter LNG markets. It has traded pipeline gas for Atlantic LNG cargos, has plans to develop LNG export facilities to serve the Atlantic market, and soon will start exporting LNG from its Pacific coast. The

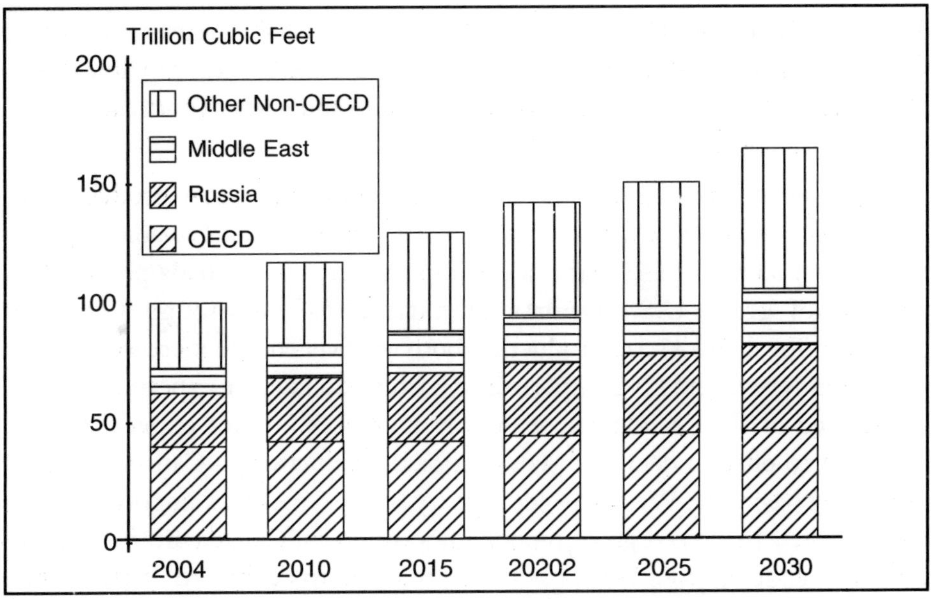

Sources: **2004:** Derived from Energy Information Administration (EIA*), International Energy Annual 2004* (May-July 2006), Website www.eia.doe.gov/iea. **Projections:** EIA, system for the Analysis of Global Energy Markets (2007).

Figure 3.3: World Natural Gas Production by Region, 2004-30

Middle East already exports significant quantities of LNG to customers in both the Atlantic and Pacific basins. In 2005, 15 percent of the LNG exports from the region went to North America and Europe and 85 percent to Asia. Qatar has several LNG export projects under construction that are targeted for sales to North America and Europe. In December 2006, however, Qatar announced that the LNG from one project originally targeted for Atlantic buyers had been sold to Asian buyers in the Pacific basin.

Africa and non-OECD Asia (excluding China and India) are expected to be important sources of natural gas production in the future. For each of the two regions, natural gas production in 2030 is projected to be some 10 trillion cubic feet above 2004 production levels. The two regions combined accounted for 14 percent of the world's natural gas production in 2004; in 2030, their combined share is projected to be 21 percent. A significant portion of the production from both regions is exported. In 2004, 26 percent of the natural gas production from the countries of non-OECD Asia (primarily from Brunei, Indonesia, Malaysia, and Myanmar [formerly Burma]) and 50 percent of the production from African countries was for export. In 2030, the export share of production from non-OECD Asia is projected to fall to 10 percent, as domestic consumption takes precedence over exports, whereas the export share of Africa's production is projected to increase. Several pipelines from North Africa to Europe are under consideration, and LNG export capacity in West Africa continues to expand.

Historically, the United States has been both the largest producer and the largest consumer of natural gas in North America, and Canada has been the primary source of U.S. natural gas imports. In 2004, Canada provided 85 percent of gross U.S. imports of natural gas. Although Canada's unconventional and Arctic production both are expected to increase over the projection period, and LNG imports into Eastern Canada are expected to begin by the end of the decade, those supply increases are not expected to be sufficient to offset a decline in conventional production in Canada's largest producing basin, the Western Sedimentary Basin. Gross U.S. imports of LNG are projected to exceed gross pipeline imports from Canada after 2015, and Canada's share of gross U.S. imports is projected to decline to 25 percent in 2030.

Rising natural gas prices are expected to make it economical for two major North American pipelines that have long been in the planning stages to come online. The first, a Canadian pipeline to transport natural gas from the MacKenzie Delta, is expected to become operational in 2012. The second, an Alaska pipeline, is expected to begin transporting natural gas from Alaska to the lower 48 States in 2018, contributing significantly to U.S. domestic supply. Alaska's natural gas production accounts for all of the projected growth in domestic U.S. conventional natural gas production from 2004 to 2030, with flows on the Alaska pipeline increasing to 2.2 trillion cubic feet in 2030. As a result, Alaskan production is projected to account for 22 percent of the increase in U.S. natural gas supply in 2030 relative to the 2004 total.

A large portion of North America's remaining technically recoverable resource base of natural gas consists of unconventional sources, which include tight sands, shale, and coalbed methane. With most of the large onshore conventional fields in the United States already having been discovered, the United States, like Canada, must look to these costlier sources of supply to make up for declines in conventional production. Unconventional production, especially from tight sands formations, is expected to be a significant source of U.S. incremental supply, increasing from 40 percent of total domestic production in 2004 to 50 percent in 2030 and accounting for 28 percent of the increase in U.S. natural gas supply in 2030 relative to the 2004 total.

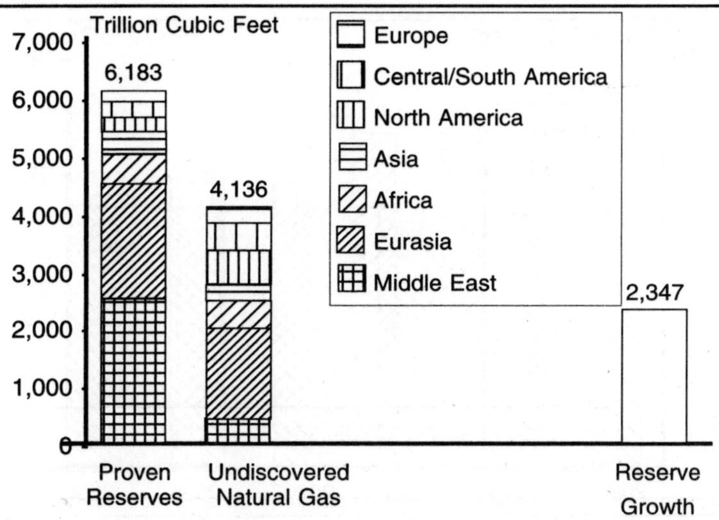

Sources: U.S. Geological Survey, WorldPetroleum Assessment, 2000, website http://greenwood.cr.usgs.gov/energy/WorldEnergy/DDS-60; "Worldwide Look at Reserves and Production," Oil & Gas Journal, Vol. 104, No. 47 (December 18, 2006), pp. 22-23; and Energy Information Administration estimates.

Figure 3.4: World Natural Gas Resources by Geographic Region, 2006-26

World Natural Gas Demand

OECD North America

Natural gas consumption in North America is projected to increase at an average annual rate of 1.0 percent from 2004 to 2030. The average annual growth rate for natural gas demand in the United States is projected to be 0.6 percent, significantly less than in Canada and Mexico, largely because of the impact of higher natural gas prices and supply concerns in U.S. natural gas markets. As North America's largest consumer, the United States accounted for more than 80 percent of the 27.6 trillion cubic feet of natural gas consumed in North America in 2004. As a result of the relatively slow growth in U.S. demand and robust growth in Canada and Mexico, the U.S. share of North America's total natural gas consumption in 2030 falls to 74 percent.

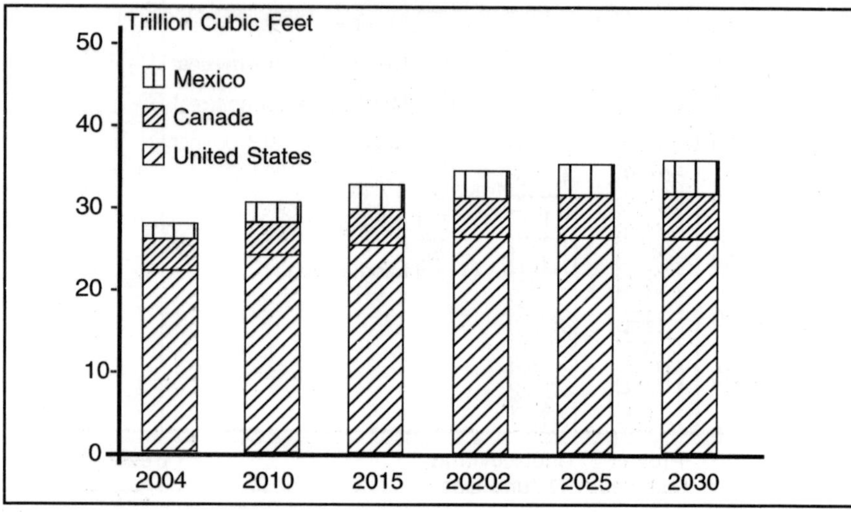

Sources: **2004:** Derived from Energy Information Administration (EIA), *International Energy Annual 2004* (May-July 2006), Website www.eia.doe.gov/iea. **Projections:** EIA, system for the Analysis of Global Energy Markets (2007).

Figure 3.5: Natural Gas Consumption in North America by Country, 2004-30

OECD Europe

Natural gas is expected to be the fastest growing fuel source in OECD Europe, with demand increasing at an annual average rate of 1.4 percent, from 18.8 trillion cubic feet in 2004 to 23.0 trillion cubic feet in 2015 and 26.9 trillion cubic feet in 2030 (Figure 3.6). Growth in natural gas use for power generation is projected to account for the majority of total incremental gas use to 2030. Natural-gas-fired generation is less carbon-intensive than oil- or coal-fired generation and is expected to remain more cost-competitive than renewable energy, making natural gas the fuel of choice for new generating capacity in OECD Europe.

OECD Asia

In Japan, natural gas consumption is projected to grow on average by 1.4 percent per year over the projection period, from 3.0 trillion cubic in 2004 to 4.3 trillion cubic feet in 2030 (Figure 3.7). The strongest growth in consumption is projected for the electric power sector, averaging 1.7 percent annually from 2004 to 2030.

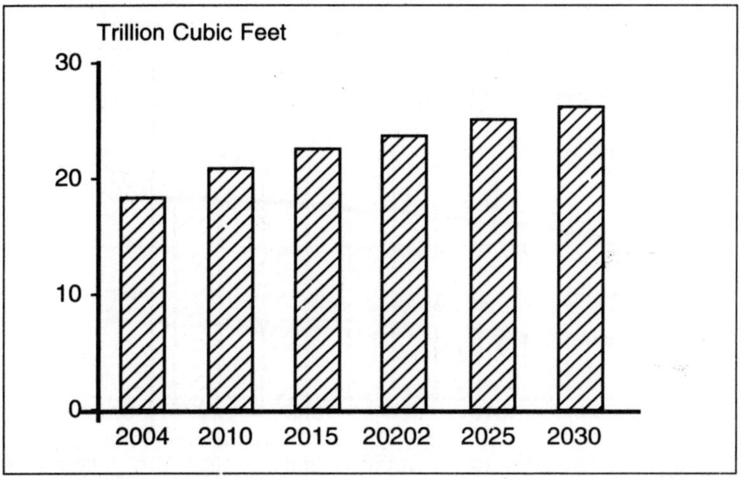

Sources: **2004:** Derived from Energy Information Administration (EIA*), International Energy Annual 2004* (May-July 2006), Website www.eia.doe.gov/iea. **Projections:** EIA, system for the Analysis of Global Energy Markets (2007).

Figure 3.6: Natural Gas Consumption in OECD Europe, 2004-30

Total natural gas consumption in South Korea is projected to grow at an average annual rate of 1.6 percent from 2004 to 2030. In 2004, the residential sector was the country's predominant source of demand for natural gas, accounting for 39 percent of the total. The electric power sector was a close second at 33 percent of total natural gas use, followed by the industrial sector at 20 percent of the total.

South Korea has large seasonal swings in demand for natural gas, importing more than twice as much LNG at its annual winter peak as at its lowest point during the summer—primarily to meet demand for heating in the residential sector. For a country that imports all its natural gas supplies as LNG and has no underground storage facilities, this can be an expensive undertaking. Korea Gas Corporation paid as much as $26 per million Btu for LNG on the spot market in 2005 and 2006, when it faced steep competition for winter cargoes. In the reference case projection, however, with nearly flat population growth, South Korea is expected to see the growth of natural gas consumption in its electric power and industrial sectors outpace growth in the residential sector, potentially moderating seasonal swings in overall demand.

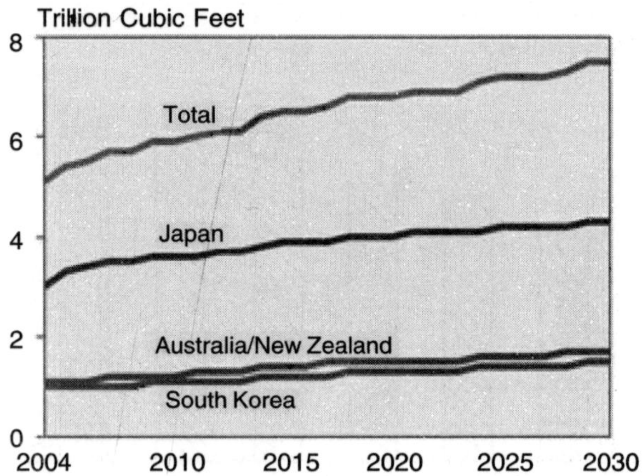

Sources: **2004:** Derived from Energy Information Administration (EIA), *International Energy Annual 2004* (May-July 2006), Website www.eia.doe.gov/iea. **Projections:** EIA, system for the Analysis of Global Energy Markets (2007).

Figure 3.7: Natural Gas Consumption in OECD Asia by Country, 2004-30

Non-OECD Europe and Eurasia

The non-OECD Europe and Eurasia region is more reliant on natural gas than any other region in the world. Russia is second only to the United States in total natural gas consumption, with demand totaling 16.0 trillion cubic feet in 2004 and representing 55 percent of Russia's total energy consumption (Figure 3.8). The other countries of non-OECD Europe and Eurasia met 44 percent of their combined total energy needs with natural gas in 2004, consuming 8.4 trillion cubic feet.

Natural gas intensity (defined as the amount consumed per dollar of GDP) in non-OECD Europe and Eurasia is greater than in any other region of the world, although it has improved in recent years from 9.7 thousand Btu per dollar of GDP in 1996 to 7.5 thousand Btu per dollar in 2004. In the IEO2007 reference case, natural gas intensity in the region is projected to continue improving (decreasing) at an average rate of 2.8 percent per year from 2004 to 2030. Even at that rate, however, natural gas intensity in non-OECD Europe and Eurasia is not projected to equal the 2004 level of North America's natural gas intensity until after 2030.

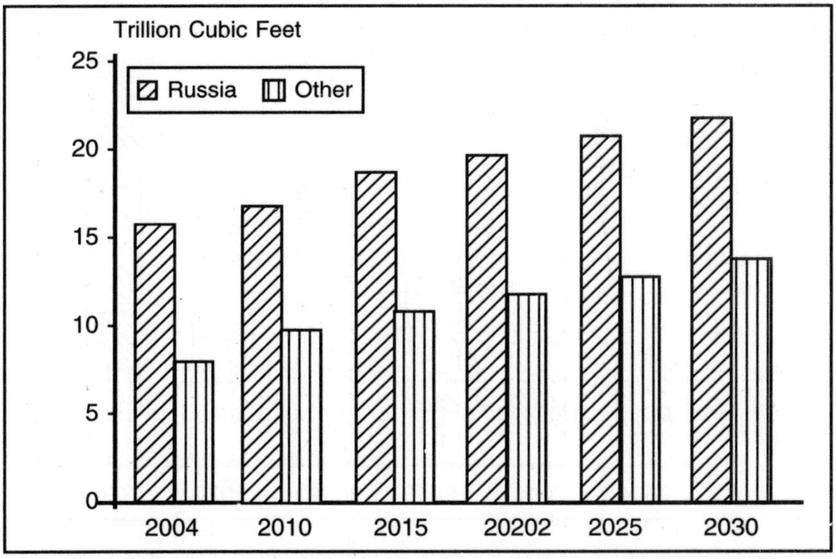

Sources: **2004:** Derived from Energy Information Administration (EIA*), International Energy Annual 2004* (May-July 2006), Website www.eia.doe.gov/iea. **Projections:** EIA, system for the Analysis of Global Energy Markets (2007).

Figure 3.8: Natural Gas Consumption in Non-OECD Europe and Eurasia, 2004-2030

Non-OECD Asia

The fastest growth in natural gas consumption among all regions is projected for non-OECD Asia, which accounted for only 8.5 percent of the world total in 2004 but is projected to account for almost 30 percent of the increase in total natural gas consumption from 2004 to 2030. Natural gas consumption in non-OECD Asia more than triples in the IEO2007 reference case, from 8.5 trillion cubic feet in 2004 to 27.4 trillion cubic feet in 2030 (Figure 3.9).

Led by demand in China and India, natural gas consumption in non-OECD Asia is projected to expand by 4.6 percent per year on average from 2004 to 2030. In both China and India, natural gas currently is a minor fuel in the overall energy mix, representing only 3 percent and 8 percent, respectively, of total primary energy consumption in 2004; however, both countries are rapidly expanding infrastructure to serve demand.

India increased its spot and short-term LNG purchases in 2006, reportedly paying more than $9 per million Btu for one cargo (a year earlier,

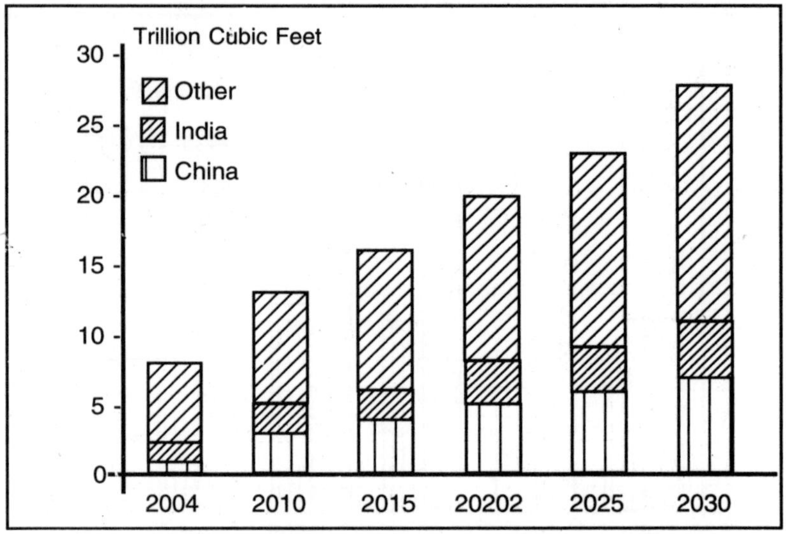

Sources: **2004:** Derived from Energy Information Administration (EIA*), International Energy Annual 2004* (May-July 2006), Website www.eia.doe.gov/iea. **Projections:** EIA, system for the Analysis of Global Energy Markets (2007).

Figure 3.9: Natural Gas Consumption in Non-OECD Asia, 2004-2030

Royal Dutch/Shell could not find customers for LNG from its Hazira regasification terminal at a price of about $8 per million Btu). Natural gas shortages in India have reportedly left natural-gas-fired electric power plants and fertilizer plants underutilized in the past few years. In the IEO 2007 reference case, India's natural gas consumption is projected to rise rapidly in the mid-term, growing by 6.2 percent per year on average from 2004 to 2015. As international natural gas prices gain acceptance in India, and as supplies from the Krishna-Godavari basin come on line around 2010, domestic natural gas supply is expected to catch up with currently underserved demand and also expand to serve new demand.

NATURAL GAS TRADING

There are two primary types of natural gas marketing and trading: physical trading and financial trading. Physical natural gas marketing is the more basic type, which involves buying and selling the physical commodity. Financial trading, on the other hand, involves derivatives and sophisticated financial instruments in which the buyer and seller never take physical delivery of the natural gas.

Like all commodity markets, the inherent volatility of the price of natural gas requires the use of financial derivatives to hedge against the risk of price movement. Buyers and sellers of natural gas hedge using derivatives to reduce price risk. Speculators, on the other hand, assume greater risk in order to profit off of changes in the price of natural gas. Some marketers who actively buy and sell in either the physical or financial markets are referred to as natural gas 'traders'; trading natural gas on the spot market to earn as high a return as possible, and trading financial derivatives and other complex contracts to either hedge risk associated with this physical trading, or speculate about market movements. Most marketing companies have elaborate trading floors, including televisions and pricing boards providing the traders with as much market information as possible.

Physical Trading

Physical trading contracts are negotiated between buyers and sellers. There exist numerous types of physical trading contracts, but most share some standard specifications including specifying the buyer and seller, the price, the amount of natural gas to be sold (usually expressed in a volume per day), the receipt and delivery point, the tenure of the contract (usually expressed in number of days, beginning on a specified day), and other terms and conditions. The special terms and conditions usually outline such things as the payment dates, quality specifications for the natural gas to be sold, and any other specifications agreed to by both parties.

Physical contracts are usually negotiated between buyers and sellers over the phone. However, electronic bulletin boards and e-commerce trading sites are allowing more physical transactions to take place over the internet.

There are three main types of physical trading contracts: swing contracts, base-load contracts, and firm contracts. Swing (or 'interruptible') contracts are usually short-term contracts, and can be as short as one day and are usually not longer than a month. Under this type of contract, both the buyer and seller agree that neither party is obligated to deliver or receive the exact volume specified. These contracts are the most flexible, and are usually put in place when either the supply of gas from the seller, or the demand for gas from the buyer, are unreliable.

Base-load contracts are similar to swing contracts. Neither the buyer nor seller is obligated to deliver or receive the exact volume specified. However, it is agreed that both parties will attempt to deliver or receive the specified volume, on a 'best-efforts' basis. In addition, both parties generally agree not to end the agreement due to market price movements. Both of these understandings are not legal obligations - there is no legal recourse for either party if they believe the other party did not make its best effort to fulfill the agreement—they rely instead on the relationship (both personal and professional) between the buyer and seller.

Firm contracts are different from swing and base-load contracts in that there is legal recourse available to either party, should the other party fail to meet its obligations under the agreement. This means that both parties are legally obligated to either receive or deliver the amount of gas specified in the contract. These contracts are used primarily when both the supply and demand for the specified amount of natural gas are unlikely to change or drop off.

The daily spot market for natural gas is active, and trading can occur 24 hours a day, seven days a week. However, in the natural gas market, the largest volume of trading occurs in the last week of every month. Known as 'bid week', this is when producers are trying to sell their core production and consumers are trying to buy for their core natural gas needs for the upcoming month. The core natural gas supply or demand is not expected to change; producers know they will have that much natural gas over the next month, and consumers know that they will require that much natural gas over the next month. The average prices set during bid week are commonly the prices used in physical contracts.

The Financial Market

In addition to trading physical natural gas, there is a significant market for natural gas derivatives and financial instruments in the United States. In fact, it has been estimated that the value of trading that occurs on the financial market is 10 to 12 times greater than the value of physical natural gas trading.

Derivatives are financial instruments that 'derive' their value from an underlying fundamental; in this case the price of natural gas. Derivatives can range from being quite simple, to being exceedingly complex. Traditionally, most derivatives are traded on the over-the-counter (OTC) market, which is essentially a group of market players interested in exchanging certain derivatives among themselves, as opposed to through a market like the

NYMEX. Basic types of derivatives include futures, options, and financial swaps.

A forward contract is an agreement between two parties to buy or sell an asset (which can be of any kind) at a pre-agreed future point in time. Therefore, the trade date and delivery date are separated. It is used to control and hedge risk, for example currency exposure risk (e.g., forward contracts on USD or EUR) or commodity prices (e.g., forward contracts on oil).

One party agrees (obligated) to sell, the other to buy, for a forward price agreed in advance. In a forward transaction, no actual cash changes hands. If the transaction is collateralized, exchange of margin will take place according to a pre-agreed rule or schedule. Otherwise no asset of any kind actually changes hands, until the maturity of the contract.

The forward price of such a contract is commonly contrasted with the spot price, which is the price at which the asset changes hands (on the spot date, usually two business days). The difference between the spot and the forward price is the forward premium or forward discount.

A standardized forward contract that is traded on an exchange is called a futures contract.

Example of how the Pay off of a Forward Contract Works

Suppose that Bob wants to buy a house in one year's time. At the same time, suppose that Andy currently owns a $100,000 Crude oil stocks that he wishes to sell in one year's time. Both parties could enter into a forward contract with each other. Suppose that they both agree on the sale price in one year's time of $104,000 (more below on why the sale price should be this amount). Andy and Bob have entered into a forward contract. Bob, because he is buying the underlying, is said to have entered a long forward contract. Conversely, Andy will have the short forward contract.

At the end of one year, suppose that the current market valuation of Andy's Crude oil stock is $110,000. Then, because Andy is obliged to sell to Bob for only $104,000, Bob will make a profit of $6,000. To see why this is so, one needs only to recognize that Bob can buy from Andy for $104,000 and immediately sell to the market for $110,000. Bob has made the difference in profit. In contrast, Andy has made a loss of $6,000.

Example of how Forward Prices should be Agreed Upon

Continuing on the example above, suppose now that the initial price of Andy's Crude oil stock is $100,000 and that Bob enters into a forward contract to buy the Crude oil stock one year from today. But since Andy knows that he can immediately sell for $100,000 and place the proceeds in the bank, he wants to be compensated for the delayed sale. Suppose that the risk free rate of return R (the bank rate) for one year is 4%. Then the money in the bank would grow to $104,000, risk free. So Andy would want at least $104,000 one year from now for the contract to be worthwhile for him - the opportunity cost will be covered.

Bob, as any other buyer would, will seek the lowest price he can for the contract—although as we've seen, there is an invisible lower limit of $104,000 that Andy will not go below. As a result, the contract price would be at least $104,000 or it will not happen at all.

A **futures contract** is a standardized contract, traded on a futures exchange, to buy or sell a certain underlying instrument at a certain date in the future, at a specified price. The future date is called the **delivery date** or **final settlement date**. The pre-set price is called the **futures price**. The price of the underlying asset on the delivery date is called the **settlement price**.

A futures contract gives the holder *the obligation* to buy or sell, which differs from an options contract, which gives the holder *the right, but not the obligation.* In other words, the owner of an options contract **may** exercise the contract, but both parties of a "futures contract" **must** fulfill the contract on the settlement date. The seller delivers the commodity to the buyer, or, if it is a cash-settled future, then cash is transferred from the futures trader who sustained a loss to the one who made a profit. To exit the commitment prior to the settlement date, the holder of a futures position has to offset their position by either selling a long position or buying back a short position, effectively closing out the futures position and its contract obligations.

Futures contracts, or simply *futures,* are exchange traded derivatives. The exchange's clearinghouse acts as counterparty on all contracts, sets margin requirements, and crucially also provides a mechanism for settlement.

Futures traders are traditionally placed in one of two groups: hedgers, who have an interest in the underlying commodity and are seeking to *hedge out* the risk of price changes; and speculators, who seek to make a profit by predicting market moves and buying a commodity "on paper" for which they have no practical use.

Hedgers typically include producers and consumers of a commodity.

For example, in traditional commodities markets, farmers often sell futures contracts for the crops and livestock they produce to guarantee a certain price, making it easier for them to plan. Similarly, livestock producers often purchase futures to cover their feed costs, so that they can plan on a fixed cost for feed. In modern (financial) markets, "producers" of interest rate swaps or equity derivative products will use financial futures or equity index futures to reduce or remove the risk on the swap.

The social utility of futures markets is considered to be mainly in the transfer of risk, and increase liquidity between traders with different risk and time preferences, from a hedger to a speculator for example.

Options are financial instruments that convey the right, but not the obligation, to engage in a future transaction on some underlying security, or in a futures contract. In other words, the holder does not have to exercise this right, unlike a forward or future. For example, buying a call option provides the right to buy a specified quantity of a security at a set strike price at some time on or before expiration, while buying a put option provides the right to sell. Upon the option holder's choice to exercise the option, the party who sold, or wrote, the option must fulfill the terms of the contract.

The theoretical value of an option can be determined by a variety of techniques. These models, which are developed by quantitative analysts, can also predict how the value of the option will change in the face of changing conditions. Hence, the risks associated with trading and owning options can be understood and managed with some degree of precision.

Exchange-traded options form an important class of options which have standardized contract features and trade on public exchanges, facilitating trading among independent parties. Over-the-counter options are traded between private parties, often well-capitalized institutions, that have negotiated separate trading and clearing arrangements with each other. Another important class of options, particularly in the U.S., are employee stock options, which are awarded by a company to their employees as a form of incentive compensation.

Other types of options exist in many financial contracts, for example real estate options are often used to assemble large parcels of land, and prepayment options are usually included in mortgage loans. However, many of the valuation and risk management principles apply across all financial options.

In many cases, *options* are traded on futures. A put is the option to sell a futures contract, and a call is the option to buy a futures contract. For both, the option strike price is the specified futures price at which the future is traded if the option is exercised. See the Black model, which is the most popular method for pricing these option contracts.

Types of Options

The primary types of financial options are:

Exchange traded options (also called "listed options") are a class of exchange traded derivatives. Exchange traded options have standardized contracts, and are settled through a clearing house with fulfillment guaranteed by the credit of the exchange. Since the contracts are standardized, accurate pricing models are often available. Exchange traded options include:

1. stock options,
2. commodity options,
3. bond options and other interest rate options,
4. index (equity) options, and
5. options on futures contracts.

Over-the-counter options (OTC options, also called "Trader options") are traded between two private parties, and are not listed on an exchange. The terms of an OTC option are unrestricted and may be individually tailored to meet any business need. In general, at least one of the counterparties to an OTC option is a well-capitalized institution. Option types commonly traded over the counter include:

1. interest rate options,
2. currency cross rate options, and
3. options on swaps or swaptions.

Options Styles

Naming conventions are used to help identify properties common to many different types of options. These include:

European option—an option that may only be exercised on expiration.

American option—an option that may be exercised on any trading day on or before expiration.

Bermudan option—an option that may be exercised only on specified dates on or before expiration.

Barrier option—any option with the general characteristic that the underlying security's price must reach some trigger level before the exercise can occur.

A swap is a derivative in which two counterparties agree to exchange one stream of cash flows against another stream. These streams are called the *legs* of the swap.

The cash flows are calculated over a notional principal amount, which is usually not exchanged between counterparties. Consequently, swaps can be used to create unfunded exposures to an underlying asset, since counterparties can earn the profit or loss from movements in price without having to post the notional amount in cash or collateral.

Swaps can be used to hedge certain risks such as interest rate risk, or to speculate on changes in the underlying prices.

Most swaps are traded Over The Counter (OTC), "tailor-made" for the counterparties. Some types of swaps are also exchanged on futures markets, for instance Chicago Mercantile Exchange Holdings Inc., the largest U.S. futures market, the Chicago Board Options Exchange and Frankfurt-based Eurex AG. David Swensen, a Yale Ph.D. at Salomon Brothers, engineered the first swap transaction according to "When Genius Failed: The Rise and Fall of Long-Term Capital Management" by Roger Lowenstein.

The five generic types of swaps, in order of their quantitative importance, are: interest rate swaps, currency swaps, credit swaps, commodity swaps and equity swaps.

A **hedge** is an investment that is taken out specifically to reduce or cancel out the risk in another investment. **Hedging** is a strategy designed to minimize exposure to an unwanted business risk, while still allowing the business to profit from an investment activity. Typically, a hedger might invest in a security that he believes is under-priced relative to its "fair value" (for example a mortgage loan that he is then making), and combine this with a short sale of a related security or securities. Thus the hedger is indifferent to the movements of the market as a whole, and is interested only in the performance of the 'under-priced' security relative to the hedge. Holbrook Working, a pioneer in hedging theory, called this strategy "speculation in the basis" where the basis is the difference between the hedge's theoretical value and its actual value (or between spot and futures prices in Working's time).

Some form of risk taking is inherent to any business activity. Some risks are considered to be "natural" to specific businesses, such as the risk of oil prices increasing or decreasing is natural to oil drilling and refining firms. Other forms of risk are not wanted, but cannot be avoided without hedging. Someone who has a shop, for example, expects to face natural risks such as the risk of competition, of poor or unpopular products, and so on. The risk of the shopkeeper's inventory being destroyed by fire is unwanted, however, and can be hedged via a fire insurance contract. Not all hedges are financial instruments: a producer that exports to another country, for example, may hedge its currency risk when selling by linking its expenses to the desired currency. Banks and other financial institutions use hedging to control their asset-liability mismatches, such as the maturity matches between long, fixed-rate loans and short-term (implicitly variable-rate) deposits.

GAS CONTRACTS

I. Henry Hub Natural Gas Futures—U.S.A

Trading Unit: 10,000 million British thermal units (mmBtu).

Price Quotation: U.S. dollars and cents per mmBtu.

Trading Hours (All times are New York time): Open outcry trading is conducted from 9:00 AM until 2:30 PM.

Electronic trading is conducted from 6:00 PM until 5:15 PM via the CME Globex® trading platform, Sunday through Friday. There is a 45-minute break each day between 5:15PM (current trade date) and 6:00 PM (next trade date).

Trading Months: The current year and the next five years. A new calendar year will be added following the termination of trading in the December contract of the current year.

Trading at Settlement (TAS): Trading at settlement is available for the front two months except on the last trading day and is subject to the existing TAS rules. Trading in all TAS products will cease daily at 2:30 PM Eastern Time. The TAS products will trade off of a "Base Price" of 100 to create a differential (plus or minus) in points off settlement in the underlying cleared product on a 1 to 1 basis. A trade done at the Base Price of 100 will correspond to a "traditional" TAS trade which will clear exactly at the final settlement price of the day.

Minimum Price Fluctuation: $0.001 (0.1¢) per mmBtu ($10.00 per contract).

Maximum Daily Price Fluctuation: $3.00 per mmBtu ($30,000 per contract) for all months. If any contract is traded, bid, or offered at the limit for five minutes, trading is halted for five minutes. When trading resumes, the limit is expanded by $3.00 per mmBtu in either direction. If another halt were triggered, the market would continue to be expanded by $3.00 per mmBtu in either direction after each successive five-minute trading halt. There will be no maximum price fluctuation limits during any one trading session.

Last Trading Day: Trading terminates three business days prior to the first calendar day of the delivery month.

Settlement Type: Physical.

Delivery: The Sabine Pipe Line Co. Henry Hub in Louisiana. Seller is responsible for the movement of the gas through the Hub; the buyer, from the Hub. The Hub fee will be paid by seller.

Complete delivery rules and provisions are detailed in Chapter 220 of the Exchange Rulebook.

Delivery Period: Delivery shall take place no earlier than the first calendar day of the delivery month and shall be completed no later than the last calendar day of the delivery month. All deliveries shall be made at as uniform as possible an hourly and daily rate of flow over the course of the delivery month.

Alternate Delivery Procedure (ADP): An alternate delivery procedure is available to buyers and sellers who have been matched by the Exchange subsequent to the termination of trading in the spot month contract. If buyer and seller agree to consummate delivery under terms different from those prescribed in the contract specifications, they may proceed on that basis after submitting a notice of their intention to the Exchange.

Exchange of Futures for Physicals (EFP) or Swaps (EFS): The commercial buyer or seller may exchange a futures position for a physical position or a swaps position of equal quantity by submitting a notice to the Exchange. EFPs and EFSs may be used to either initiate or liquidate a futures position.

Grade and Quality Specifications: Pipeline specifications in effect at time of delivery.

Position Accountability Levels and Limits: Any one month/all months: 12,000 net futures, but not to exceed 1,000 in the last three days of trading in the spot month.

Margin Requirements: Margins are required for open futures positions.

Trading Symbol: NG

NGT (TAS Code)

II. Multi commodity Exchange of India—Mumbai

Exchange: MCX

Commodity: Natural Gas

Settlement: Both cash as well as physical delivery

Duration of Contract: 3 months

Trading Unit: 500 mmBtu

Price Quotation: Rs. per mmBtu

Minimum Price Movement: Rs. 0.10 per mmBtu

Maximum Daily Price Fluctuation: 4%

Maximum Allowable Open Position: (i) For individual clients: 50,00,000 mmBtu. (ii) For a member collectively for all clients: 2,00,00,000 mmBtu or 20% of open interest, whichever is higher.

Margins: Margins are required to initiate a position on the exchange.

1. *Initial Margin:* Buyers and Sellers have to submit a 7% initial margin to initiate a position on the Exchange.
2. *Special Margin:* In case of additional volatility, a special margin at such percentage, as deemed fit, will be imposed immediately on both buy and sale side in respect of all outstanding position, which will remain in force for next 2 days, after which the special margin will be relaxed.
3. *Delivery Period Margin:* A Delivery Period Margin of 25% will be imposed during tender and delivery period on both buyers and sellers on matched quantity.

Working:

1. On the contract expiry day by 6.00 p.m. sellers and buyers will submit Notices of Intention to Deliver and Notices of Intention to Accept, respectively with the exchange.

2. Sellers will also submit copies of relevant documents as a proof of holding stock at the time of giving Notice of Intention to Deliver.

3. On the basis of Notices of Intentions to Deliver and Accept the Exchange will match the total quantity offered by the buyers and sellers and with respect to the matched quantity, the allocation of delivery between the buyers and sellers will be done.

4. *Penalty:* After receipt of intentions from the buyer and seller to take or give delivery, if any of the party fails to honor his obligations, a penalty of 1% of the DDR will be imposed on him, out of which 90% will be passed on to the other party and 10% will be retained by the Exchange.

5. Cash Settlement:
   (i) All positions that are offset before the expiry of the contract are cash settled.
   (ii) All outstanding positions on the expiry of contract where Notice of Intention to Deliver or Accept has not been received and such positions where Notices of Intention have been received but have not found the counter party for honoring the intentions, shall be closed out at due date rate and respective pay-in and pay-out of funds of such close out positions shall be take place on the following day of contract expiry day by 11.00 a.m.

6. *Physical Delivery:* Physical Delivery takes place for the open positions after the expiry date where the Exchange is able to match the Notices of Intention to Deliver and Accept.

Note: This contract is mainly used for hedging/speculation purposes by players in the market. Also, trading participants are still not doing physical trading on exchanges in India. They go for OTC market for physical trade as there they know and can choose the counter party and can negotiate the terms of contract. Hence, all the contracts are cash settled even though there is a provision for physical settlement. Moreover, the contract size is also too small to attract traders to go for physical delivery.

Due Date Rate: Due date rate shall be the settlement price of NYMEX Natural Gas (NG) near month contract on the last day (Expiry date) of the MCX Natural Gas contract. The NYMEX (NG) Natural Gas settlement price will be converted at the Rupee-US$ rate as notified by the Reserve Bank of India on that particular day.

Delivery Center: Hazira Hub.

Delivery Grades: Natural Gas should be of standard pipeline quality.

Delivery and Payment: The seller has to make the delivery by 11:00 a.m. on the 3rd day from the day of expiry of contract. The buyer submits the payment with the clearing house by 11:00 a.m. on the 2nd working day from the day of expiry of the contract. The clearing house will release this amount to the seller by 11:00 a.m. on the 3rd working day from the day of expiry of contract.

Extension of Delivery Period: As per the Exchange decision due to a force majeure or otherwise.

Endorsement of Delivery Order: The buyer member can endorse delivery order to a client or any third party with full disclosure given to MCX. Responsibility for contractual liability would be with the original assignee.

III. New York Mercantile Exchange—U.S.A

Exchange: NYMEX

Commodity: Natural Gas

Price Quote: Henry Hub

Settlement: Physical delivery

Duration of Contract: 72 consecutive months

Trading Unit: 10,000 mmBtu

Price Quotation: US dollars and cents per mmBtu

Minimum Price Movement: $0.001 (0.1¢) per mmBtu ($10.00 per contract)

Maximum Daily Price Fluctuation:

1. $3.00 per mmBtu ($30,000 per contract) is the upper limit for daily price movement.

2. If any contract is traded, bid, or offered at the limit for five minutes, trading is halted for five minutes. When trading resumes, the limit is expanded by $3.00 per mmBtu in either direction.

3. If another halt were triggered, the market would continue to be expanded by $3.00 per mmBtu in either direction after each successive five-minute trading halt. There will be no maximum price fluctuation limits during any one trading session.

Maximum Allowable Open Position: 12,000 net futures contracts (1 contract = 10,000 mmBtu) in any one month or all months combined, but not to exceed 1,000 contracts in the last three days of trading in the spot month.

Working:

1. By 11:30 a.m. on the first business day after the final day of trading, each member holding an open short position (seller) and open long position (buyer) shall file with the Exchange a properly completed and signed 'Notice of Intention to Deliver' and 'Notice of Intention to Accept', respectively.

2. The 'Notice of Intention to Deliver' shall include: the name of the seller's customer, the pipeline(s) through which the seller will transport the product to the Henry Hub, the number of contracts, and such additional information as may be required by the Exchange.

3. The 'Notice of Intention to Accept' shall include: the name of the buyer's customer, the number of contracts to be accepted, and such additional information as may be required by the Exchange.

4. The Clearing House shall allocate Notices of Intention to Deliver and Notices of Intention to Accept by matching size of positions, and the designated delivery and receiving pipelines to the extent possible.

5. The Clearing House shall pass copies of the notices to the respective Clearing Members by 2:00 p.m. on the first business day after the final day of trading. The day the notices are passed to the Clearing Members shall be referred to as the *Notice Day*.

6. Thereafter, a buyer or seller may amend the names of its pipeline(s) by providing a Notice of Revision and Clearance to the counterparty.

Clearance: Not later than 10:30 a.m. on the last business day prior to the Delivery month, the Seller shall give the Buyer a properly completed and signed Notice of Clearance in the form prescribed by the Exchange, with a copy to the Exchange, stating that the product and transportation are in place to enable the delivery to occur in accordance with the provisions of the Notice of Intention to Delivery and Notice of Intention to Accept.

Non-Clearance:

1. In the event that the Seller is unable to make delivery in accordance with the Notice of Intention to Deliver and Notice of Intention to Accept because of inability to receive clearance from the Henry Hub facility, the Seller shall, not later than 10:30 a.m. on the last business day prior to the Delivery Month, give to the Buyer a Notice of Non-Clearance with a copy to the Exchange, and state the reasons for such inability.

2. The Seller, may at its option, in the Notice of Non-Clearance suggest an alternate or preferred delivery site.

3. If the reason for the Non-Clearance is the Seller's inability to transport the product through the Henry Hub facilities, the Seller shall require, at the time the Notice of Non-Clearance is given, to post additional original margin equal to 25% of the total contract value of all contracts listed in such Notices. Such additional margin shall be posted by the Seller with the Exchange on the next business day.

4. In addition, the Seller shall, not later than 4:00 p.m. on the last business day prior to the delivery month, file with the Exchange with a copy to the Buyer, a Revised Notice of Intention to Deliver setting forth a revised designation of the pipeline(s) through which Seller will transport the product to Buyer's pipeline interconnection(s), and give the Buyer, with a copy to the Exchange, a Notice of Clearance or a Second Notice of Non-Clearance stating the reasons for the second Non-Clearance.

5. If the reason for the non-clearance is the Buyer's inability to secure transportation from the Henry Hub facilities, the Buyer shall, no later than 4:00 p.m. on the last business day prior to the delivery month, file with the Exchange with a copy to the Seller, a Revised Notice of Intention to Accept Delivery, setting forth a revised designation of the pipeline interconnection(s) at the Henry Hub from which the Buyer will accept the product and a certification that delivery shall occur pursuant to the terms of the Notice of Intention to Deliver and Revised Notice of Intention to Accept Delivery or a Second Notice of Non-Clearance stating the reasons for the second Non-Clearance.

Settlement Price: The settlement price on the final day of trading at the exchange shall be the basis of delivery.

Delivery Center: The Sabine Pipe Line Co. Henry Hub in Louisiana. Seller is responsible for the movement of the gas through the Hub; the buyer, from the Hub. The Hub fee will be paid by seller.

Delivery Grades: Natural Gas meeting the specifications set forth in the Federal Energy Regulatory Commission (FERC)-approved tariff of Sabine Pipe Line Company as then in effect at the time of delivery shall be deliverable in satisfaction of futures contract delivery obligations.

Alternate Delivery Procedure (ADP):

1. An alternate delivery procedure is available to buyers and sellers who have been matched by the Exchange subsequent to the termination of trading in the spot month contract.

2. If buyer and seller agree to consummate delivery under terms different from those prescribed in the contract specifications, they may proceed on that basis after submitting a notice of their intention to the Exchange.

3. The delivery of an executed 'Alternative Notice of Intention to Deliver' to the Exchange shall release the Clearing Members and the Exchange from their respective obligations under the Exchange contracts.

4. Upon receipt of an executed Alternative Notice of Intention to Deliver, the Exchange will return to the Clearing Members all margin monies held for the account of each with respect to the contracts involved.

Exchange of Futures for Physicals (EFP) or Swaps (EFS):

1. The commercial buyer or seller may exchange a futures position for a physical position or a swap position of equal quantity by submitting a notice to the Exchange.

2. EFPs and EFSs may be used to either initiate or liquidate a futures position.

3. At the time such EFP and EFS transactions are effected, the buyer of the futures contract must be the seller of the physical product (for EFP) or swaps contract (for EFS) and the seller of the futures contract must be the buyer of the physical product (for EFP) or swaps contract (for EFS).

4. EFP/EFS must take place during the hours of futures trading for the Natural Gas futures contract. EFP/EFS is permitted in the expiring futures contract until two hours after trading terminates on the last day of trading of the expiring futures contract.

5. Each buyer and seller must satisfy the Exchange, at its request, that the transaction is a legitimate EFP/EFS transaction.

Inspection:

1. Inspection shall be conducted in accordance with pipeline practices.

2. A buyer or seller may appoint an inspector to inspect the quality of oil delivered.

3. The buyer or seller who requests the inspection will bear its costs and will notify the other party of the transaction that the inspection will occur.

Delivery:

1. Delivery shall be F.O.B. the Buyer's interconnection point at the Henry Hub.

2. Delivery shall be considered to have occurred when product passes through the buyer's interconnection point, at such time the buyer shall bear the risk of loss.

3. The seller shall provide natural gas which is free from all liens, encumbrances, unpaid taxes, fees and other charges.

4. Delivery shall take place no earlier than the first calendar day of the delivery month and shall be completed no later than the last calendar day of the delivery month.

5. All deliveries shall be at as uniform an hourly and daily rate of flow over the course of the delivery month as is possible under the operating procedures and conditions of the transporting pipelines.

6. The seller shall give the buyer all appropriate documents to transfer title of product upon receipt of payment.

Delivery Margins:

1. On the third business day following the last day of trading, the buyer shall deposit margin equal to the full value of the product to be delivered, not including any adjustment for discounts and premiums, with the clearing house.

2. Such margin shall consist of cash, securities issued by the United States Treasury Department maturing within ten (10) years from the date of deposit and guaranteed as to principal and interest by the United States Government or a letter of credit.

3. The seller shall deposit with the Clearing House, margin in an amount fixed, from time to time, by the Exchange.

4. Such margins shall be returned on the business day following notification to the Exchange that delivery and payment have been completed.

Payment:

1. Not later than 12:00 o'clock noon on the third business day prior to the payment date, the seller shall advise his clearing member of the name and address of the bank, and the name of the account to which payment shall be made.

2. The seller's clearing member shall advise the buyer's clearing member who shall advise the buyer.

3. On the payment date, the buyer shall pay the seller contract value by federal funds wire transfer to the account of the seller at the bank nominated by the seller.

4. Not later than 12:00 noon (NY time) the buyer shall advise his clearing member of the federal funds wire transfer number and the name of the sending bank.

5. The buyer's clearing member shall advise, by telex, the seller's clearing member who shall similarly advise the seller.

6. Not later than the business day following the payment date, the seller shall advise his clearing member of receipt of payment.

7. The seller's clearing member shall deliver a notice of payment to the buyer's clearing member with a copy to the Clearing House not later than the business day following the payment date.

8. Upon receipt of such notice, the delivery shall be complete.

Note: Any payment made on payment date shall be based on Btu's actually delivered.

Payment Not Received:

1. In the event that the seller's clearing member receives notification that payment has not been received, it shall advise the Exchange and the buyer's clearing member in writing.

2. On the following business day, unless the buyer or his clearing member has advised the Exchange in writing that the seller failed to deliver, the Exchange shall liquidate the margins held and, when the liquidation is complete, shall pay the seller's clearing member which shall pay the seller.

3. If the buyer or his clearing member has advised the Exchange in writing that the seller failed to deliver, the matter shall be referred to the Petroleum Delivery Committee for resolution.

Extension of Delivery Period: Force Majeure shall be determined by a Panel of the Delivery Committee appointed by the Chairman of the Delivery Committee. "Force Majeure" shall mean any circumstance (including but not limited to a strike, lockout, national emergency, governmental action, or act of God) which is beyond the control of the buyer or seller, and which prevents the buyer or seller from making or taking delivery of product or effecting payment when and as provided for.

IV. International Commodity Exchange—London

Exchange: ICE

Commodity: Natural Gas

Settlement: Physical Delivery

Duration of Contract: 6 months

Trading Unit: Minimum of 5 lots of 1,000 therms per lot of natural gas per day

(1 therm = 100,000 Btu)

Price Quotation: Sterling and Pence per therm

Minimum Price Movement: 0.01 pence per therm

Maximum Daily Price Fluctuation: No Limit.

Maximum Allowable Open Position: No Limit.

Working:

1. The contract is deliverable unless positions are closed out prior to expiry.

2. Physical delivery takes place through the transfer of rights within the UK natural gas grid at the National Balancing Point (NBP).

3. *National Balancing Point:* This notional point is where National Grid effects a balance every day between the input and withdrawal of gas taking place on the UK National Transmission System (NTS).

4. Delivery is made equally each day throughout the delivery period.

5. The Seller shall submit a Disposing Trade Nomination (for gas delivery) in respect of the Delivery Day to BG TransCo (British Gas TransCo) for a Trade Nomination Quantity which is equal to the number of lots of Natural Gas specified in the Contract, such number of lots converted in to kWh.

6. The Buyer shall submit an Acquiring Trade Nomination (for acceptance of delivery of gas) in respect of the Delivery Day to BG TransCo for a Trade Nomination Quantity which is equal to the number of lots of Natural Gas specified in the Contract, such number of lots converted into kWh.

Delivery:

1. Matching Acquiring and Disposing Trade Nominations are input by buyer and seller to National Grid Transco before 18:30 hours (London time) on the business day prior to delivery.

2. Delivery takes place in kilowatt-hours (29.3071 kilowatt hours per therm).

Settlement Price: The weighted average price of trades during a fifteen minute settlement period starting from 16:00:00 hours, London time on ICE.

Delivery Centre: Transfer of rights of Natural Gas will take place within the UK natural gas grid at the National Balancing Point (NBP).

Payment: The Buyer shall pay the Exchange Delivery Settlement Price (EDSP) per each Therm of Natural Gas specified in the Contract.

Buyer's and Seller's Security: The Buyer and the Seller may be required to put up such security as the Clearing House may require from time to time. Such security may be in the form of a bank guarantee or cash or such other form as the Clearing House may accept.

Exchange of Futures for Physical (EFP):

1. The EFP facility allows Members to register Futures trades linked to physical and forward transactions. This allows more effective hedging opportunities for market participants with over-the-counter positions.

2. Reporting of EFP trades may take place at any time during trading hours and for 30 minutes after the close of the relevant individual Contract.

3. On an expiry day, EFP in respect of the expiring contract date may be reported up to one hour after the expiry of the contract date.

4. The Exchange may require Members to supply evidence of the underlying physical transaction either prior to or following registration of the trade and may refuse registration in its sole and final discretion.

5. In the case of EFP transactions, the underlying OTC contract must be properly documented and available for production to the ICE Futures compliance department on demand in order to validate its legitimacy.

6. The registration of the EFP should be at the current market price or within plus/minus £0.01 (1.0 pence) per lot limit (the Exchange may amend the limit at any time as necessary), otherwise the exchange must be satisfied that the transaction is a legitimate use of facility and not for money laundering

or any other purpose other than as a consequence of normal commercial activity, before EFP's registration can take place.

Force Majeure: Force Majeure shall mean the occurrence of any event which is outside the reasonable control of the Buyer (or its Transferee) or the Seller (or its Transferor), as the case may be, which totally prevents a Trade Nomination from being submitted by or on behalf of a party to BG TransCo or from being received and taken into account by BG TransCo in determining a party's "Daily Imbalance" and thereby prevents a transfer of rights in respect of Natural Gas from being made on the Delivery Day.

Neither party to a Contract shall be liable for any failure to transfer or take a transfer of rights in respect of Natural Gas under the Contract if performance of such obligation is prevented by Force Majeure. In such case, neither party shall be held to be in default under such Contract nor will any payment be made.

INTRODUCTION OF LNG

Global demand for liquefied natural gas has grown rapidly in recent years particularly in the Asia pacific region, where LNG imports are the primary source of gas in some countries. The current development of the global LNG industry will have substantial implications for the global gas industry and in particularly for security of gas supply. Tremendous cost reductions have been experienced in all parts of LNG chain in recent years. The fall in the tanker prices over the last decade led to much wider economic reach of LNG transportation. The dramatic cost reductions for LNG liquefaction trains, especially for expansion trains, but also for new trains such as the Trinidad and Tobago project made LNG projects viable even if only part of the capacity is secured by long-term sales, so that the remainder could be sold on flexible terms or spot basis.

Recently the LNG market started developing very fastly due to the sudden increase in demand in Atlantic and Pacific basins. U.S. and Europe had started developing new LNG terminals and expanding the capacities of old terminals with increasing demand of natural gas in their economy.

As most of so far undeveloped gas reserves are located far away from OECD markets, it is clear that LNG will play a key role to bring this gas to the market, when distance or natural and political obstacles make pipeline transport impossible.

At the same time, the increasing use of gas in power generation is creating a market able to absorb very substantial new gas volumes, opening the perspective for many gas-reserves owning countries to monetize their gas reserves via LNG sales. The decreasing cost of LNG chain, as well as there is increase in number of buyer and sellers side. And all these events are helping the LNG industry overall by overcoming the past rigidities in the business.

The growing supply of LNG has enabled the supplier to get price arbitrage by selling the LNG to the highest value market. Spot and flexible LNG purchases are increasingly used to cover part of peak and gas demand. Even global LNG market is already linking different markets together, by allowing shifting volumes between regions, benefiting from differences in their supply and demand balance. Key part of LNG trade is that it should be developed without market barriers, by considering the geo-political factor and ensuring high safety and environmental.

In recent years, it had been seen that spot trading in international trade of gas has significantly gained importance. Traditionally gas trade was used to done through long-tram contract basis because there was limited region and due to lack of pipeline infrastructure but as the technology advances industry found the LNG method of transporting gas to different regions of the world. Growing intra continent trade e.g. within North America and Europe/ Russia and the development of LNG tanker trade have led to an increasing integration of world markets. In the early years of this decade there were some arbitrage with LNG tankers between the volatile markets of North America and Europe (Source: Deutsche Bank). Thus, one would expect to see increasing price convergence in coming years.

The objective of this project paper is intended to have an overview of global LNG market and India's contribution in Natural gas and Liquefied Natural Gas (LNG) market and the impact of worldwide liberalization of the natural gas industry. The paper examines some of the barriers to the workably competitive model for this extremely rigid commodity cross-border trade and speculation about the likely future structure of the industry and also the study of OECD countries production and consumption of LNG. This study also gives a short overview on the deregulation of the gas markets and LNG shipments.

Liquefied natural gas or LNG is natural gas that has been processed to remove either valuable components e.g. helium, or those impurities that could cause difficulty downstream, e.g. water, and heavy hydrocarbons and then condensed into a liquid at almost atmospheric pressure (Maximum transport pressure set around 25kPa) by cooling it to approximately −163 degree Celsius. LNG is transported by specially designed cryogenic sea vessels and cryogenic road tankers; and stored in specially designed tanks. LNG is about $1/614^{th}$ volume of natural gas at standard temperature and pressure (STP), making it much more cost efficient to transport over long distances where pipelines are not able to access the regions. Transporting the natural gas by pipelines is not possible or economical; it can be transported by LNG vessels, where the most common tank types are membrane (prismatic), Moss Rosenberg (spheres), or self-supporting prismatic type.

Basic Facts on LNG

LNG offers an energy density comparable to petrol and diesel fuels and produces less pollution, but its relatively high cost of production and the need to store it in expensive cryogenic tanks have prevented its widespread use in commercial applications.

Conditions required to condense natural gas depend on its precise composition, the market that it will be sold to and the process being used, but typically involve temperatures between −120 and −170 degrees Celsius (pure methane liquefies at −161.6 degree Celsius) and pressures of between 101 and 6000 kPa (14.7 and 870 lbf/in^2 [approx 1-60 atm]). By this way high pressure natural gas which is condensed now it can be used for storage and shipping.

The density of LNG is roughly 0.41 to 0.5 kg/L, depending on temperature, pressure and composition. In comparison water has a density of 1.0 kg/L.

LNG does not have specific heat value as it is made from natural gas, which is a mixture of different gases. The higher heating value of LNG is estimated to be 24 MJ/L at −164 degrees Celsius. This corresponds to a lower heating value of 21 MJ/L.

The natural gas fed into the LNG plant will be treated to remove water, hydrogen sulfide, carbon dioxide and other components that will freeze (e.g. benzene) under the low temperatures needed for storage or be destructive to the liquefaction facility. Purified LNG typically contains more than 90% methane. It also contains small amounts of ethane, propane, butane and some heavier alkanes.

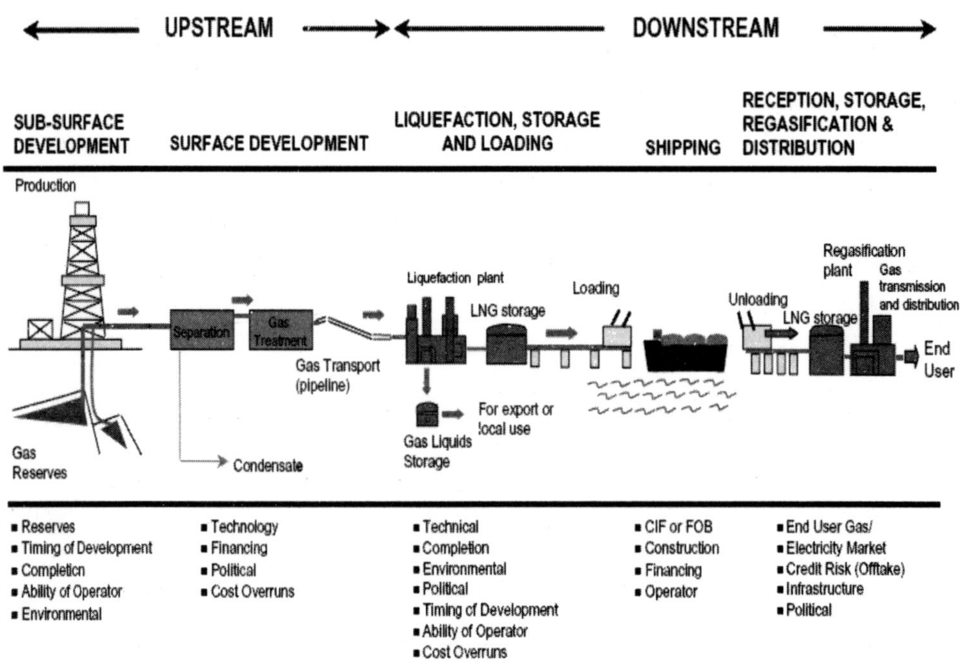

Figure 3.10: Value Chain LNG

The most important infrastructure needed for LNG production and transportation is an LNG plant consisting of one or more LNG trains each of which is an independent unit for gas liquefaction. Other facilities needed are load-out terminals for loading the LNG onto vehicles, LNG vessels for transportation, and a receiving terminal at the destination for discharge and Regasification, where the LNG is reheated and turned into gas for use. Regasification terminals are usually connected to a storage and pipeline distribution network to distribute natural gas to local distribution companies or independent power plants.

In 1964 the UK and France were the LNG buyers under the world's first LNG trade from Algeria witnessing the new era of energy. The construction of an LNG plant costs USD 1-3 billion, a receiving terminal costs USD 0.5-1 billion, and LNG vessels cost USD 0.2-0.3 billion. Compared with the crude oil, the natural gas market is small but mature. Commercial development of LNG is completely different because in this first producer confirms with the downstream industry, then have a long-term contract for 20-25 years with strict terms and structures for gas pricing. Thus, the LNG business has been regarded as the costly affair because it needs lot of capital investment and political sources for cross border trade permissions. Major international oil companies such as BP, Exxon Mobil, Royal Dutch Shell; and national oil companies like Pertamina, Petronas are active players. Japan, South Korea and Taiwan import large sums of LNG due to their shortage of energy.

In recent years, as more players take part in investment, both in upstream and downstream and new technologies are adopted because of this the prices for construction of LNG plants, receiving terminals and vessels have fallen, making LNG more competitive means of energy distribution. The standard price for a 125,000 cubic meter LNG vessel built in European and Japanese shipyards used to be USD 250 million.

When Korean and Chinese shipyards entered the race, increased competition reduced the profit margins and improved efficiency, reducing costs 60%. Since 2004, ship costs have increased due to a large number of orders increasing demand for shipyard slots. The per-ton construction cost of a LNG liquefaction plant fell steadily from the 1970's through the 1990's, with the cost reduced approximately 35%.

INFRASTRUCTURE OF LNG VALUE CHAIN

The LNG "value" or "supply" chain consists of four highly linked, interdependent segments—exploration and production; liquefaction; shipping—from the point of liquefaction to the final destination; and receiving Storage and Regasification at the final destination.

Exploration and Production

The first segment in the LNG value chain is exploration and production E&P activity ranges from the finding of gas (prospective blocks), to the mobilization of financial capital to support drilling and field development to ultimate production. The E&P segment incorporate geological risk. In this it is explained that whether the extraction of gas is economical or not. Natural gas reserve of U.S. was increased by more than 11%, from 183.5 to 204.4 tcf, between 2001 and 2005. To a large extent, this increase in reserves reflects the impact of high natural gas prices since 1999.

For the year 2005, worldwide proved reserves of natural gas were 6,348 Tcf, an increase of 25% over the year 1995, and more reserves of natural gas continue to be discovered. Much of this natural gas is stranded a long way from market, in countries that do not need large quantities of additional energy. The leading countries producing natural gas and selling it to world markets in the form of LNG are Indonesia, Malaysia, Qatar and Algeria. Trinidad and Tobago is an example of a small country that has benefited hugely from its LNG export strategy. Several countries are growing rapidly as Natural Gas producers and LNG exporters, such as Nigeria and Australia. Countries like Angola and Venezuela are striving to reach their full potential in the global LNG market place, and countries like Saudi Arabia and Iran, that have vast reserves of Natural gas would also participate as LNG exporter.

LNG Liquefaction

Currently liquefaction capacity to serve the Atlantic and Pacific Basin is about the same all together, including Middle East facilities, about 170mn tons per year (MTPA) of capacity is in place (as of March 2007). Another 91 MTPA is under construction and 285 MTPA are planned. Egypt joined the club of LNG exporter in May 2005 by shipping a first cargo from newly constructed Idku terminal on the Mediterranean sea.

In 2006 two liquefaction projects came into operation: Australia started its second LNG project in Timor Sea, and Qalhat terminal in Oman shipped first cargoes to Japan and Spain.

During liquefaction contaminants which are found while at time of production of natural gas are removed by the freezing up and damaging equipment when the gas is cooled to LNG temperature (−256 Fahrenheit) and to meet pipeline specification at delivery point.

The liquefaction process entails cooling the clean feed gas by using refrigerators. The liquefaction plant may consist of several parallel units (trains). By liquefying the gas, its volume is reduced by a factor of 600 which means that LNG at -256 Fahrenheit use 1/600th of the space required for a comparable amount of gas at room temperature and atmospheric pressure.

LNG is a cryogenic liquid, it is clear liquid, with a density of about 45%, the density of water. At both liquefaction and receiving and Regasification facilities, the LNG is stored in double-walled tanks at atmospheric pressure.

LNG Shipping

LNG tankers are double—hulled ships specially designed and insulated to prevent leakage or rupture in an accident. The LNG is stored in a special containment system within the inner hull where it is kept at atmospheric pressure and cryogenic temperature.

Those ships are:

1. The spherical (Moss) design;
2. The membrane design; and
3. The structural prismatic design.

Historically most of the LNG ships used spherical (moss) tanks. Moss type ships are easily identifiable as LNG ships because the top half of the tankers are visible above deck. However, the trend is toward membrane design. The Figure 3.11 below shows 44% of LNG was spherical design in 2006; this compares to 52% of LNG ships in 2002.

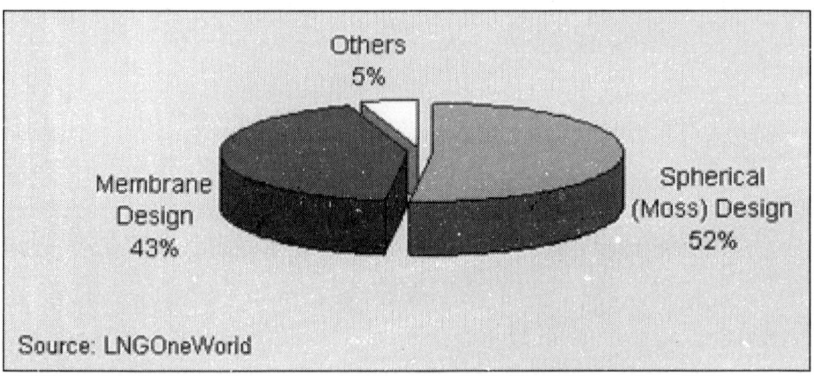

Figure 3.11: LNG Containers

To shift toward membrane design is even more obvious by analyzing the structure of orders for LNG carrier.

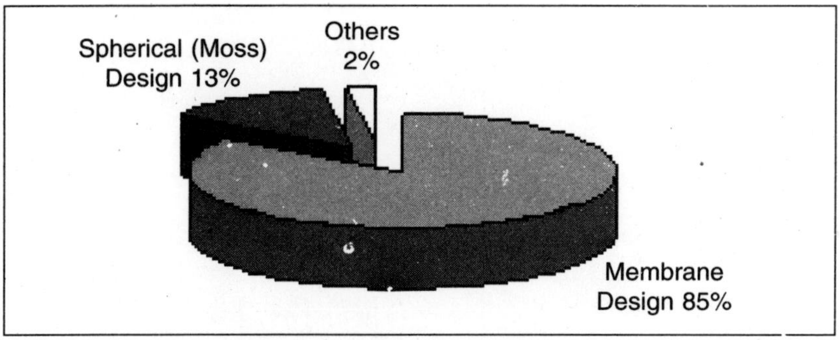

Source: Maritime Business Strategies, LLC.

Figure 3.12: LNG Fleet Containment System—Order Book 2005-10 (No. of Ships)

The typical LNG carrier can transport about 125,000 - 138,000 cubic meter of LNG.

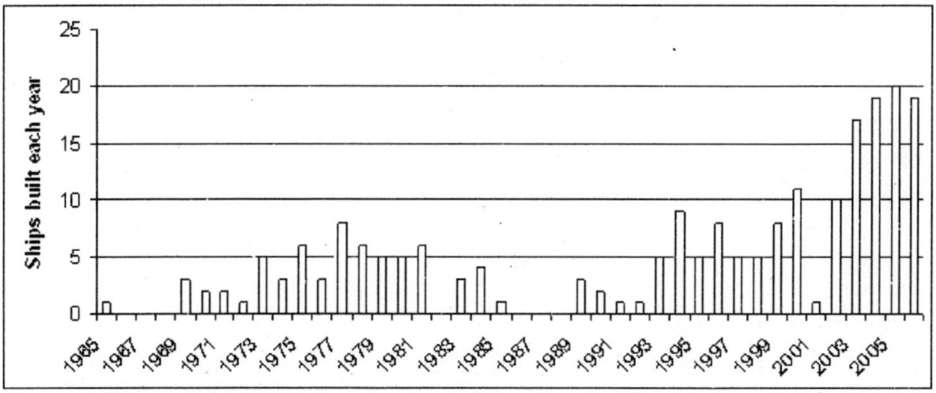

Source: Maritime Business Strategies, LLC.

Figure 3.13: Number of LNG Ships Built 1965-2006

The LNG shipping market has been expanding. Accordingly to maritime business strategies, as of March 2007, there were 224 LNG tankers in operation with 145 on order. The LNG tanker fleet size is estimated to continue to grow well over 300 tankers by 2010.

Note: World LNG tanker fleet at the end of report as Appendix B.

Storage and Regasification

Last point of value chain is storage and Regasification for its end use. LNG may be used in various ways, for instance LNG may be used as a transportation fuel for truck and bus fleets; in these cases, LNG import receiving terminals will include facilities to dispense LNG into tanker trucks for distribution to central re-fuelling locations. Sometimes LNG import terminals located with electric power generation stations, allowing use of the cryogenic properties of LNG to help cool the power plant natural gas vapor is burned for power production.

To return LNG into a gaseous state, it is fed into a Regasification facility. On arrival at the receiving terminal in its liquid state, LNG is pumped at atmospheric pressure first to a double-walled storage tank, similar to those used I the liquefaction plant where LNG is stored at atmospheric pressure until needed. LNG is then pumped at higher pressure through various receiving terminal components where it is warmed in a controlled environment. The LNG can be warmed by passage through pipes heated by direct-fired heaters, or pipes warmed by seawater, or through pipes that are in heated water.

In last five to ten years LNG industry has changed a lot in respect to supply cost. Now LNG industry, have come largely from increases in train size, imported fuel efficiency in liquefaction and Regasification (mainly from high efficiency gas turbines in on-site co-generation facilities), improved equipment design, the elimination of gold plating and optimum utilization of available capacity. Since 1999 cost of liquefaction fallen down steeply by 25% to 30% and shipping cost by 20% to 30%.

	Cost Estimate Early 1990s	*Cost Estimate Early 2000s*
Upstream development cost	0.5-0.8	0.5-0.8
Liquefaction	1.3-1.4	1.0-1.1
Shipping (LNG tanker)	1.2-1.3	0.9-1.0
Regasification	0.5-0.6	0.4-0.5
Total cost	3.5-4.1	2.8-3.4

LNG MARKET

Cedigaz forecasts that world LNG demand could increase by about 6.9% year over the next 15 years, approaching 375 Mt/year (506 Bcm) in 2020. Atlantic basin and Pacific basin markets shows glaring contrast in its demand.

Pacific Basin LNG demand could account for about 45% of the world total in 2020, posting an increase of about 4%/year over the period. In the short-to-medium term Japan is likely to provide a significant impetus to LNG tanker trade in the region. The "S-curve" price formula that limits the impact

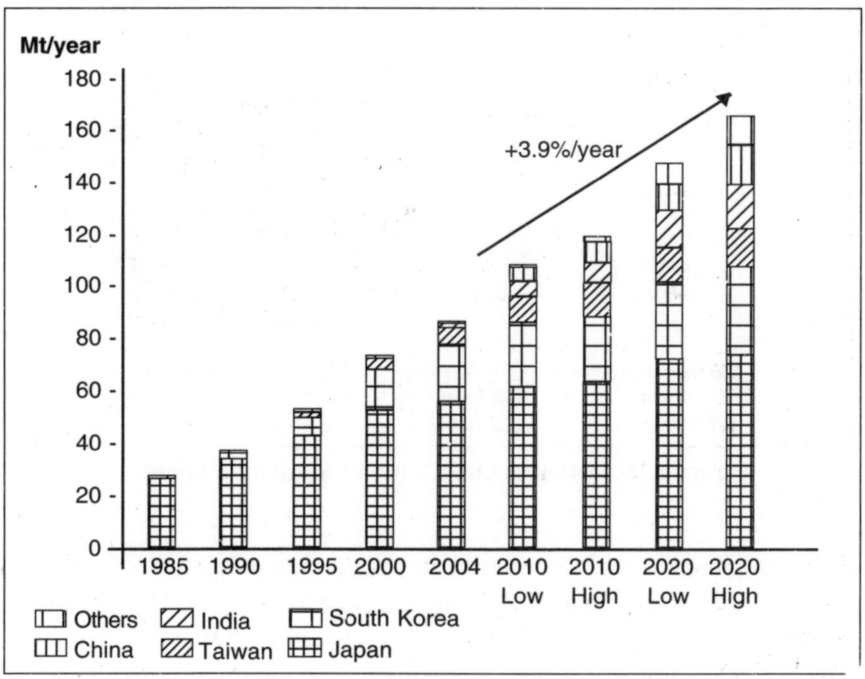

Figure 3.14: LNG Demand of Pacific Basin

of high oil price increase for the buyer makes LNG more competitive. In South Korea, sales to city gas are increasing steadily, while demand from the power sector is more volatile, in line with price fluctuations. There are many new LNG receiving terminal projects had initially being announced in India and in China, but most of them have been cancelled due to the rising prices. In India, where a "moderate" LNG prices is probably the key to its expansion, at least in the medium-term because local prices are heavily subsidized, only the capacity extension of the Dahej terminal (Petronet LNG) to 10 Mt/year seems realistic by 2010-11. Since cargoes received at Hazira terminal (Shell/ Total) remained unsold because local customers were asked to pay too high prices, the capacity of the facility is barely exploited. In China two terminals (Guangdong and Fujian) will receive their first cubic meters of LNG price that importing companies will be able to get. In Indonesia, the planned construction of two receiving terminals in Java responds to the government strategy to priortise the supply of the domestic market.

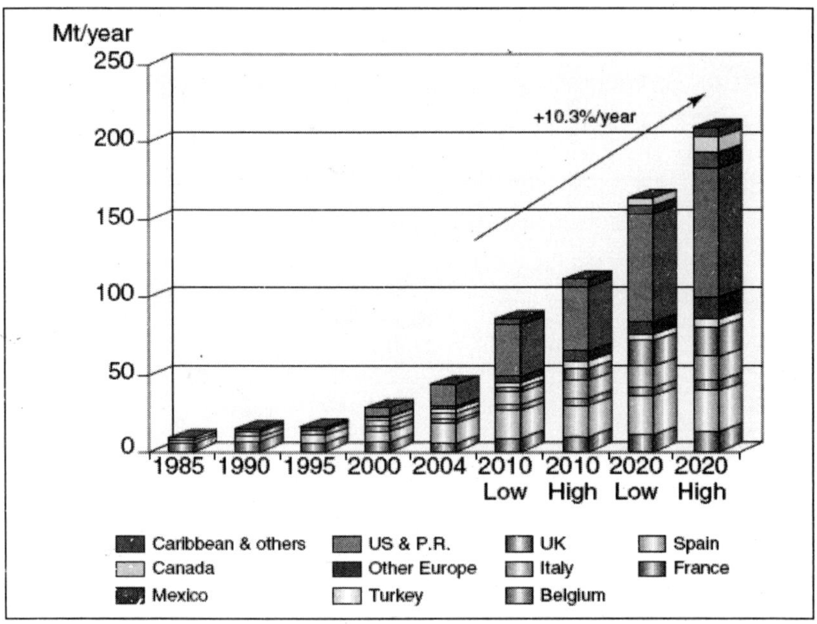

Figure 3.15: Potential LNG Demand of Atlantic Basin

Atlantic Basin could experience faster growth of about 10%/year and account for about 55% of world LNG demand by 2020. In the Atlantic Basin, which already has receiving capacity of about 80 Mt/year, some fifty Regasification terminals are being built or planned. Most of them are extremely unlikely to materialize, these projects attest to the dynamism and the optimistic vision for LNG that the companies show in these markets.

Table 3.3. LNG Receiving Capacities in Atlantic Basin

Mt/Year

	Existing capacity	*Under construction & approved*	*Planned*	*Total (existing & potential)*
North America	33.8	+ 172	+ 280	485.8
Europe	46.4	+ 42	+ 90	178.4
Total	80.2	+ 214	+ 370	664.2

Even if the scale of the demand growth rate is still uncertain, LNG will very likely have a major and increasing role in the Atlantic. The main uncertainty surrounds the impact which price arbitrage could have on the distribution of volumes between the two markets, American and European.

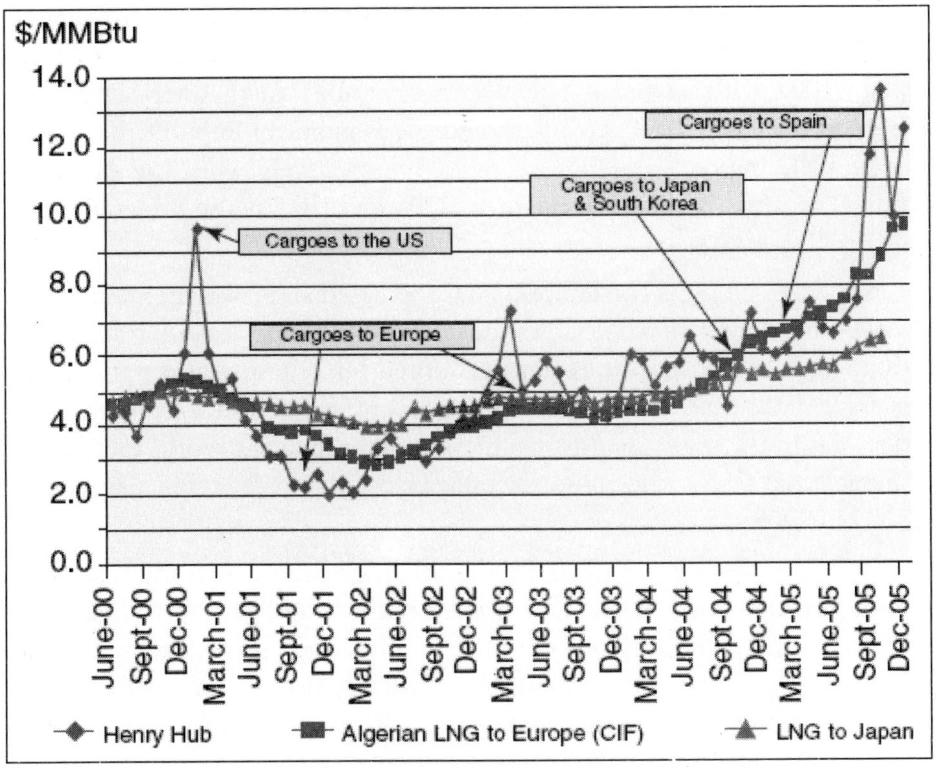

Figure 3.16: Price Arbitrage Develops Among Market

It is becoming the "benchmark" already determining the final destination "spot" LNG in particular, as producers and importers shuttle their cargoes to the most lucrative market. In the future, there will be shift of LNG volumes to North America could force European terminals to operate well under capacity.

The trades of LNG in recent years have seen massive of growth; world LNG demand reached 125 mt in 2003. Of this total 67% was concentrated in the Asia-Pacific region, 24% in Europe, and 9% in the Americas. European LNG imports totaled nearly 30 mt in 2003, with largest importers being Spain and France. LNG provides 7.6% of European gas supply.

Although the USA is the world's largest gas market, LNG imports forms a comparatively low proportion of gas supply, 10 mt in 2003 representing only 2% of US supply. However, the 2003 level was a record, following a dramatic increase over recent years from the level of 0.5 mt in 1996. These increases are due to surplus cargoes from the Asia-Pacific market, high US gas prices since 2000, and the commissioning of the Atlantic LNG facility in Trinidad, which is much closer to the US east cost than the other LNG plants. Expansion of the four current US LNG terminals should bring import capacity at least 40 mtpa by 2008, with around 40 new terminals around North America planned or proposed to be built. Puerto Rico and the Dominican Republic have also become LNG importers in 2000 and 2003 respectively, with the Altamira Terminal in Mexico commencement in 2006 and the Energy Bridge project Offshore Gulf of Mexico.

World natural gas consumption has increased at an average annual rate of 2.6% over the past two decades, due to its economic and environmental advantages. The asia pacific region accounted for 13% of world natural gas consumption in 2002 or around 338 billion cubic meters. Consumption of natural gas in the region has grown more rapidly than the world average, at an annual rate of 7.5% since 1980. the table below shows the trade movements of LNG in 2006.

However, despite prospects for durably high prices, a steady economic growth rate of about 2.5%/year, combined with the obligations to fulfill the national pledges made at Kyoto, continue to offer bright growth prospects for natural gas. World gas demand should accordingly rise at a rate of about 2%/year to reach 3800 billion cubic meters by 2020, accounting for 26 to 27% of world primary energy demand.

Table 3.4: Trade Movement of LNG

(Billion cubic metres)

To	From													Total imports
	USA	Trinidad & Tobago	Oman	Qatar	UAE	Algeria	Egypt	Libya	Nigeria	Aus-tralia	Brunei	Indo-nesia	Malay-sia	
North Ameria														
USA	-	10.85	-	-	-	0.49	3.60	-	1.62	-	-	-	-	16.56
Mexico	-	0.16	-	0.08	-	-	0.16	-	0.54	-	-	-	-	0.94
S. & Cent. America														
Dominican Republic	-	0.25	-	-	-	-	-	-	-	-	-	-	-	0.25
Puerto Rico	-	0.72	-	-	-	-	-	-	-	-	-	-	-	0.72
Europe														
Belgium	-	0.16	-	0.36	-	3.35	0.25	-	0.16	-	-	-	-	4.28
France	-	-	-	-	-	7.35	2.30	-	4.23	-	-	-	-	13.88
Greece	-	-	-	-	-	0.45	0.04	-	-	-	-	-	-	0.49
Italy	-	-	-	-	-	3.00	0.10	-	-	-	-	-	-	3.10
Portugal	-	-	-	-	-	-	-	-	1.97	-	-	-	-	1.97
Spain	-	3.00	1.00	5.00	-	2.80	4.80	0.72	7.10	-	-	-	-	24.42
Turkey	-	-	-	-	-	4.60	-	-	1.12	-	-	-	-	5.72
United Kingdom	-	0.60	-	-	-	2.00	0.96	-	-	-	-	-	-	3.56
Asia Pacific														
China	-	-	-	-	-	-	-	-	-	1.00	-	-	-	1.00
India	-	-	0.24	6.80	0.08	0.08	0.55	-	0.08	0.08	-	-	0.08	7.99
Japan	1.72	0.44	3.04	9.87	7.00	0.24	0.80	-	0.22	15.68	8.65	18.60	15.60	81.86
South Korea	-	0.07	7.10	8.98	-	0.32	1.25	-	0.16	0.87	1.16	6.72	7.51	34.14
Taiwan	-	-	0.16	-	-	-	0.16	-	0.38	0.40	-	4.25	4.85	10.20
Total Exports	1.72	16.25	11.52	31.09	7.08	24.68	14.97	0.72	17.58	18.03	9.87	25.57	28.24	211.08

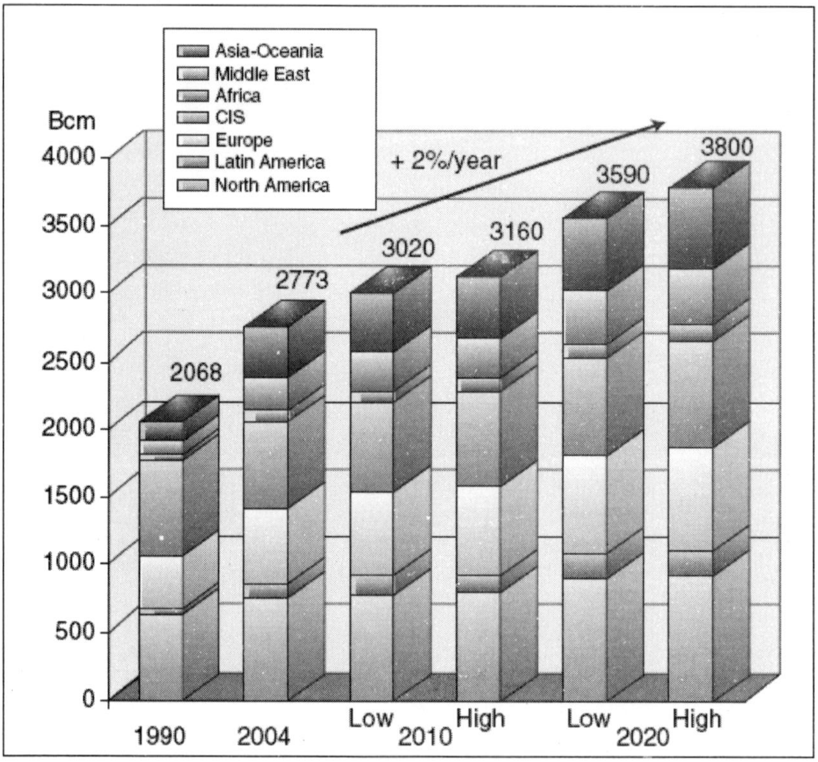

Figure 3.17: Gas Demand Prospects by Region

Global LNG liquefaction capacity is expected to increase from 6.6 tcf (139 million metric tons) per year in 2003 to 9.4 tcf (197 million metric tons) per year 2007 based on facilities currently under construction.

As of late 2003, there were 151 LNG tankers in the world LNG fleet with 55 tankers under construction. The addition of the new ships to the fleet will raise the total fleet capacity to 44 percent from 17.4 million cubic meters of liquid (equivalent to 366 Bcf of natural gas) in October 2003to 25.1 million cubic meters of liquid (equivalent to527 Bcf of natural gas) in 2006.

Short-term trading has grown from 1 percent of the LNG market in 1992 to 8 percent in 2002. Then it again raised to 15% in the year 2005 and now it is approximately 30% in the year 2007. Short term trading will continue growing especially in Atlantic Basin.

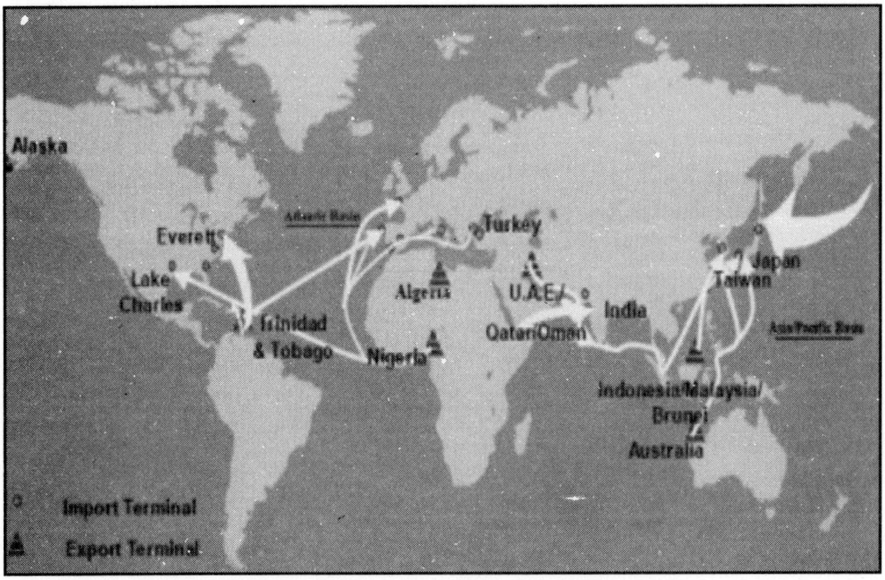

Figure 3.18: World LNG Trade Flows

LNG Exports and Supply

LNG supplier located in the Asia-Pacific region exported 59 million tonnes of LNG in 2003. the region is the world's largest LNG producer, supplying close to half of global LNG trade in that year. Indonesia alone supplied 21 percent of world LNG exports. The three exporters in Middle East supplied 26 million tonnes of LNG in 2003, equivalent to 23 percent of total world LNG trade. In 2003, 12 countries exported 5.4 tcf of natural gas as LNG.

Potential new exporters such as Iran, Yemen, Equatorial Guinea, Angola, Venezuela, Bolivia (via Peru or Chile), and Peru are looking to LNG exports as a way of monetizing their natural gas resources.

New projects under construction in Australia, Russia, Norway, and Egypt, together with expansions of existing facilities throughout the world, will increase annual liquefaction capacity by 2.8 Tcf (58 million tons) by 2007, increasing global capacity to 9.4 Tcf (197 million tons) per year, which represents 10 percent of 2002 global natural gas consumption.

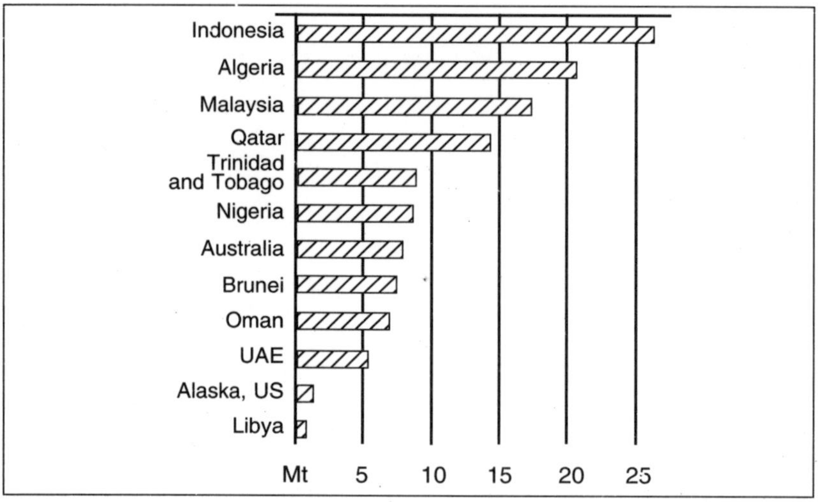

Figure 3.19: World LNG Exports, by Country, 2003

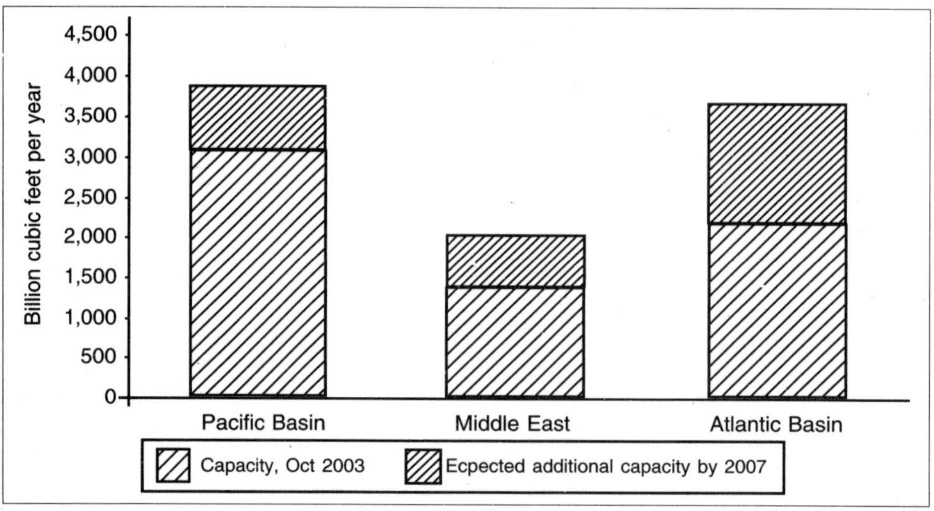

Source: Data from IEA 2003 *Natural Gas Information*, and updated based on trade press reports as accomodate by the Gas Technology Institute.

Figure 3.20: Global LNG Liquefaction Capacity, October 2003

Pacific Basin Exporters

Pacific Basin LNG exporters produced 2.6 Tcf (55 million tons) in 2002, about 49 percent of total world LNG production. As of late 2003, five Pacific Basin exporters had 3.1 Tcf (63 million tons) of annual liquefaction capacity. Liquefaction capacity in the Pacific Basin is expected to increase by 780 billion cubic feet (Bcf) or 16 million tons of annual capacity over the next few years to more than 3.8 Tcf (80 million tons) per year by 2007.

- Indonesia is the world largest LNG producer and exporter. In 2002, Indonesia exported 1.1 Tcf (23 million tons) of LNG or 21 percent of the world's total LNG exports. Most of Indonesia's LNG is imported by Japan with smaller volumes going to Taiwan and South Korea.
- Indonesia's annual liquefaction capacity is 1.4 Tcf (30 million tons) from the two exporting complexes at Bontang and Arun. An additional train at Bontang is under consideration but has yet to contract for the capacity. BP is leading development of a two-train, 341-Bcf-per-year (7.0-million-tpy) project at Tangguh scheduled to start up in 2007. The Tangguh LNG is destined for China, other Asian markets, and potentially the United States.
- Malaysia the world's third largest LNG exporter after Indonesia and Algeria, exported 741 Bcf (15.6 million tons) in 2002. These exports went primarily to Japan, with smaller volumes to Taiwan and South Korea. Three liquefaction terminals have been developed at the Bintulu LNG complex in Sarawak, Malaysia Satu, Dua, and Malaysia Tiga, the first train of which went on-stream in mid-2003. A second train will come online in November 2003, raising the total capacity of the Bintulu complex to an annual 1.1 Tcf (22.7 million tons).
- Australia exported 367 Bcf (7.7 million tons) of LNG from the Northwest Shelf project in 2002, primarily to Japanese utilities. The project owners have started construction on an additional 205-Bcf-per-year (4.2-million-tpy) train scheduled to come online in 2004. An additional train is under consideration.

Three new projects are also in various stages of development. ConocoPhillips has begun construction on a 175-Bcf-per-year (3.6-million-tpy) Darwin LNG project, to monetize reserves in the Timor Sea shared by Australia and East Timor.

Conoco Phillips is also working with Shell, Osaka Gas, and Woodside Petroleum to develop the 258-Bcf-per-year (5.3-million-tpy) Greater Sunrise project via a floating LNG facility. ChevronTexaco, in partnership with ExxonMobil and Shell, is spearheading a two-train Gorgon project with an annual capacity of 487 Bcf (10.0 million tons) to monetize reserves discovered offshore Northwest Australia.

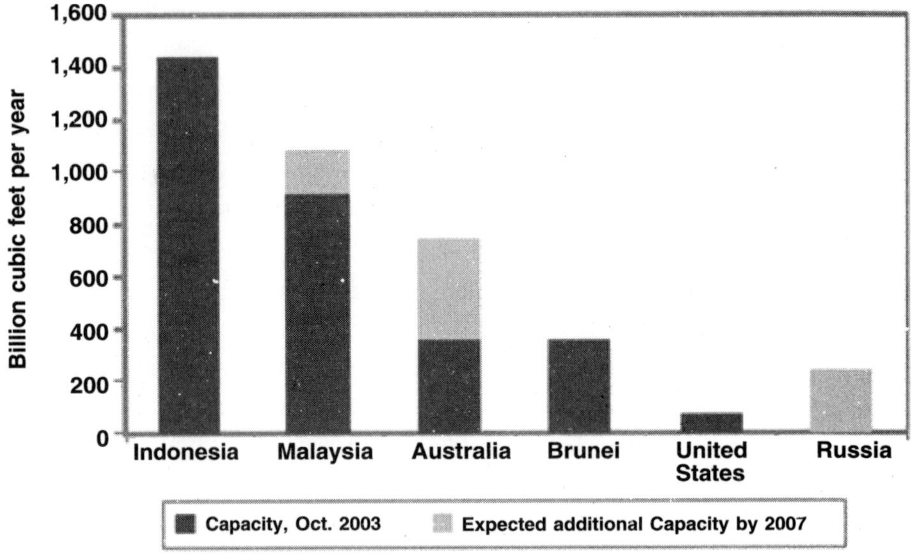

Source: Data from IEA 2003 *Natural Gas Information*, and updated based on trade press reports as accomodate by the Gas Technology Institute.

Figure 3.21: Pacific Basin Liquefaction Capacity, October 2003

Atlantic Basin Exporter

Atlantic Basin exporters produced 1.5 Tcf (32 million tons) in 2002, about 29 percent of total world LNG production. As of late 2003, Atlantic Basin LNG producers had 2.1 Tcf (43 million tons) of annual capacity. Expansions in Nigeria and Trinidad and Tobago, as well as new facilities in Egypt and Norway, would increase annual Atlantic Basin liquefaction capacity to 3.3 Tcf (73 million tons) by 2007.

- Algeria was the second largest LNG exporter in 2002, shipping 935 Bcf (19.6 million tons) mainly to Europe (France, Belgium, Spain, and Turkey) and the United States.
- Nigeria exported 394 Bcf (8.2 million tons) of LNG in 2002, mainly to Turkey, Italy, France, Portugal, and Spain. Nigeria has also delivered more than 20 cargos under short-term contracts to the United States over the past three years. The total annual capacity of Nigeria's Bonny Island LNG plant is 463 Bcf (9.5 million tons), and Nigeria LNG has begun construction of two additional 200-Bcf-per-year (4.1-million-tpy) trains that are scheduled to begin operation in 2005.

- Trinidad and Tobago exported 189 Bcf (4.0 million tons) of LNG in 2002. Trinidad and Tobago's LNG facility at Point Fortin has three trains and an annual capacity of 482 Bcf (9.9 million tons).
- Libya exported 21 Bcf (0.4 million tons) of LNG in 2002. The plant at Marsa El Brega has an annual capacity of about 131 Bcf (2.7 million tons).
- Norway plans to export LNG from a 200-Bcf-per-year (4.1-million-tpy) liquefaction terminal now being built on Melkøye Island in the Norwegian Sea. Exports are targeting markets in Spain, France, and the United States.

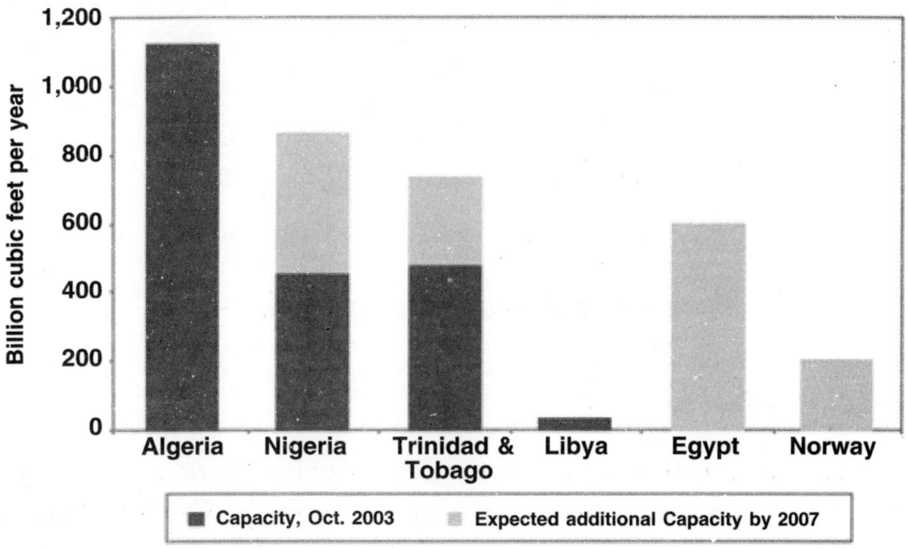

Source: Data from IEA 2003 *Natural Gas Information*, and updated based on trade press reports as accomodate by the Gas Technology Institute.

Figure 3.22: Atlantic Basin Liquefaction Capacity, October 2003

Supply of LNG

The growth potential of LNG demand combined with the discovery of large gas resources in new areas (Egypt, Peru, Barents Sea) is encouraging national and international companies to invest massively in liquefaction plants. Shared among thirteen countries, current world liquefaction capacity of 176 mt/year (238 Bcm) is therefore slated to increase sharply. Many projects representing additional capacity of about 220 mt/year, are under construction or planned to meet future requirements.

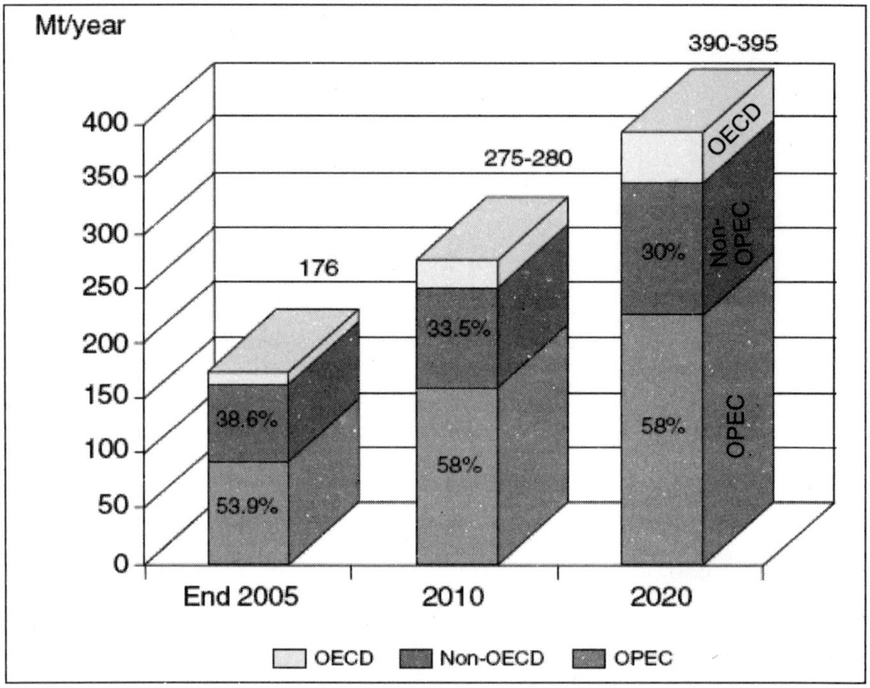

Figure 3.23: World Potential Supply of LNG

Atlantic Basin Producers

Five Atlantic basin countries currently have liquefaction capacity of 62 mt/year. New plants under construction in Norway (Snovhit LNG) and Equatorial Guniea and new trains and debottleneckings on existing plants, will add about 20 Mt/year capacity by 2010. Beyond 2010, new projects in Angola, Russia (Shtokman, Ust-Luga) and Nigeria (Brass LNG, Olokola LNG), as well as further extensions to existing plants, could boost total production capacity in the basin to about 150 Mt/year by 2020.

Pacific Basin Producers

Although its share has decreased significantly in the recent years, Asia still hosts 40% of the world's liquefaction capacity. Liquefaction capacity in the Atlantic basin, currently amounting 72 Mt/year and mainly shared among four countries (Australia, Brunei, Indonesia and Malaysia), will continue to grow to reach 96 to 98 Mt/year by 2010, or even 120 to 125/Mt/year in 2020.

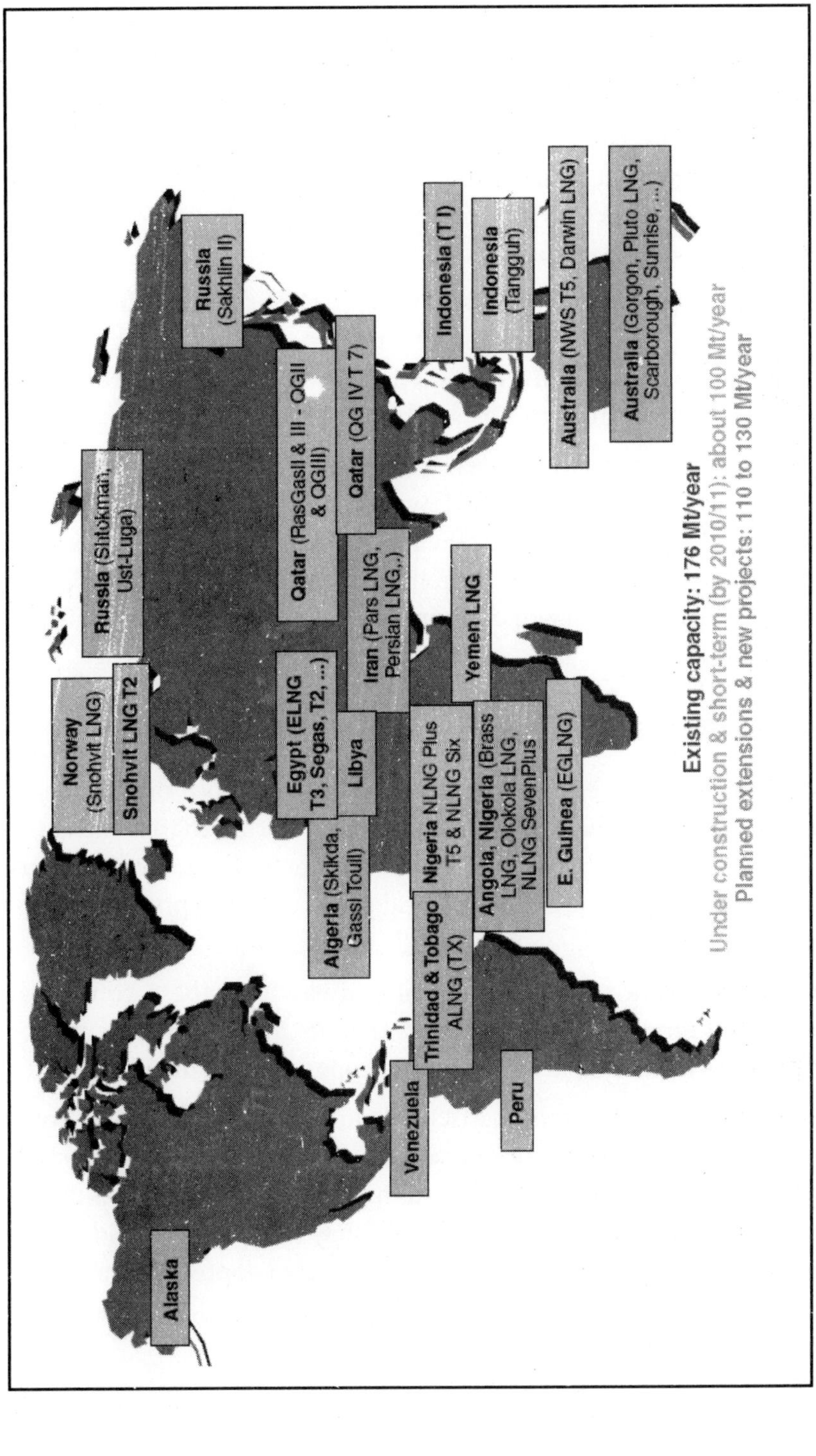

Figure 3.24. World Liquefaction Projects

ROLE OF GAS EXPORTING COUNTRIES AND FORUM

Like the members of OPEC, the GECF members are united by a common interest, namely their status as producers of hydrocarbons and the resultant motivation to maximize revenues. Within this context though, they are in fact very different with regard to gas production capabilities, reserves, the role gas plays in their economies, and the markets they sell into. This diversity of interests and motivations creates the potential for conflicting interests, as has been seen over the years in the oil markets with OPEC.

So far these differences have presented little problem other than occasionally diverging rhetoric, though potential exists for more significant and divisive differences of opinion if the GECF evolves into a more structured organization beyond its current role as a debating forum.

Since its formation there have been a number of concerns, particularly from consuming countries, that the GECF will evolve into a gas cartel similar to that of OPEC in the oil markets. The GECF has consistently made strenuous efforts (despite recent conflicting signals from some parts of the group) to deny this in an effort to allay fears among consumers of any plans to squeeze either supply or prices.

Opposition to Shift from Long-term Purchase Contracts

One of the key themes of the GECF meetings has been both the existence of long term contracts and the pricing formulas used within these contracts. The GECF has been keen to see these long-term contracts maintained in order to assist with the underwriting of large capital projects and to provide stable incomes to its members.

It has not been in favor of the movement away from these contracts towards the shorter term spot-type contracts that are increasingly becoming more widespread as markets, particularly in Europe, are liberalized.

Despite significant discussions, particularly in the form of proposals from Egypt, little (if any) progress has been made by the GECF towards devising an alternative gas pricing formula delinked from oil. The lack of progress made on this issue at recent meetings means that it is likely to be some considerable time before a formula is determined and subsequently adopted, particularly given the difficulties in accommodating the disparate agendas and positions of the various GECF members.

Factors against OPEC-style Development

There are several factors that explain why it is unlikely that GECF will emerge as the gas equivalent to OPEC.

Differing Agendas and Difficulties in Reaching Consensus

Like OPEC, the GECF has a highly diverse and disparate membership. These differences have in the past lead to a lack of cohesion within OPEC and there are increasingly signs that this issue is beginning to emerge within the GECF.

The Disparate Nature of the Membership

The members of the GECF have widely differing reserves, production and GDP profiles that ultimately give them differing agendas and motivations. If the GECF were to operate as a gas cartel along the lines of OPEC, big producers such as Russia, which accounts for 22% of global gas production and 54% of GECF production, would be unlikely to have sufficient motivation to hold back supply to boost prices, given that its huge gas resource endowments allow it to make money on volume rather than on price. Qatar is in a similar position.

The Existence of Long-term Contracts

Gas is largely currently traded on long term contracts, often 10 or even 20 years in length. Only when the gas market has predominantly moved away from long term contracts towards a more spot market-based system would there be scope for a gas OPEC to influence gas prices through production programming in the way that OPEC influences the oil market. In Datamonitor's opinion, it will be a number of years before sufficient spot market liquidity exists to back out long term contracts and create the conditions needed for such a system.

Gas is not a Global Market

Unlike oil, and despite the growing role of long distance LNG, gas is not a global market. Instead it operates largely on a regional basis, with comparatively little movement outside a handful of regional supply zones. This, combined with the fact that just 18% of global gas demand is met by imported supplies, compared to 59% of oil demand, means that there is less scope for consumers to be influenced by production programming and supply side management by producers.

Difficulties in Allocating Production Quotas

Intense, and often bitter, wrangling and negotiation characterize the agreement of an overall OPEC quota, while various attempts to allocate quotas amongst the members on a structured basis over organization's 44-year history have all been unsuccessful. A gas cartel would face exactly the same problem with little to suggest that both overall and individual quotas could be easily or successfully agreed upon.

The Threat of International Anti-cartel Laws

Any attempts by the GECF to adopt the structure and policies of a formalized cartel would be likely to meet with severe resistance from the consuming countries. The European Union would potentially be one of the key dissenting voices in this context, and the potential for retaliatory trade sanctions could not be ruled out.

Despite its dominance of the world gas markets through its reserve and production levels, the GECF is far from being a dominant or influential force in gas pricing.

Developing, agreeing on and implementing a gas price formula delinked from oil has shown little sign of progress despite significant debate and discussion over the past few years. With the various proposals still under discussion, there are few indications that an agreement will be reached, let alone implemented, in the short-term.

Instead the GECF is likely to continue to serve a role as a debating forum for its members and will seek to promote their interests, particularly with regard to market liberalization. Even if the GECF does evolve itself into a more structured and organized grouping, its ability to radically influence the gas markets will be curtailed by the wide-ranging, and sometimes conflicting, positions, viewpoints and agendas of its membership. 'End Intelliext.

PRICING

A more flexible approach to and a wider range of pricing is emerging in the LNG industry. Suppliers are adopting different pricing policies according to the buyers' market. For instance, Qatar, which sells on the three main LNG markets, has pegged its LNG sales to *crude oil prices in Japan, to Henry Hub spot prices in the US, to NBP spot prices in the UK and to fuel oil prices in continental Europe.*

In Japan, cif LNG prices are based on a basket of crude oils imported into the country, known as the Japanese Crude Cocktail (JCC), which are adjusted on a monthly basis. In the past, this "cocktail" was a convenient basis for gas pricing because the main competitor of gas was light crude oils, whose prices are reflected in the JCC. However, as gas in electricity generation – the major user of gas in Japan – is no longer competing with crude oil, Japanese buyers require more flexibility in volume and pricing. Moreover, the contract signed by Australian North West Shelf (NWS) with Chinese buyers has set a new benchmark for LNG pricing in Asia. The price formula is reported to be similar to that used for the NWS Japanese contracts, i.e. an S-curve formula based on the average price of a cocktail of imported crudes, designed to protect the parties against sharp swings in oil prices. However, based on a reference barrel of $18, NWS partners have lowered the cif price to China to around $3/mBtu, or about 15% below the current Japanese price. Moreover, the slope of the S-curve is not as steep as under the Japanese formula. This means that for a price of $25/b, China would pay 25% less than Japanese buyers.

This price cut will greatly affect renegotiation of the Asian contracts which come up for renewal before the end of the decade (about 25 Mt including Japanese contracts with NWS partners). A decrease in prices is expected; ToP obligations are expected to be relaxed and more pricing flexibility should be introduced in renewed contracts. European LNG contracts are still predominantly linked to the evolution of gasoil and heavy fuel oil prices, with a reference period usually of six months to one year.

European LNG contracts are less rigid than those in Japan, as they include renegotiation clauses and opportunities to reopen price discussions. In some contracts, other indices, such as electricity pool prices, have now been included to reflect the new competitive situation of gas in power generation, for instance in the formula negotiated between Trinidad and Tobago and Spain's Gas Natural. As gas trading develops and new gas market indices appear, future LNG contracts could be pegged to them. This is the case for LNG imports to the UK, which will be pegged to the National Balancing Point (NBP) prices.

In the US market, LNG prices are generally linked to the Henry Hub prices. Ex-ship prices tend to represent 80% to 90% of the futures prices at Henry Hub, as they are adjusted for the location of the LNG terminal. LNG supply will seek highest differential compared with Henry Hub spot prices first: Everett; Cove Point; Elba Island and then Lake Charles. However, the arrival of sudden large LNG supplies flowing directly into the US gas grid has an impact on the basis to Henry Hub prices and sometimes completely annihilates it. Expanding pipeline connections from the terminals is an obvious tactic for operators striving to preserve the differentials to Henry Hub.

With increasing short-term trading and physical arbitrage in the Atlantic basin, inter-regional pricing links may evolve. Although some arbitrage exists, and more is anticipated, there is as yet little sign that movements from one area to another really have much effect on prices in the market left behind. Given the limited volume scale of price arbitrage so far, it is not surprising that LNG cargo diversions have had little effect on the markets from which they have been diverted.

In the Pacific basin, such arbitrage is not possible as long as no regasification capacity is available on the US west coast or Mexico. Even when such capacity becomes available, transportation distances may be a limiting factor for the development of arbitrage possibilities. Such a development would involve much larger differences in shipping distances than in the Atlantic basin. For example, it would take three times more ships to deliver an equivalent amount of LNG from Indonesia's Bontang to California as it now does to Japan. However, as the LNG market evolves, the Middle East is going to act as a swing supplier. The Atlantic basin market will be connected to the Pacific basin via Middle East producers, which may export to both markets.

The Main Factors that are Affecting the Natural Gas and LNG Price

General Situation of the Country

- Whether it is gas short or gas rich country
- Sharing of risk
- Share of the gas compared with the competing fuel
- Penetration strategy and penetration speed

The quality of the product:

- Reliability of gas
- Flexibility of deliveries
- Quality

Market Conditions

- Which competing fuels
- Shares of the competing fuel
- Changes of the competing fuels over time or by price development
- Any premium may be subject to change or by price development
- Changes in the market structure

The price of the gas will take account the extraction cost, as well as transportation and distribution costs. For example usually the formula which is stated in the contract linked to the movement in the price of competing fuels, including provision of periodic adjustments.

It is usual to use "Netback value", which is the maximum price of gas at the consuming markets less all intermediate costs (Regasification, transportation, liquefaction etc.).

The Principle of Gas Pricing

The gas pricing is very controversial issue from many years. Basic things which are considered are:

1. From setting producers prices high enough to tempt the risk takers into exploration and production.
2. To creaming of some of the resources rent for the government.
3. To find equitable transfer prices between gas producers and utilities.
4. To devising complex tariff structures to reward large consumers for shifting off-peak.
5. To protecting small consumers from monopoly exploitation by the utility.
6. The whole chain of prices, from the gas producer to the small consumer, must reflect.
7. And properly distribute the economic gains from gas development.

Objectives of Gas Pricing

Prices set by the central authority are generally based implicitly or explicitly, on three sets of objectives they are as follows:

1. The efficiency of resource allocation, economic efficiency requires

that the real cost of energy to the society be reflected in the prices that guide the decisions of producers and consumers of that energy.

2. The satisfaction of specific financial targets, because the investment in exploration and distribution is so high that it is usually happens that there is set of tariff devised structures so they can satisfy efficiency criteria and whose average level meets the financial needs.
3. Consideration of social equity, this may be contradicting with the previous objectives and may lead to contradictory results.

Subsidies should be the last resource to correct the deficiencies of direct income transfer mechanisms and must be rigorously limited in order to safeguard the objective of financial viability.

The Level of Gas Prices

The overriding criteria for the gas pricing should be economic efficiency the first step insetting or changing gas prices is to determine the economic price of gas in the particular country or region.

Upstream Gas Pricing

Framework of gas pricing is illustrated in the below figure.

- Elements of upstream gas pricing are: Base prices, indexation, floor prices, capacity charge (load factor), currency adjustment, lag periods and price preview clauses.
- Gas pricing indexation yardsticks differs as established by bilateral agreements.

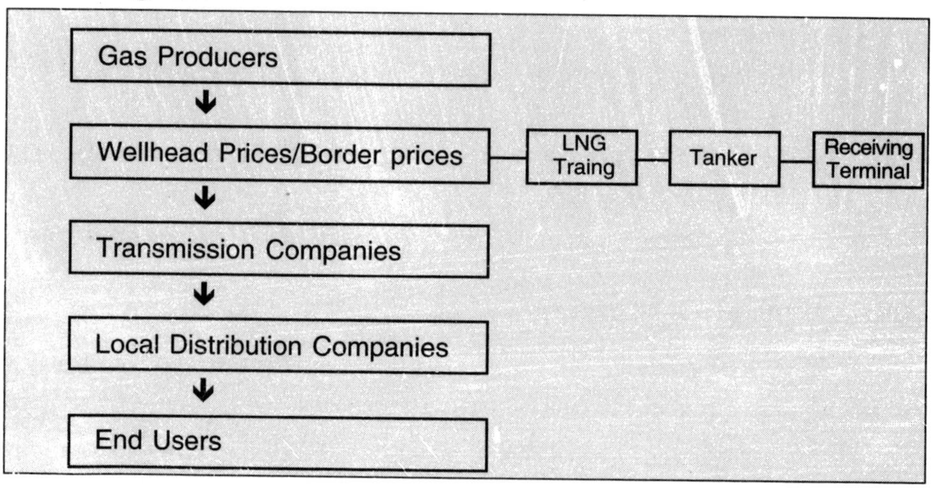

Figure 3.25

Pricing Formula

LNG is usually sold on the basis of pricing formula which usually links pricing of LNG to the price of the crude oil. The exact formula are usually considered commercial secrets, typical formula will have the following structure:

$$\text{Price Paid on Day 1} = \frac{\text{Base price} * (\text{MPI-1}) + A}{\text{MP}}$$

Where **MPI-1** is the market price of specified cocktail of crude oils imported on a specific day.

MP is the market price of the specified cocktail of crude oils imported on a day of the contract.

A is an adjustment factor often specified with limits.

Two Distinct Formula are used in Arabian Gulf Region

Qatar pricing formula in contracts with Japan calculates LNG price by taking the Japanese custom cleared price of a basket of crude and multiplying with a factor of 0.1845 or $6.73 MMBTU/bbl of oil.

A fixed factor is then added to the price which is between $0.6 - $0.9/ MMBTU to take account for the relatively fixed transportation costs for the gas.

Oman price formula calculates LNG prices on the basis of Japanese customs clearing price of the crude oil on a FOB basis to be multiplied by the factor of 0.1515 or a conversion factor of 6.6 MMBTU/bbl of oil. It does not contain a fixed element nor does it specify a minimum price.

LNG Pricing in Europe

The European gas industry, which witnessed stable and steady growth for nearly four decades, is in the throes of profound change. Restructuring the gas market is leading to emergence of new players. Third party access rules are being developed for LNG import facilities and natural gas transmission. The introduction of competition in the gas markets will imply fundamental changes in commercial and contractual relationships, affecting pricing, and therefore prices. As overall competitiveness is a determinant feature of future gas expansion, price accordingly becomes the crucial factor for success.

Gas Pricing Mechanisms

LONG-TERM CONTRACTS, NETBACK APPROACH AND NOW SPOT PRICES

Since natural gas developed as a regional business, gas and LNG pricing regimes and formula structures developed to meet local constraints and already specified to the end-user markets for gas. Unlike oil market, gas don't have international benchmark price.

However, the prices of gas are influenced particularly by crude oil and oil product, on all the regional markets. Natural gas does not have a captive market, and is always in competition with other energies: electricity, gas-oil and LPG's in the residential/ tertiary sectors, electricity, coals and heavy fuel oil in the industrial sector, and coal, fuel oil and nuclear power in the power sector. Thus its price cannot deviate too much from competing energies, which always offer a satisfactory replacement.

Long-term Contract and Netback Approach in Europe

Looking at the basic principle of gas pricing, the formula incorporated two factors:

- The base price, which splits the risk between the two parties, sellers and buyers
- Indexing, this ensures gas competitiveness and helps to integrate the changes occurring in the energy market, without having to renegotiate the contract.

Although the marketing of the gas on a "spot" basis continues to grow, a major share of the international contracts in force on the European continent largely remain indexed either directly to the price of crude oil or petroleum products imported by the buyer country, or indirectly through the use of crude oil netback prices. The netback market value approach has been the basis of gas pricing in Europe. The price paid by the importing company to the producer at the border or beach is negotiated on the basis of the weighted average value of the gas in competition with other fuels (gas-oil, low sulphur, high sulphur, heavy fuel oil) on the end user market, adjusted to allow for transportation and storage costs from the beach or border and any taxes on gas.

$$Pt = Po\,[a\,(Gt/Go) + b\,(Ft/Fo)]$$

Have been adopted, where:

Pt is the price of gas at time t,

Po is the price of gas at time o,

Gt is the price of gas oil at time t,

Go is the price of gas oil at time o,

Ft is the price of fuel oil at time t,

Fo is the price of fuel oil at time o.

Since LNG competes directly with pipeline gas on the end user market, LNG prices are indexed to a similar mix of product prices. Due to this method of calculating the gas price (indexed to the average price of a basket of crude oil or petroleum products over several months), European LNG and pipeline prices are generally lower than crude oil prices.

Short-term Sales

In recent years there has been a pronounced shift towards spot and short term contracts (one-day to one-year duration), mainly in LNG supplies. In that case, short-term contracts typically specify a fixed price for gas supplied, the price being determined by market conditions.

The Move Towards Spot Gas Price Indexation in Mid-terms Contracts

As it occurred in US in the mid –Eighties, short term spot trading has emerged in Europe as a key aspect of restructuring the market. Spot trading began to develop in the United Kingdom in 1993. The notional delivery point for gas is the National Balancing Point, a fact which limits the basis risk for hedging spot NBP trading. In 2003, 50 players were active at the NBP and the traded volume was estimated to amount to 675 Bcm/year. IPE prices have started to be used as the basis for pricing indexing in mid-term pipeline contracts:

1. In 2002, Statoil and British Gas trading signed a ten-year (2205-2015) supply contract for a plateau volume of 5 Bcm/year, indexed to the spot gas price at the National Balancing Point (UK).

The development of gas trading has gradually led to a spot market in Europe, with specific price quotations appearing in the British market and at the Zeebrugge hub in Belgium, where the arrival of the UK-Continent Interconnector and the Zeepipe Pipelines and the LNG receiving terminal provided platforms for the establishment of an active spot market. In 2003,

20 players were active at Zeebrugge and the traded volumes were estimated at about 70 Bcm/year. In 2002, another trading centered started operating in Emdem/Bunde in northern Germany.

LNG Pricing in Asia-Pacific Region

In the Asian market 97% of the gas comes in the form of LNG and Japan alone imports over 50% of the world production (BP, 2003). The Asia-pacific LNG prices are typically indexed to crude oil prices, either in Japan or Indonesia, specifically the Japan Custom Cleared also known as Japan Crude Cocktail (JCC) Crude prices in some cases shaped with "S" curves to limit the impact of extreme oil price movements.

JCC ids the average price of the crude imported into Japan every month, because of the linkage of crude prices and the LNG, the price of LNG go up or down with the price of JCC.

In 1969 the first cargoes were shipped from Kenai, Alaska to Japan at a fixed price of $ 0.52/MMBtu. This is substantial premium to crude oil as crude's price averaged $0.33/MMBtu in equivalent terms.

The current Asian LNG price formula revolves around crude oil linkage.

The traditional formula breaks down in the following manner:

PLNG = A* Pcrude oil + B

The variables are defined below:

PLNG = Price of LNG in cents/MMbtu

A = Slope of line (Shows crude linkage)

Pcrude oil = Price of crude $/bbl

B = a constant in cents/MMbtu.

Most LNG sold in Asia uses this formula, where A= 14.85and B = 70-90 cents. The slope is critical because it shows the linkage between LNG prices and crude oil prices. A slope of 14.85 has an 85 percent of crude oil linkage, meaning that if the price of crude increases by 10 percent, the price of LNG will increase by 8.5 percent.

LNG Pricing in USA

In the US competitive gas markets is firmly ensconced and prices are generally linked to the market price at Henry Hub which, is a physical point in Louisiana where 17 gas pipelines are interconnected, thereby creating a competitive reference point.

The price of the gas at various points in the continental US is derived from the differentials (+/–) from Henry Hub. The differentials are based on demand patterns and distance of end-users. LNG sales into the U.S., whether they are spot sales or long –term trades, are linked to Henry Hub prices because LNG is competing with pipeline gas.

It is interesting to note that the high volume at Henry Hub allows a transparent market which has enabled the futures market to develop on the NYMEX. This future market allows to sellers and buyers to hedge their sales and purchases, there by guaranteeing future prices.

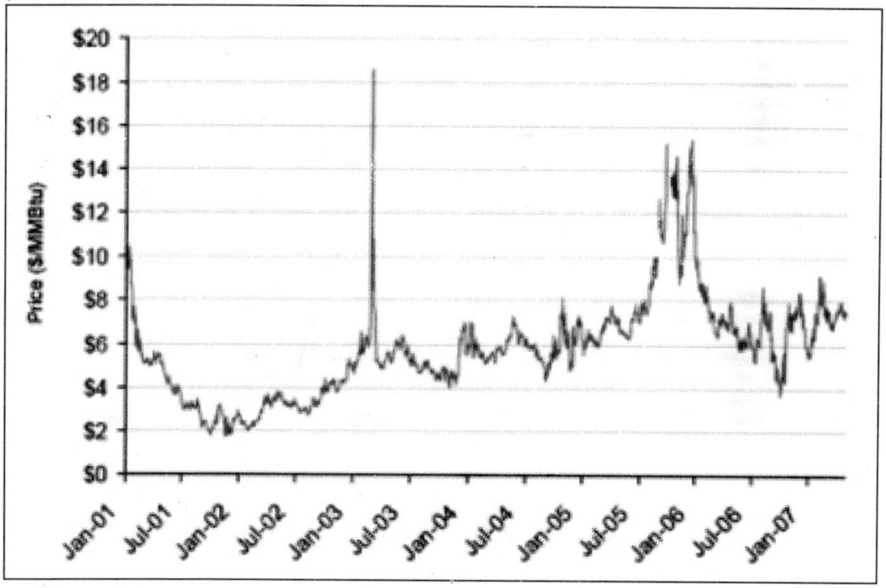

Figure 3.26: Prices of Gas at Henry Hub

LNG ECONOMICS

The typical size of investment for setting up a LNG import and export facility, with a capacity of 5 MMtpa, is estimated at $2.5-3 billion; $1.5-2 billion for the gas treatment and liquefaction plant, $ 500 million for two LNG carriers, and $ 500 million for an import terminal and re-gasification plant. Given the investment required, it is necessary that all the elements of the chain (gas production, liquefaction, transport and consumers) are tied-up simultaneously, in order to ensure the bankability of the projects.

In addition, LNG has to compete with domestically available gas and other fuels, on the basis of price. As liquefaction, transportation and regasification involve significant processing costs over the cost of production of Natural Gas, LNG would cost more than domestically available gas. In order to ensure LNG demand, it has to be priced competitively. Hence, it is necessary to examine the various elements of the LNG cost chain (liquefaction, transportation and regasification).

Typical Capital Costs of 2.5 MMtpa LNG Project

	Capital Cost (US $ million)	*Cost per unit gas (US $/MMBtu)*
Upstream	400	0.60
Liquefaction	750	1.10
Shipping	500	0.6
Regasification	400	0.6

As can be seen from the table the over all capital costs for a single LNG project can be in excess of $2bn, which when included with a gas fired power plant of 2000 MW would be a gross capital cost approaching $4bn.

Assumptions

Capital Costs for Generic LNG Liquefaction Terminal

LNG Liquefaction	*2.5 MMtpa*	*5 MMtpa*
Liquefaction, Utilities, Storage etc.	460	921
EPC	103	154
Marine	28	28
Infrastructure	47	47
Owners	112	112
Total	750	1262

Cost Date for Typical LNG Ship

LNG Tanker	
Vessel size (cum LNG)	138.0
Ship speed (Knots)	17
Capital Expenditure ($million)	250
Operating Costs ($ million)	6 per annum
Insurance	1% Capital Expenditure

Capital Costs for Generic LNG Receiving Terminal in $ million

	2.5 MMtpa	*5 MMtpa*
Unloading/ Marine	49	49
Storage, vaporization, utilities etc.	148	268
Fuel Oil storage, Building, Facilities	34	135
Direct Field Costs	231	352
Field Distributable	31	44
Field Costs	262	396
Project Mgt., Engineering + Contingency	137	190
Total	339	586

The operating and maintenance and insurance costs for a liquefaction plant are taken to be 2.50% of the capital cost. These costs for a receiving terminal are taken to be 1.50% of the total capital cost.

There are significant economies of scale to be realized in LNG projects as incremental size increases come at a fraction of the new cost. For example to add a new train to a liquefaction plant there will be the costs for the new train, for additional storage and for some additional utilities but much of the infrastructure developed for a single train plant is good for a two train plant e.g. marine facilities loading facilities. These economies of scale are also present in the regasification facilities.

The optimization of LNG economics comes in the sizing of the project to optimize the unit rate of gas delivered ($/MMBtu). Matching the quantity delivered to shipping sizes and distance will make significant saving. For example a typical single train LNG project is 2.5 – 3.3 MMtpa. However because of the distance to India from the Gulf, two standard large LNG boats (138000 tonnes) would be required to deliver this volume. However by reducing the volume delivered a project could be supported by a single boat resulting in lower delivered cost of gas.

The overall capital cost for LNG projects are enormous and such projects require enormous skill and resources in matching each link of the chain together. An LNG project chain is supported by the end user contract, which is a gas sales agreement with the offtaker and often ultimately the power purchase agreement the offtaker has with its customers.

Implicit in these high capital projects are long payback periods, which necessitate the use of long tern supply contracts back to back throughout the LNG chain. The assets of an LNG project are typically locked in to a project for 20-25 years. Due to the high debt service requirements associated with the financing of the various project components, take or pay contacts are the norm, where the offtaker pays for the sales quantity whether it can be used or not. There are various contract mechanisms whereby the offtaker may defer the delivery of a shipment to a later date known as make up delivery – but the essence of LNG supply contracting to date has been the take or pay mechanism.

Delivered Price of LNG

As per a study conducted by Asian Development Bank, the delivered cost of LNG varies between $2.55/MMBtu and $3.65/MMBtu depending upon the terminal and sources used. LNG can be delivered most cheaply to the west coast of India from the Gulf, the netbacked pricing calculation indicating that this gas could be delivered and revapourized at less than $3.25/MMBtu. Supplies from Malaysia would be landed at a similar price.

Supply to the central eastern coast would be marginally cheaper from Malaysia. Gas from Australia would be relatively more expensive due to the substantial shipping cost involved. The closest source of LNG to the west coast and southern India could be from Arun in northern Sumatra, Indonesia. If a swap arrangement could be enacted, such that LNG from another South East Asian source was substituted for Arun LNG to Japan, revapourized LNG could be supplied to Gujarat at a higher rate than at other locations due to the higher costs involved in constructing the appropriate marine facilities

CHAPTER 4

Power Trading

INTRODUCTION OF POWER TRADING

Power can be defined as the rate of doing work or energy transferred per unit time. Electric power generation is the process of converting any form of energy to electrical energy. Depending upon the fuel used for generating power it can be named as nuclear power (radioactive elements), solar power (sun), wind power, wave power, tidal power, geothermal power (coal, natural gas), hydropower (water).

Alessandro Volta was first to produce electricity in 1800, with the help of electrolytic cell later on the cell was known as voltaic cell. In voltaic cell electricity is produced as a result of the chemical reactions that take place in an electrolytic cell. But its production by this means was, expensive. In 1831, Michael Faraday devised a machine that generated electricity from rotary motion, but it took almost 50 years for the technology to reach a commercially viable stage. In 1878, in the US, Thomas Edison developed and sold a commercially viable replacement for gas lighting and heating using locally generated and distributed direct current electricity.

The world's first public electricity supply was provided in late 1881, when the streets of the Surrey town of Godalming in the UK were lit with electric light. This system was powered from a water wheel on the River Wey, which drove a Siemens alternator that supplied a number of arc lamps within the town. This supply scheme also provided electricity to a number of shops and premises.

Coincident with this, in early 1882, Edison opened the world's first steam-powered electricity generating station at Holborn Viaduct in London, where he had entered into an agreement with the City Corporation for a period of three months to provide street lighting. In time he had supplied a number of local consumers with electric light. The method of supply was direct current (DC).

It was later on in the year in September 1882 that Edison opened the Pearl Street Power Station in New York City and again it was a DC supply. It was for this reason that the generation was close to or on the consumer's premises as Edison had no means of voltage conversion. The voltage chosen for any electrical system is a compromise. Increasing the voltage reduces the current and therefore reduces resistive losses in the cable. Unfortunately it increases the danger from direct contact and also increases the required insulation thickness. Furthermore some load types were difficult or impossible to make for higher voltages.

Additionally, Robert Hammond, in December 1881, demonstrated the new electric light in the Sussex town of Brighton in the UK for a trial period. The ensuing success of this installation enabled Hammond to put this venture on both a commercial and legal footing, as a number of shop owners wanted to use the new electric light. Thus the Hammond Electricity Supply Co. was launched. Whilst the Godalming and Holborn Viaduct Schemes closed after a few years the Brighton Scheme continued on, and supply was in 1887 made available for 24 hours per day.

Nikola Tesla, who had worked for Edison for a short time and appreciated the electrical theory in a way that Edison did not, devised an alternative system using alternating current. Tesla realised that while doubling the voltage would halve the current and reduce losses by three-quarters, only an alternating current system allowed the transformation between voltage levels in different parts of the system. He went on to develop the overall theory of his system, devising theoretical and practical alternatives for all of the direct current appliances then in use, and patented his novel ideas in 1887, in thirty separate patents.

In 1888, Tesla's work came to the attention of George Westinghouse, who owned a patent for a type of transformer that could deal with high power and was easy to make. Westinghouse had been operating an alternating current lighting plant in Great Barrington, Massachusetts since 1886. While Westinghouse's system could use Edison's lights and had heaters, it did not have a motor. With Tesla and his patents, Westinghouse built a power system for a gold mine in Telluride, Colorado in 1891, with a water driven 100 horsepower (75 kW) generator powering a 100 horsepower (75 kW) motor over a 2.5-mile (4 km) power line. Almarian Decker finally invented the whole system of three-phase power generating in Redlands, California in 1893. Then, in a deal with General Electric, which Edison had been forced to sell, Westinghouse's company went on to construct a power station at the Niagara Falls, with three 5,000 horsepower (3.7 MW) Tesla generators supplying electricity to an aluminum smelter at Niagara and the town of Buffalo 22 miles (35 km) away. The Niagara power station commenced operation on April 20 1895.

Tesla's alternating current system remains the primary means of delivering electrical energy to consumers throughout the world. While high-voltage direct current (HVDC) is increasingly being used to transmit large quantities of electricity over long distances or to connect adjacent asynchronous power systems, the bulk of electricity generation, transmission, distribution and retailing take place using alternating current.

Need for Deregulation

The **electrical power industry** provides the production and delivery of **electrical power** (electrical energy), often known as **power**, or **electricity**, in sufficient quantities to areas that need electricity through a grid. Many households and businesses need access to electricity, especially in developed nations, the demand being scarcer in developing nations. Demand for electricity is derived from the requirement for electricity in order to operate domestic appliances, office equipment, industrial machinery and provide sufficient energy for both domestic and commercial lighting, heating, cooking and industrial processes. Because of this aspect of the industry, it is viewed as a public utility as infrastructure.

The electrical power industry is commonly split up into four processes. These are electricity generation such as a power station, electric power transmission, electricity distribution and electricity retailing. In many countries, electric power companies own the whole infrastructure from generating stations to transmission and distribution infrastructure. For this reason, electric power is viewed as a natural monopoly. The industry is generally heavily regulated, often with price controls and is frequently government-owned and operated. The nature and state of market reform of the electricity market often determines whether electric companies are able to be involved in just some of these processes without having to own the entire infrastructure, or citizens choose which components of infrastructure to patronise. In countries where electricity provision is deregulated, end-users of electricity may opt for more costly green electricity.

Restructuring of the power industry aims at abolishing the monopoly in the generation and trading sectors, thereby, introducing competition at various levels wherever it is possible. Generating companies may enter into contracts to supply the generated power to the power dealers/distributors or bulk consumers or sell the power in a pool in which the power brokers and customers also participate. In a power-exchange, the buyers can bid for their demands along with their willingness to pay. Power generation and trading will, thus, become free from the conventional regulations and become competitive. Electricity sector restructuring, also popularly known as deregulation is expected to draw private investment, increase efficiency, promote technical growth and improve customer satisfaction as different parties compete with each other to win their market share and remain in business. Open access is the key to a free and fair electricity market. Power producers (sellers) and dealers/customers (buyers) have to share a common transmission network for wheeling the power from the point of generation to the point of consumption. Thus, interconnected transmission system is considered to be a natural monopoly so as to avoid the duplicity, the problem of right-of-the-way, and huge investment for new infrastructure and to take the advantage of the interconnected network viz. reduced installed capacity, increased system reliability and improved system performance.

Development and Deregulation—Electricity Market

An electricity market is a system for effecting the purchase and sale of electricity using supply and demand to set the price. Wholesale transactions in electricity are typically cleared and settled by the grid operator or a special-purpose independent entity charged exclusively with that function. Markets for certain related commodities required by (and paid for by) various grid operators to ensure reliability, such as spinning reserve, operating reserves, and installed capacity, are also typically managed by the grid operator. In addition, for most major grids there are markets for electricity derivatives, such as electricity futures and options, which are actively traded. These markets developed as a result of the deregulation of electric power systems around the world. This process has often gone on in parallel with the deregulation of natural gas markets.

Early History

The earliest introduction of market concepts and privatization to electric power systems took place in Chile in the late 1970s, in parallel with other market-oriented reforms associated with the Chicago Boys. The Chilean model was generally perceived as successful in bringing rationality and transparency to power pricing, but it contemplated the continuing dominance of several large incumbents and suffered from the attendant structural problems. Argentina improved on the Chilean model by imposing strict limits on market concentration and by improving the structure of payments to units held in reserve to assure system reliability. One of the principal purposes of the introduction of market concepts in Argentina was to privatize existing generation assets (which had fallen into despair under the government-owned monopoly, resulting in frequent service interruptions) and to attract capital needed for rehabilitation of those assets and for system expansion. The World Bank was active in introducing a variety of hybrid markets in other Latin American nations, including Peru, Brazil and Colombia, during the 1990s, with limited success.

A key event for electricity markets occurred in 1990 when the UK Government under Margaret Thatcher privatised the UK Electricity Supply Industry. The process followed by the British was then used as a model or at least a catalyst for the deregulation of several other Commonwealth countries, notably Australia and New Zealand, and regional markets such as Alberta. However, in many of these other instances the market deregulation occurred without the widespread privatisation that characterised the UK example.

In different deregulation processes the institutions and market designs were often very different but many of the underlying concepts were the same. These are: separate the contestable functions of generation and retail from the natural monopoly functions of transmission and distribution; and establish a **wholesale electricity market** and a **retail electricity market**. The role of the wholesale market is to allow trading between generators, retailers and other financial intermediaries both for short-term delivery of electricity (spot price) and for future delivery periods (forward price).

Wholesale Electricity Market

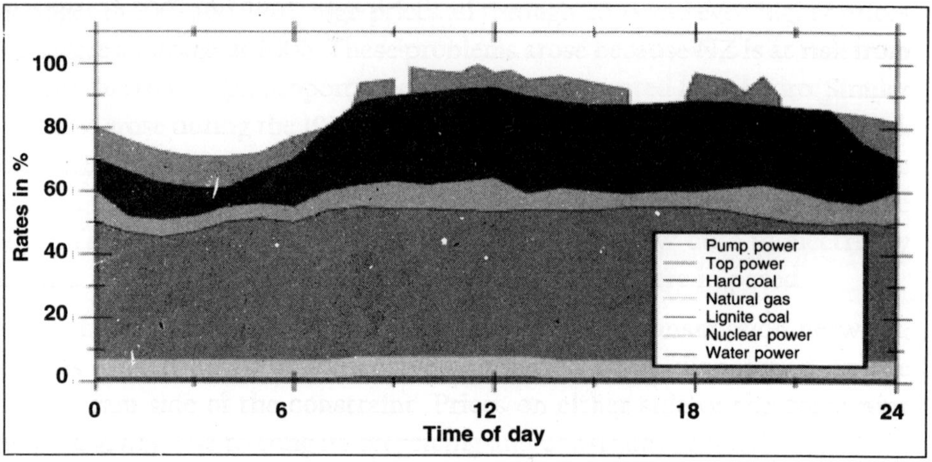

Figure 4.1: Typical Daily Consumption of Electrical Power in Germany

A **wholesale electricity market** exists when competing generators offer their electricity output to retailers.

Electricity is by its nature difficult to store and has to be available on demand. Consequently, unlike other products, it is not possible, under normal operating conditions, to keep it in stock, ration it or have customers queue for it. Demand and supply vary continuously. There is therefore a physical requirement for a controlling agency, the transmission system operator, to coordinate the dispatch of generating units to meet the expected demand of the system across the transmission grid. If there is a mismatch between supply and demand, the generators speed up or slow down causing the system frequency (either 50 or 60 hertz) to increase or decrease. If the frequency falls outside a predetermined range the system operator will act to add or remove either generation or load.

In addition, the laws of physics determine how electricity flows through an electricity network. Hence the extent of electricity lost in transmission and the level of congestion on any particular branch of the network will influence the economic dispatch of the generation units.

For an economically efficient electricity wholesale market to flourish, it is essential that a number of criteria are met. Professor William Hogan of Harvard University has identified these. Central to his criteria is a coordinated spot market that has "bid-based, security-constrained, economic dispatch with nodal prices". Other academics such as Professors Shmuel Oren and Pablo

Spiller of the University of California, Berkeley have proposed other criteria. Variants of Professor Hogan's model have largely been adopted in the US, Australia and New Zealand.

Bid-based, Security-constrained, Economic Dispatch with Nodal Prices

The theoretical price of electricity at each node on the network is a calculated "shadow price", in which it is assumed that one additional kilowatt-hour is demanded at the node in question, and the hypothetical incremental cost to the system that would result from the optimized re-dispatch of available units establishes the hypothetical production cost of the hypothetical kilowatt-hour. This is known as Locational Marginal Pricing (LMP) or *nodal pricing* and is used in some deregulated markets, most notably in the PJM, New York and New England markets in the USA and in New Zealand. However, many established markets do not employ nodal pricing, examples being the UK, Powernext and Nord Pool (Scandinavia and Finland). While in theory the LMP concepts are useful and not evidently subject to manipulation, in practice system operators have substantial discretion over LMP results through the ability to classify units as running in "out-of-merit dispatch", which are thereby excluded from the LMP calculation. In most systems, units that are dispatched to provide reactive power to support transmission grids are declared to be "out-of-merit" (even though these are typically the same units that are located in constrained areas and would otherwise result in scarcity signals). System operators also normally bring units online to hold as "spinning-reserve" to protect against sudden outages or unexpectedly rapid ramps in demand, and declare them "out-of-merit". The result is often a substantial reduction in clearing price at a time when increasing demand would otherwise result in escalating prices. Hogan and others have noted that a variety of factors, including energy price caps set well below the putative scarcity value of energy, the impact of "out-of-merit" dispatch, the use of techniques such as voltage reductions during scarcity periods with no corresponding scarcity price signal, etc., results in a "missing money" problem. The consequence is that prices paid to suppliers in the "market" are substantially below the levels required to stimulate new entry. The markets have therefore been useful in bringing efficiencies to short-term system operations and dispatch, but have been a failure in what was advertised as a principal benefit: stimulating suitable new investment where it is needed, when it is needed.

Since the introduction of the market, New Zealand has experienced shortages in 2001 and 2003, high prices all through 2005 and even higher prices and severe shortage in 2006. These problems arose because NZ is at risk from drought due to its high proportion of electricity generated from hydro. Similar shortages arose during the 1970s before the electricity market was introduced. The absence of shortages during the 1980s appears to be due to the large increase in capacity as a result of the "Think Big" projects started during the 1970s. The difference the market has made is that now cuts in electricity demand are made voluntarily while in the 1970s cuts were imposed.

In LMP markets, where constraints exist on a transmission network, there is a need for more expensive generation to be dispatched on the downstream side of the constraint. Prices on either side of the constraint separate giving rise to congestion pricing and constraint rentals.

A constraint can be caused when a particular branch of a network reaches its thermal limit or when a potential overload will occur due to a contingent event (e.g., failure of a generator or transformer or a line outage) on another part of the network. The latter is referred to as a *security constraint*. Transmission systems are operated to allow for continuity of supply even if a contingent event, like the loss of a line, were to occur. This is known as a *security constrained system*.

The system price in the day-ahead market is, in principle, determined by matching offers from generators to bids from consumers at each node to develop a classic supply and demand equilibrium price, usually on an hourly interval, and is calculated separately for subregions in which the system operator's load flow model indicates that constraints will bind transmission imports. In practice, the LMP algorithm described above is run, incorporating a security-constrained, least-cost dispatch calculation with supply based on the generators that submitted offers in the day-ahead market, and demand based on bids from load-serving entities draining supplies at the nodes in question. In most systems the algorithm used is a "DC" model rather than an "AC" model, so constraints and redispatch resulting from thermal limits are identified/predicted, but constraints and redispatch resulting from reactive power deficiencies are not. Some systems take marginal losses into account. The prices in the real-time market are determined by the LMP algorithm described above, balancing supply from available units. This process is carried out for each 5-minute, half-hour or hour (depending on the market) interval at each node on the transmission grid. The hypothetical re-dispatch calculation that determines LMP must respect security constraints and the re-dispatch calculation must leave sufficient margin to maintain system stability in the event of an unplanned outage anywhere on the system. This results in a spot market with "bid-based, security-constrained, economic dispatch with nodal prices".

Wholesale Electricity Markets

- Australia—NEMMCO the Australian Market Administrator
- Canada—Independent Electricity System Operator (IESO) Ontario Market and Alberta Electric System Operator (AESO)
- Chile
- Scandinavia—Nord Pool
- France—Powernext
- Germany—European Energy Exchange (EEX)
- Great Britain—Elexon
- India
- New Zealand—New Zealand Electricity Market
- Philippines—Philippine Wholesale Electricity Spot Market
- USA—ERCOT Market, PJM Market, New York Market, Midwest Market, and California ISO
- Singapore—Energy Market Authority, Singapore and Energy Market Company (EMC)

Retail Electricity Market

A **retail electricity market** exists when end-use customers can choose their supplier from competing electricity retailers; one term used in the United States for this type of consumer choice is 'energy choice'. A separate issue for electricity markets is whether or not consumers face real-time pricing (prices based on the variable wholesale price) or a price that is set in some other way, such as average annual costs. In many markets, consumers do not pay based on the real-time price, and hence have no incentive to reduce demand at times of high (wholesale) prices or to shift their demand to other periods. Demand response may use pricing mechanisms or technical solutions to reduce peak demand.

Generally, electricity retail reform follows from electricity wholesale reform. However, it is possible to have a single electricity generation company and still have retail competition. If a wholesale price can be established at a node on the transmission grid and the electricity quantities at that node can be reconciled, competition for retail customers within the distribution system beyond the node is possible. In the German market, for example, large, vertically integrated utilities compete with one another for customers on a more or less open grid.

Although market structures vary, there are some common functions that an electricity retailer has to be able to perform, or enter into a contract for, in order to compete effectively. Failure or incompetence in the execution of one or more of the following has led to some dramatic financial disasters:

— Meter reading
— Meter rental
— Billing
— Credit control
— Customer management via an efficient call centre
— Distribution use-of-system contract
— Reconciliation agreement
— "Pool" or "spot market" purchase agreement
— Hedge contracts - contracts for differences to manage "spot price" risk

The two main areas of weakness have been risk management and billing. In the USA in 2001, California's flawed regulation of retail competition led to the California electricity crisis and left incumbent retailers subject to high spot prices but without the ability to hedge against these. In the UK a retailer, Independent Energy, with a large customer base went bust when it could not collect the money due from customers.

Mechanics of Power Trading

What is Power Trading?

- POWER TRADERS were incorporated in the system to act as an entity which could undertake trading of power to achieve economic efficiency and security of supply.
- POWER TRADERS have a two-fold mandate:
  - To develop a full fledged, efficient and competitive market mechanism for trading in power, and

  - To facilitate the development of generation projects including through private investment, both resulting in reliable, economic and quality power in the long-term.
- A vibrant power market, which is deep and liquid, needs to be developed in the long-term, and POWER TRADERS would continue to play a frontrunner's role towards this objective and strive to add value to its customers' operations through providing services that serve their evolving needs.
- Develop power market for optimal utilization of energy. Develop the power system on regional basis into five Electricity regions i.e. Eastern, North-Eastern, Southern, western and Northern.
- Promote power trading to optimally utilize the existing resources. Excess of the Eastern region must be utilized to cover the deficit of the Southern and western region.
- Catalyze development of Power Projects particularly environment friendly hydro projects. The energy thus generated must be utilized to fulfill the peak load deficit and short-term demands.
- Promote exchange of power with neighboring countries.

Power Trading draws its special nature due to specific characteristics of electric energy viz. It requires to be consumed as it is being produced. Further, it is not possible to produce electrical energy at the point of consumption due to various factors viz. fuel and technology being some of these.

There is a need to, also, regulate demand by adopting measures such as differential tariffs based on the time-of-day and the season. SEBs can also shift the agricultural load to the nights by regulating the distribution to this sector.

NTPC is investing Rs. 41,500 crore in this period which will see the company add 9,370 MW, 43 per cent of its existing capacity of 21,435 MW. NHPC is implementing projects adding up to 4,300 MW — almost twice its existing installed capacity of 2,475 MW. Others such as Neyveli Lignite Corporation are also investing aggressively in capacity expansion.

Interestingly, while the SEBs managed to almost achieve their targeted capacity addition in the Ninth Plan, it was the central utilities and the private sector that failed, achieving just 37 per cent and 28 per cent of their targets.

Private players such as Reliance Energy and Tata Power are planning big projects that will add about 5,000 MW in the next four years. Reliance has signed an agreement with the Uttar Pradesh Government for a 3,500 MW plant to be fuelled by gas from the Krishna-Godavari basin while the Tatas' are planning a 1,500 MW plant near Delhi, again gas-based.

The Indian electricity sector has grown manifold since independence making India the third largest producer of electricity in Asia. The installed capacity has increased from 1362 MW in 1947 to about 108000 MW as at end March 2002.

Substantial growth in terms of installed capacity and power supply has been achieved. However, it is a long way before India can be called as self sufficient in bridging the gap between demand and supply.

Inter-regional power transfer capacity of around 6000 MW is currently available, which is expected to increase further to about 9500 MW in the coming few years. With transmission capacity being put in place for large size inter-State projects, the inter-regional transfer capacity is likely to get further enhanced. Substantial opportunities therefore exist to improve the economic efficiency and security of supply through trading of power.

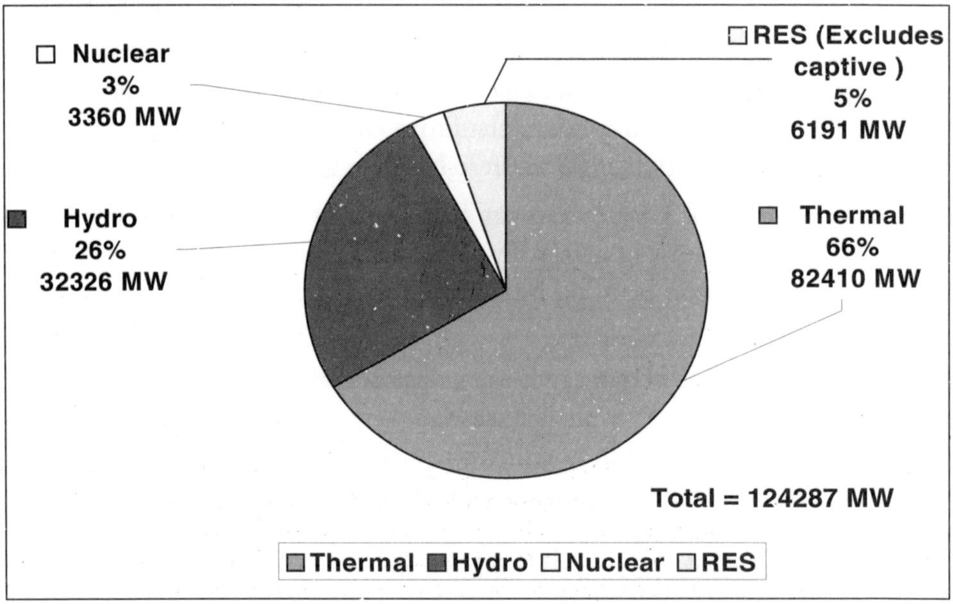

Figure 4.2: All India Installed Capacity (MW) (as on 31-3-2006)

In order to meet the growing demand for power, potential for large-sized private projects has been recognized. Alongside this the Govt. of India also developed the Mega Power Policy through which, the development of large

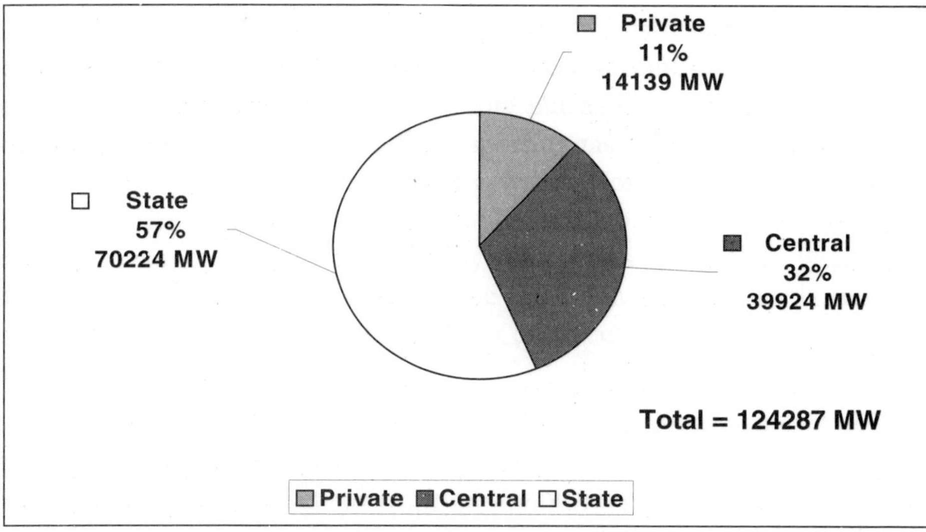

Figure 4.3: All India Installed Capacity (MW) Sector-wise (as on 31-3-2006)

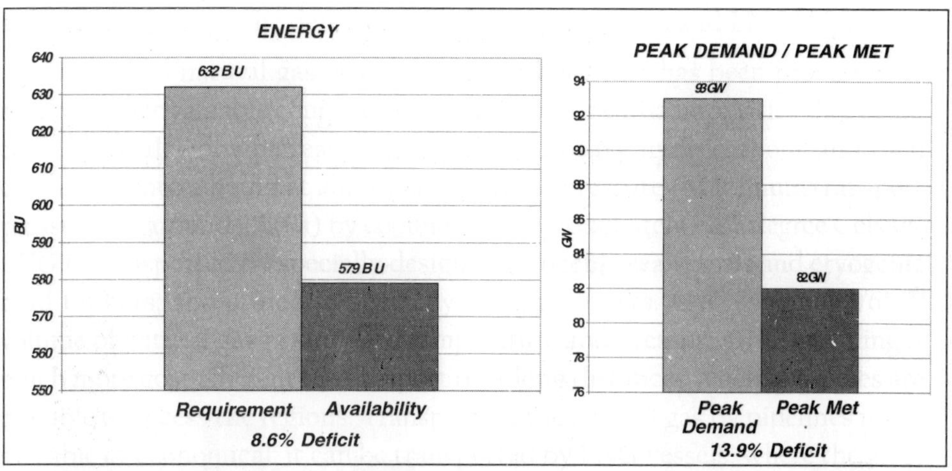

Figure 4.4: All India Power Supply Scenario *(April, 2005–March, 2006)*

private power projects was foreseen. These projects are to supply power to multiple states and this usually leads to difficulties in reaching agreement on risk sharing as well as on payment security mechanisms, reducing the credit-worthiness of the project. Therefore, a single credit-enhancing agency, which could buy power from these private power stations and sell to the State Utilities and other buyers, was felt inevitable. Such an entity could manage the risks effectively to provide adequate comfort to investors and lenders.

Power Trading Corporation of India Limited, incorporated in 1999, under the Companies Act was setup to achieve the aforementioned objective and also to act as an entity, which could undertake trading of power to achieve economic efficiency and security of supply.

One of the mandates for PTC is to develop a full fledged, efficient and competitive market mechanism for *trading in power, resulting in reliable, economic and quality power in the long-term.* Essentially an integrated national power market needs to be developed in the long-term, and this is what PTC has taken as the core of its statement of purpose.

The increase in the volumes calls for a higher capitalized venture (started with an authorized capital of Rs 1500 Million and paid up capital of Rs. 60 Million and presently at Rs. 915 Million) and PTC has made plans to increase its paid up capital base to Rs 1 billion in the current financial year and eventually to Rs 7.5 billion in the next few years. It is a reflection of the market confidence in the PTC concept that leading FIs (IDBI, IDFC, IFCI, GIC and LIC) and Power Sector Majors viz DVC, Tata Power and NHPC (presently one of the promoters) have picked up equity in PTC in addition to the original promoters (NTPC, POWERGRID and PFC).

Set up in year 1999, PTC was set up as a Nodal agency for exchange of power with neighboring countries. Clearly Mandated for power trading to optimally utilize the existing resources in the country.

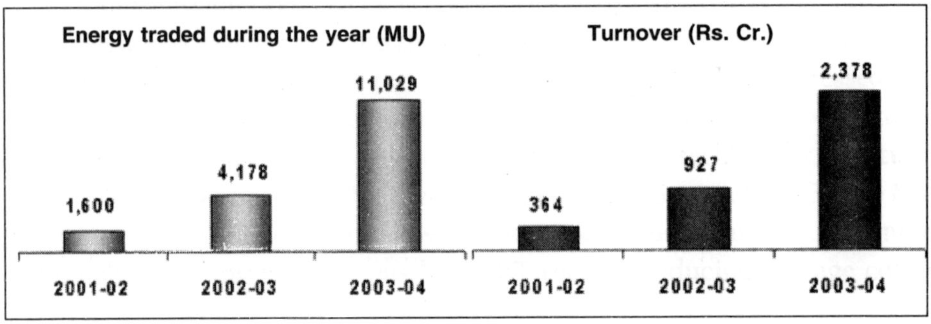

Figure 4.5

There are enough indicators and reasons to go for trading in power in a regulated and free manner so as to achieve the national objective of Power for everyone in a reliable and secured manner.

Rationale Behind Power Trading

- Optimum Utilization of Existing resources in power sector would be affected since the deficit of one region would be made up by the surplus of the other.
- The reforms in the power sector can be implemented more rigorously through regulations.
- Shortages in the deficit locations would be minimized.
- It can allow deferment of fresh investment required to augment the generating and transmission capacities.
- Average cost of power can be brought down by bringing in competition and utilizing the surplus power.
- Schedule exchanges will increase and un-scheduled exchanges would reduce bringing in the grid discipline.

MAIN ISSUES FOR POWER TRADING

1. Financial Viabilities of the Utilities: Operation of the Divided Utilities must be financially viable. The tariff structure, payment mechanism, PBT and PAT must be ensured. This requires the regulation which has to balance out the interests of the utilities and the consumers both.
2. Power Trading will be able to address the issue regarding lack of adherence to commitments by the Utilities. Currently, utilities do not guarantee to provide adequate service. Disconnection is favored over any other mechanism of payment realization. Non-payment of electricity bills is also not followed vigorously. Over a period of time, this results in the sickness of the utility leading to its ultimate collapse.
3. Power trading also needs to address the issue of adequacy of transmission capacity. HVDC has not been a success for the fact that optimum capacity utilization has not been achieved so far thereby resulting in high costs of transmission. Inter-regional interconnections of the transmission networks are necessary for power transfer. Resource sharing arrangements (Transmission or wheeling price) need to be formulated and regulated either bilaterally or through some nodal agency. Most of the transmission networks have outlived their lives and need replacement / augmentation. They cause higher T&D losses and cost over runs.

4. Outside the state trading needs statutory provisions for direct sale by the IPPs/CPPs/Licensees. Taxation, cap on the margins etc are the issues that must be addressed before allowing trading.
5. Market should exist with well defined market mechanisms. Power exchanges etc can serve the objective. Dispute redressal mechanisms must exist.
6. Demand-Supply mismatch should be used for the benefit of the user in making the power pricing economical through trading the surplus or time of the day concepts or any other method. The prices should match the intrinsic vale of power.
7. Grid discipline should be maintained for improving the quality of power (Frequency excursions and voltages).These measures could bring down the average cost of power.

Key Drivers for Power Trading

Power Trading requires free trading regime. Therefore, the utilities need to commercialize their operations in order to sustain for themselves in the open market. All opportunities of revenue generation need to be tapped to their fullest extent. At the same time, need for tapping power at lower cost should not be overlooked. These measures are bound to turn the financial conditions of these utilities round and make the economically and financially viable.

Transmission needs to be accorded due credit since it is the most vital link between the generator and the consumer. Age old transmission links need augmentation. Inter-regional transmission capacity should be addressed with due seriousness. It must be enhanced for regional transfer of power to the destination through HVDC links or any other relevant technology. A national grid has been envisaged by 2012 with an inter-regional capacity of 30000 MW (currently 4850 MW). Intrinsic value of power, thus, would be recognized through balancing mechanisms like ABT thereby reducing average cost of power.

Intermediaries, thus introduced, would grow in numbers bringing in the management and technical skills in Power Sector. Potential of Power Exchanges can be explored to its peak. State utilities would be able to negotiate long-term commercial contracts to the benefit of all. Surplus revenue can be utilized for augmenting the infrastructure and facilities to the consumer and the staff.

Open access to the facilities of transmission and distribution should be allowed with a definite time frame. Intermediate step of payment of surcharge kept towards meeting cross-subsidy levels, should be phased out. Distribution, trading and transmission should become licensed activities. Trading should be allowed to the distributor. These should, further, be allowed to franchise the distribution and generation and also allowed to utilize the assets of other businesses. Cross subsidy on open access and retail tariff must be phased out in a regulated manner to maintain stability and improve the health of the power sector. CTU/STU must be barred from trading in power.

Thermal power generation is de-licensed. This mode constitutes the major source of power generation. General Companies are free to choose their buyers which may either be a licensee (Distribution Companies) or a consumer. Captive power and co-generation is being encouraged with a greater emphasis on renewable energy resources. Regulator has a special role to play to oversee the operations of the market and apply appropriate controls whenever necessary.

Risk is an inherent component of any system which, if not addressed with due care and seriousness, may result in ultimate failure. Regulatory Risk, for instance, indicates that the project turns un-viable if the charges levied for wheeling power make the power delivery difficult for the operators. Similarly government's willingness to implement policies is embedded with political risk.

Payment security is another highly sensitive issue. How to ensure the accurate and complete payment at the right time? Though, there are a number of payment options ensuring implementation of the policies, still, other risks play their role and turn this issue as the only one to be addressed at priority. Tools like Bank Guarantee, Letter of credit or Cash etc, though preferred, have their own operational liabilities.

A. Electricity as a Commodity

Similar to any products, the trading of electricity consists of buying and selling of energy. The trading of electricity exists since utilities companies were originally formed. Nevertheless, the main difference between trading of electricity during that time and now is that consumers have freedom of choice between suppliers. Since electricity cannot be differentiated (all electron are physically the same), it is defined as a commodity. This "commodization" of electricity applied mainly at the wholesale level. The wholesale market for electricity can be seen as the direct result of the separation between transport and production. This new status of electricity involves the development of novel types of contracts for electricity trading. These contracts can either be sold on the bilateral market or on an organized market. They can also be physical contracts (for delivery) or financial contracts (hedging). However, all of them share three characteristics: a defined period, a certain amount of electricity, and a price. The other characteristics can differ widely. For the purpose of this paper we will focus on the physical trading of electricity.

Electricity can be bought and sold according to a variety of factors, such as how it is generated and when it is used. Utility companies can use power trading to better manage their price risks, for example by buying gas-generated electricity on the market if the costs of generating their cwn energy from other sources are too high. As well as by speculating on future prices, companies can generate additional revenues by selling risk-management services to smaller utilities and other firms.

A robust trading system is very important for free and fair competitive electricity market operation. Trading system should be capable of risk hedging associated with price volatility and other unexpected changes. Operating behavior of a competitive power market is significantly affected by the trading arrangements, strategic bidding, market model and rule. Trading arrangement is properly designed in every country to take care of other abuse of market. These arrangements are kept on changing from time to time depending on the requirement for transparent and non-discriminatory electricity market.

Managing risk is primary tasks of any trading system. This task is perceived harder for electricity being a non-storable commodity. In competitive environment, the price is determined by stochastic supply and demand functions. The price can change at any time. As a consequence of increased volatility, a market participant could make trading contracts with other parties to hedge possible risks and get better returns. Congestion occurs when transmission lines or transformers are overloaded and this prevents the system operators from dispatching additional power from a specific generator. This may be prevented to some extent by means of reservations or rights. These rights are used to guarantee an efficient use of transmission system capacity and to allocate transmission capacity to users who value it most.

B. Physical Trading

The physical contracts can differ between long-term (one to twenty years), forward (using current or forecast price with delivery in the future) and spot ones (very short term, mainly day ahead). Since electricity cannot be stored, this range of contracts is necessary to keep supply and demand in balance. Consumers buy in advance long-term and forward contract in order to cover their consumption. Nevertheless, players also need daily and even hourly contracts to fulfill their consumption's requirements because real consumption is not completely predicable.

In most European countries, all these contracts are negotiated on a bilateral basis. However due to the transaction cost related to spot trading, spot markets are usually organized by a power exchange. It does not mean that spot trading can not occur on a bilateral basis, but that for this kind of contract power exchange are generally preferred by market participants. In all countries, power trading is growing at an impressive rate. The Nordic region so far is the most important in terms of absolute volume. Nevertheless, the traded volumes within others European countries, such as Germany, the United Kingdom and the Netherlands are increasing very quickly. The aggregate of these volumes may soon overtake the Nordic market.

C. Trading on a Power Exchange

Electricity spot prices are volatile due to the unique physical attributes of electricity such as non-storability, uncertain and inelastic demand and a steep supply function. Uncontrolled exposure to market price risks could lead to devastating consequences. During the summer of 1998, wholesale power prices in the Midwest of US surged to a stunning $7,000 per MWh from the normal price range of $30-$60 per MWh, causing the defaults of two power marketers in the east coast. In February 2004, persistent high prices in Texas during a 3-day ice storm led to the bankruptcy of a retail energy provider that was exposed to spot market prices. And of course, the California electricity crisis of 2000-01 and its devastating economic consequences are largely attributed to the fact that the major utilities were not properly hedged through long-term supply contracts. Such expensive lessons have raised the awareness of market participants to the importance and necessity of risk management practices in competitive electricity market.

An electricity power exchange provides a spot market (mainly day-ahead) for electricity, which like any other market matches demand and supply for each hour, while providing a public price index. It can be viewed as a competitive wholesale spot trading arrangement that facilitates the selling and buying of electricity. An exchange is absolutely neutral toward the market because its rules apply to both sides of the transactions. A power exchange is therefore a voluntary marketplace in full competition with the classic bilateral market (Over The Counter, OTC).

Competition in an electricity power exchange's spot market occurs by generators, distributors, traders, and large consumers submitting bids for buying and selling electricity. Each sale bid specifies the quantity and its minimum price at which they are willing to supply energy. Conversely, each buy bid specifies the desired quantity and the maximum price at which they are willing to buy energy. The power exchanges match supply and demand along with publishing a market-clearing price.

The exchanges play an essential role in the new structure of the electricity industry, especially within the pan-European wholesale spot market which was until now dominated by bilateral trade. All these power exchanges share the same goals. They aim to facilitate trading of electricity, foster the development of competition, insure transparency and become recognized as "a" European market place. Finally, each power exchange aims to develop volume and the credibility of its price index.

Derivative Instruments—Power Trading

This section reviews various electricity financial/physical instruments traded on the exchanges and over the counters. Most of the electricity futures and options on futures are traded on the New York Mercantile Exchange (NYMEX). However, the trading volume of electricity futures is less than electricity forwards traded in the over-the-counter (OTC) markets. A large variety of electricity derivatives are traded among market participants in the OTC markets, including forward contracts, swaps, plain vanilla options, and exotic (i.e., non-standard) options like spark spread options, swing options and swap options. Other important trading vehicles for hedging the price risk of long-term revenue streams and service obligations are termed as structured transactions, including tolling agreements and load-serving full requirement contracts. The institutional details of these instruments are given below.

A derivative is a financial instrument (contract) between two parties with opposite views on the market, who are willing to exchange certain risks. Many derivative instruments are used in electricity trading, but the most common ones applied to energy risk management strategies are future, forward and option contracts. In some instances, these financial contracts can be used to accomplish what might be termed as virtual divesture.

Electricity Forwards, Futures and Swaps

The plainest forms of electricity derivatives are forwards, futures and swaps. Being traded either on the exchanges or over the counters, these power contracts play the primary roles in offering future price discovery and price certainty to generators and LSEs.

Electricity Forwards

Electricity forward contracts represent the obligation to buy or sell a fixed amount of electricity at a pre-specified contract price, known as the forward price, at certain time in the future (called maturity or expiration time). In other words, electricity forwards are custom-tailored supply contracts between a buyer and a seller, where the buyer is obligated to take power and the seller is obligated to supply. The payoff of a forward contract promising to deliver one unit of electricity at price F at a future time T is:

$$\textbf{Payoff of a Forward Contract} = (S_T - F) \qquad (1)$$

where S_T is the electricity spot price at time T. Although the payoff function (1) appears to be the same as for any financial forwards, electricity forwards differ from other financial and commodity forward contracts in that the underlying electricity is a different commodity at different times. The settlement price S_T is usually calculated based on the average price of electricity over the delivery period at the maturity time T.

Consider a forward contract for the on-peak electricity on day T. "On-peak electricity" refers to the electricity delivered over the daily peak-period, traditionally defined by the industry as 06:00 - 22:00. The daily "off-peak" period is the remaining hours of the day. In this case, S_T is obtained by averaging the 16 hourly prices from 06:00 to 22:00 on day T.

Based on the delivery period during a day, electricity forwards can be categorized as forwards on on-peak electricity, off-peak electricity, or "around-the-clock" (24 hours per day) electricity. As almost all electricity derivatives have such categorization based on the delivery time of a day, we will not repeat this point.

Generators such as Independent Power Producers (IPPs) are the natural sellers (or, shortside) of electricity forwards while LSEs such as utility companies often appear as the buyers (or, long-side). The maturity of an electricity forward contract ranges from hours to years although contracts with maturity beyond two years are not liquidly traded. Some electricity forwards are purely financial contracts, which are settled through financial payments based on certain market price index at maturity, while the rest are physical contracts as they are settled through physical delivery of underlying electricity. Examples of financially settled electricity forwards include the Contract for Differences in the United Kingdom and Australian power markets.

Electricity forwards with short maturity like one hour or one day are often physical contracts, traded in the physical electricity markets such as the Pennsylvania-New Jersey- Maryland (PJM) power pool market and the energy balancing market operated by the California Independent System Operator (CAISO) in the U.S. Those with maturity of weeks or months can be either physical contracts or financial contracts and they are mostly traded through brokers or directly among market participants (namely, traded in the OTC markets).

Electricity forward contracts are the primary instruments used in electricity price risk management. LSEs (e.g., local distribution companies) typically combine several months of forward/futures contracts to form a close match to the long-term load shape of their customers. Other power marketers usually use forwards to hedge their positions in electricity options and other complex electricity derivatives.

Electricity Futures

First traded on the NYMEX in March 1996, electricity futures contracts have the same payoff structure as electricity forwards. However, electricity futures contracts, like other financial futures contracts, are highly standardized in contract specifications, trading locations, transaction requirements, and settlement procedures. The most notable difference between the specifications of electricity futures and those of forwards is the quantity of power to be delivered. The delivery quantity specified in electricity futures contracts is often significantly smaller than that in forward contracts. For example, a Mid-Columbia electricity futures traded on the NYMEX specifies a delivery quantity of 432 MWh of firm electricity, delivered to the Mid-Columbia hub at a rate of 1 megawatt per hour, 16 on-peak hours per day during delivery month, while a corresponding forward contract has a delivery rate of 25 MW per hour for the same delivery periods in a month.

Electricity futures are exclusively traded on the organized exchanges while electricity forwards are usually traded over-the-counter in the form of bilateral transactions. This fact makes the futures prices more reflective of higher market consensus and transparency than the forward prices. The majority of electricity futures contracts are settled by financial payments rather than physical delivery, which lower the transaction costs. In addition, credit risks and monitoring costs in trading futures are much lower than those in trading forwards since exchanges implement strict margin requirements to ensure financial performance of all trading parties. The OTC transactions are vulnerable to financial non-performance due to counterparty defaults. The fact that the gains and losses of electricity futures are paid out daily, as opposed to being cumulated and paid out in a lump sum at maturity time, as in trading forwards, also reduces the credit risks in futures trading.

In summary, as compared to electricity forwards, the advantages of electricity futures lie in market consensus, price transparency, trading liquidity, and reduced transaction and monitoring costs while the limitations stem from the various basis risks associated with the rigidity in futures specification and the limited transaction quantities specified in the contracts.

FUTURE CONTRACTS

I. Power Contract on NYMEX

Trading Unit: 40 megawatt hours (Mwh) per peak day (between 19 and 23 days) depending on the month. Depending on the number of peak days in the month, the number of megawatt hours will vary (between 760 Mwh and 920 Mwh).

Price Quotation: U.S. dollars and cents per Mwh.

Minimum Price Fluctuation: $0.05 per Mwh.

Maximum Price Fluctuation: No price limits.

Trading Hours (All times are New York time): The contract is available for trading on the NYMEX ClearPort® trading platform from 6:00 PM Sundays through 5:15 PM Fridays, with a 45-minute break each day between 5:15 PM and 6:00 PM. Off-Exchange transactions can be submitted solely for clearing to the NYMEX ClearPort® clearing website as an exchange of futures for swaps (EFS) or exchange of futures for physicals (EFP) transaction until 5:15 PM, Monday through Friday, and the day preceding a holiday.

Trading Months: The current year plus the next five calendar years. A new calendar year will be added following the termination of trading in the December contract of the current year.

Peak Days: Monday through Friday, excluding North American Electric Reliability Council (NERC) holidays.

Termination of Trading: One business day before the last peak day of the month.

Settlement: Financial, based on the arithmetic average of the PJM western hub real-time locational marginal price (LMP) for the peak hours of each day provided by PJM Interconnection LLC. At the close of trading each day, starting with the last business day of the month prior to the contract month, 40 Mwh (a day's equivalent) will be subtracted from the quantity of the contract for the balance of the contract month.

For peak days that are not also business days, cash-settlement will take place on the business day immediately preceding these days, separately, in chronological succession, if there is more than one such day in a row.

In the event a business day is not also a peak day, no cash-settlement will be performed on the business day before. Cash-settlement will be resumed on the business day that immediately precedes the next coincident peak day and business day.

Trading Symbol: JM

II. ICE Electricity Contract

Together with ICE's natural gas market, the availability of an electric power market on one platform provides an important advantage in speed and price information. More electric power is traded on ICE than any other electronic exchange in the world. ICE offers a broad range of futures and OTC products for baseload, peak and off-peak periods, including products through 18 unique power hubs in North America and Europe. Both physically delivered and cash settled power products are traded at a fixed price or differential to daily power indices. Power contract forms include swaps, futures, location spreads, time spreads and options.

ICE Futures offers the UK Electricity futures, and ICE's OTC markets offer trading in cleared or bilateral North American power hubs. Use the Product Search for more information about ICE's power contract.

ICE OTC Power: Cleared and Bilateral

Today, 18 hubs—or delivery points—can be traded throughout the major FERC power regions in North America. Available both cleared and bilaterally, power contract forms include swaps, location spreads, time spreads, and options. Hundreds of standard time strips are available, from same-day hourly power to full calendar years. Custom user-defined time strips are also available for some products.

Power products settle either financially in cash or with physical delivery at designated points and times. Both physical and financial power products can be traded at a fixed price or, for some products, at a differential to ICE's daily published power price indices.

UK Electricity Futures

The UK Electricity Futures contract is a deliverable contract offering all the benefits of exchange transparency and clearing in addition to the following key features:

- Baseload and Peakload **contracts** will be listed based on the EFA (Electricity Forwards Agreement) calendar and settlement cycle favoured by the industry with 12 months, 6 quarters and 4 seasons;
- No requirement to be a Balancing and Settlement Code party;
- Margin offset between ICE UK Electricity Futures and ICE Natural Gas Futures;

- Each contract will be physically deliverable and will be cleared by one central counterparty, LCH.Clearnet;
- Minimum **trading size** will be **10 lots**;
- Months, Quarters and Seasons will be listed in parallel – no cascading;
- All positions will be held as months for maximum flexibility for participants;
- There will be **50% margin** offsets between Peak and Base Load contracts;
- Inter-month spreads will be available and there will be price implication down the curve;
- **Outright margin** rates are envisaged to be **£1.70 per MWh** for baseload contracts and **£3.10 per MWh** for peakload contracts. Inter-month spread rates are envisaged to be £2.25MWh for baseload contracts and £3.75 per MWh for peakload contracts;
- The Contracts will initially be available for trading through WebICE and will then be rolled out to ISV solutions

Cessation of Trading

Month, Quarter and Season Contracts cease trading at the close of business (17:00 hours London Time) on the second business day prior to the day on which electricity is to be delivered.

Electricity Swap

Electricity swaps are financial contracts that enable their holders to pay a fixed price for underlying electricity, regardless of the floating electricity price, or vise versa, over the contracted time period. They are typically established for a fixed quantity of power referenced to a variable spot price at either a generator's or a consumer's location. Electricity swaps are widely used in providing short- to medium-term price certainty up to a couple of years. They can be viewed as a strip of electricity forwards with multiple settlement dates and identical forward price for each settlement.

Electricity locational basis swaps are also commonly used to lock in a fixed price at a geographic location that is different from the delivery point of a futures contract. That is, a holder of an electricity locational basis swap agrees to either pay or receive the difference between a specified futures contract price and another locational spot price of interest for a fixed constant cash flow at the time of the transaction. These swaps are effective financial instruments for hedging the basis risk on the price difference between power prices at two different physical locations.

Electricity Options

The power industry had been utilizing the idea of options through embedded terms and conditions in various supply and purchase contracts for decades, without explicitly recognizing and valuing the options until the beginning of the electricity industry restructuring in the U.K., the U.S. and the Nordic countries in the 1990s. The emergence of the electricity wholesale markets and the dissemination of option pricing and risk management techniques have created electricity options not only based on the underlying price attribute (as in the case with plain vanilla electricity call and put options), but also other attributes like volume, delivery location and timing, quality, and fuel type.

Basically, a counterpart of each financial option can be created in the domain of electricity options by replacing the underlying of a financial option with electricity. Here, we describe a sample of electricity options that are commonly utilized in risk management applications in generation and distribution sectors. These options usually have short- to medium maturity times such as months or a couple of years. Options with maturity times longer than 3 years are usually embedded in long-term supply or purchase contracts, which are termed as structured transactions.

Plain Call and Put Options

Electricity call and put options offer their purchasers the right, but not the obligation, to buy or sell a fixed amount of underlying electricity at a pre-specified strike price by the option expiration time. They have similar payoff structures as those of regular call and put options on financial securities and other commodities. The payoff of an electricity call option is:

$$\text{Payoff of an electricity call option} = \max(S_T - K, 0) \qquad (2)$$

where S_T is the electricity spot price at time T and K is the strike price. The underlying of electricity call and put options can be exchange-traded electricity futures or physical electricity delivered at major power transmission inter-ties, like the ones located at California-Oregon Border and Palo Verde in the Western U.S. power grid. The majority of the transactions for electricity call and put options occur in the OTC markets. Electricity call and put options are the most effective tools available to merchant power plants and power marketers for hedging price risk because electricity generation capacities can be essentially viewed as call options on electricity, particularly when generation costs are fixed.

Spark Spread Options

An important class of non-standard electricity options is the spark spread option (or, spark spread). Spark spreads are cross-commodity options paying out the difference between the price of electricity sold by generators and the price of the fuels used to generate it. The amount of fuel that a generation asset requires to produce one unit of electricity depends on the asset's fuel efficiency or heat rate (Btu/kWh). The holder of a European- spark spread call option written on fuel G at a fixed heat rate K_H has the right, but not the obligation, to pay at the option's maturity K_H times the fuel price at maturity time T and receive the price of one unit of electricity. Thus, the payoff at maturity time T is

$$\textbf{Payoff of a spark spread call} = \max (S_T - K_H \cdot G_T, 0) \qquad (3)$$

where S_T and G_T are the electricity and fuel prices at time *T*, respectively.

Abstracting away the operational characteristics of a fossil fueled power generator (e.g. startup cost and ramping constraints), the per kW benefit of owning the right to use the generator is equivalent to having one kW spark spread call option with a strike heat rate matching the generator's operating heat rate. Based on this observation, it is clear that spark spread call options play important roles in hedging the price risk of the output electricity of fossil fueled power plants and further serve as key instruments in valuing those generation assets.

Callable and Putable Forwards

Two interesting types of electricity derivatives termed as callable forward and putable forward are introduced to mimic the interruptible supply contracts and the dispatchable independent power producer contracts. In a callable forward contract, the purchaser of the contract longs one forward contract and shorts one call option with a purchaser-selected strike price. The seller of the forward contract holds opposite positions and can exercise the call option if the electricity price exceeds the strike price, effectively canceling the forward contract at the time of delivery. The purchaser gets an "interruptibility" discount on the forward price, which is equal to the option premium at the time of contracting continuously compounded to the delivery time.

In a putable forward, the purchaser longs one forward contract and one put option with a seller-selected strike price. The seller holds the corresponding short positions. The purchaser exercises the put option if the electricity price drops below the strike price at the maturity time, effectively canceling the forward contract. At the time of contracting, the purchaser needs to pay a "capacity availability" premium over the forward energy price, which equals the put option price at that time, continuously compounded to the maturity time.

One variation of the callable forwards is proposed by adding an earlier notification date for exercising the call option in a callable forward before the contract matures. This emulates an interruptible service contract with early notification.

Swing Options

Electricity swing options are adopted from their well-known counterparts in the natural gas industry. Also known as flexible nomination options, swing options have the following defining features. First, these options may be exercised daily or up to a limited number of days during the period in which exercise is allowed. Second, when exercising a swing option, the daily quantity may vary (or, swing) between a minimum daily volume and a maximum volume.

However, the total quantity taken during a time period such as a week or a month needs to be within certain minimum and maximum volume levels. Third, the strike price of a swing option may be either fixed throughout its life or set at the beginning of each time period based on some pre-specified formula. Last, if the minimum-take quantity of any contract period is missed by the buyer, then a lump sum penalty or a payment making up the seller's revenue shortfall needs to be paid (i.e., take-or-pay).

Structured Transactions

Structured bilateral transactions are powerful tools for power market participants to share and control a variety of risks including price and quantity risks over a potentially long time horizon.

Tolling Contracts

Tolling is one of the most innovative structured transactions embraced by the power industry. A tolling agreement is similar to a common electricity supply contract signed between a buyer (e.g., a power marketer) and an owner of a power plant (e.g., an IPP) but with notable differences. For an upfront premium paid to the plant owner, it gives the buyer the right to either operate and control the scheduling the power plant with the ISO or simply take the output electricity during pre-specified time periods subject to certain constraints. In addition to inherent operational constraints of the underlying power plant, there are often other contractual limitations in the contract on how the buyer may operate the power plant or take the output electricity. For instance, a tolling contract almost always has a clause on the maximum allowable number of power plant restarts. These constraints make the pricing of tolling contracts a very challenging task. The analogy between holding a tolling contract and owning the underlying merchant power plant, however, leads to a numerical approach for valuing and hedging tolling contracts. Alternatively, one may use a statistical approach for benchmarking the price reasonableness of tolling contracts based on historical electricity price and fuel costs.

Load-serving full-requirement Contracts

Most large electricity consumers prefer a power supply contract with flexible consumption terms. Specifically, they desire to pay a fixed rate per unit of energy for the actual consumption quantity, regardless of the quantity being high or low. Such a contract is termed as a load-serving full-requirement contract.

Suppose an electricity supplier (or, LSE) signs a full-requirement contract with a customer and then utilizes futures contracts to lock in a fixed quantity of electricity supply at a fixed cost for hedging the expected energy consumption of the customer. The LSE is then at the risk of either under- or over-hedging, as the consumption quantity of the customer will almost surely deviate from the amount hedged by the futures contracts. When the electricity spot price is high (low), the total demand for electricity is likely to be high (low) as well. A case in point is the periods of unusual cooling/heating needs. Hence, if the market price of electricity is higher than the fixed contract rate for serving electricity, chances are that the customer's energy consumption level is significantly higher than the hedged quantity. As a result, the LSE is under-hedged relative to its load obligation and must purchase electricity in the open market to serve its customer at a loss because the wholesale spot price most likely exceeds the contracted price paid by consumers. Conversely, when the electricity spot price is low, the LSE faces the risk of being over-hedged and having to sell the surplus in the spot market or settle it financially at a price below its long-term contract price.

The above illustrates the under- and over-hedging exposures faced by an LSE due to the volumetric uncertainty in customers' load and the positive price-load correlation. To hedge the volumetric risk, the LSE would need to buy an electricity option on the consumption quantity of its customers. Unfortunately, such an option is usually unavailable in the marketplace. Although perfect hedging may not be possible, weather derivatives that exploit the correlation between load and temperature can be used.

Financial Derivatives on Electricity Transmission Capacity

Open access to, efficient utilization of, and adequate investment in transmission networks are critical for the electricity wholesale markets and retail competitions to be workable and efficient. Intuitively, rights are required for using transmission networks and rules are needed for rationing transmission usage when networks become congested. There are two major proposals for using financial instruments as transmission rights in the U.S.: (a) the point-to-point financial transmission rights (FTRs); and (b) the flowgate rights (FGRs), as outlined in the Standard Market Design (SMD) put forth by the Federal Energy Regulatory Commission (FERC). FTRs and FGRs are electricity derivatives, with their values derived from the network transmission capacity.

FTR and FTR Options

In an electricity market such as the PJM that employs locational market price (LMP), a point-to-point FTR is specified over any two locations in the power transmission grid. An FTR entitles its holder to receive compensation (or pay) for transmission congestion charges that arise when the grid is congested. The congestion charge/payment (or, payoff) associated with one unit of FTR is equal to the difference between the two locational prices of one unit of electricity resulting from the re-dispatch of generators out of merit order to relieve transmission congestion. The primary markets for the FTR trading are auctions held by the independent system operators (ISOs) of power markets.

An FTR option offers the right to the FTR settlement without the obligation to pay when that settlement is negative. Hence the settlement of an FTR option equals to the positive part of the corresponding two-sided point-to-point FTR.

FGRs

Flowgates are defined over all transmission elements such as lines, transformers, or linear combinations of them. Each transmission element has two elemental flowgates, one in each direction. An elemental flowgate has a rated capacity in megawatts in its pre-specified direction corresponding to the capacity of an underlying transmission element. Thus, flowgate rights are link-based transmission rights for hedging transmission risks. The values of flowgate rights can be established through auctions conducted by the ISOs. The spot price upon which the settlement of flowgate rights is based is given by the real time shadow price on the corresponding constrained element, determined by the security constrained economic dispatch algorithm employed by an ISO. Since these shadow prices are nonnegative, FGRs are inherently defined as options.

PRICING ELECTRICITY DERIVATIVES

Since the value of electricity derivatives are based on the underlying electricity prices, modeling electricity price is the most critical component in pricing electricity derivatives. Due to the unique physical and operational characteristics of electricity production and transmission processes, electricity price exhibits different behaviors than other financial prices which can be often described by Geometric Brownian Motion. There has been a growing literature addressing mainly two competing approaches to the problem of modeling electricity price processes:

(a) "Fundamental approach" that relies on simulation of system and market operation to arrive at market prices; and
(b) "Technical approach" that attempts to model directly the stochastic behavior of market prices from historical data and statistical analysis.

While the first approach provides more realistic system and transmission network modeling under specific scenarios, it is computationally prohibitive due to the large number of scenarios that must be considered. Such analysis may be necessary for pricing financial transmission rights (in particular, flowgate rights) but not for the other electricity derivatives. Therefore, we shall focus our attentions on the second approach and review the corresponding methodologies for pricing electricity derivatives.

Approaches to characterize market prices include discrete-time time series models such as GARCH and its variants, Markov regime-switching models, continuous-time diffusion models such as mean-reversion, jump-diffusion, and other diffusion models. There are also models proposed for direct modeling of electricity forward curves.

While a straightforward application of the maximum likelihood estimation (MLE) method yields the parameter estimates of a discrete-time time series model, it does not yield analytic expressions for derivative prices. In fact, Monte Carlo simulation and lattice-based approaches are the only feasible derivative pricing methods under time-series price models. For continuous-time diffusion models, model parameters can be estimated by applying moment-based methods, such as the generalized method of moments, which may not be as efficient as the MLE method. Nonetheless, more option pricing methods (e.g., the analytic solution approach and the Partial Differential Equation (PDE) approach) become applicable under the diffusion price models.

The binomial/multinomial lattice and Monte Carlo simulation methods are powerful numerical tools for pricing electricity options with complex structures and/or under a complicated model for the electricity price process. For instance, given the complex structure of a swing option or a tolling contract, it is impossible to obtain prices of such contracts either in closed-forms or through PDEs. Thus, swing options are priced by lattice models, or by approximation methods for obtaining price lower bounds. The pricing of tolling contracts requires a combination of Monte Carlo simulation with dynamic programming.

RISK MANAGEMENT APPLICATIONS

Hedging a Generator's Output

Albeit having simple payoff structures, forwards, swaps, and call options are effective tools for a generator with fixed per unit cost to lock in profits by selling forwards, fixed-price swaps, and call options on electricity. When the forward/swap rate or the strike price of the call options is higher than the fixed cost, the generator's profits are guaranteed.

However, if the generating costs are market-based (e.g., a natural gas fired merchant power plant that burns natural gas at market price), the selling forwards, swaps and calls will expose the generator to potential fuel cost increases. In such a case, a properly constructed portfolio of spark spread calls would be the right tool for hedging a generator's revenue stream over a given time period.

The operational efficiency of a natural gas fired power plant is characterized by its operating heat rate. Therefore, the financial benefit of owning a portfolio of spark spread calls with strike heat rates identical to the operating heat rate of the plant is the same as owning the power plant during the time period of the options' maturity times. When taking into account the operational characteristics, lattice-based method and simulation method are necessary to determine pricing and hedging strategies of generation capacity.

In the case where the electricity forward market at the generator's location is not liquidly traded, electricity forwards from adjacent trading hubs or even forwards on the input fuel, which are liquidly traded, can be utilized to cross-hedge the electricity output price.

Ensuring Generation Adequacy

Oren and Chao and Wilson proposed a new role for options with long maturity to address the resource adequacy problem. They propose a scheme for ensuring generation adequacy via call options as obligations imposed on the LSEs. Call options provide an attractive alternative to artificial capacity products such as installed capacity (ICAP) employed in New York, New England, and PJM, whose demand is based only on administrative requirements and which have no intrinsic value. By requiring LSEs to purchase a proper portfolio of options, a regulator can achieve spot price volatility reduction by implementing price insurance while using the premium to stabilize generators' income and enhance investment incentives.

Callable Forwards and Interruptible Service Contracts

The restructured electricity markets have shown little demand response to price spikes. The enormous price volatility affirms the need for demand responsiveness to make these markets workable. As load curtailment can provide an efficient substitute for generation capacity in meeting balancing energy and reserves needs, flexible loads are viable and valuable resources in taming price volatility.

Consider the traditional utility interruptible service contracts utilized in demand-side management (DSM) to mitigate supply shortages. These interruptible contracts are readily implementable through standard electricity derivatives. For instance, a synthetic interruptible service contract offered by an LSE is a callable forward under which the LSE sells a forward to and buys a call option from its customer. Furthermore, with a liquid electricity derivative market, the discounts offered to the interrupted services would be set through market trading instead of bilateral negotiations thus making the pricing of the interruptible services more transparent and efficient.

Hedging Congestion Risk of Bilateral Transactions

From the perspective of new power network transmission users, FTRs can be viewed as an instrument for hedging their exposure to congestion cost risk. A one-megawatt (MW) bilateral transaction between two points in a transmission network is charged (or credited) the nodal price difference between the point of withdrawal and the point of injection. At the same time (assuming that transmission rights are fully funded), a one MW FTR between two points is an entitlement (or obligation) for the difference between the nodal prices at the withdrawal node and the injection node. Thus regardless of how the system is dispatched, a one MW FTR between two nodes is a perfect hedge against the uncertain congestion charge between the same two nodes.

The hedging properties of FTRs make them ideal instruments for converting historical entitlements to firm transmission capacity into tradable entitlements that hold the owners of such entitlements harmless, while enabling them to cash out when someone else can make more efficient use of the transmission capacity covered by these entitlements. In other words, FTRs make it relatively easy to preserve the status quo while opening up the transmission system to new and more efficient use. A word of caution is that the hedging function of FTRs may not be perfect due to changing network operating conditions and potential inherent trading inefficiency. Some ISOs de-rate FTR settlements in order to cover congestion revenue shortfalls due to transmission contingencies not accounted for in the FTR auction. In such cases, depending on the de-rating approach, FTRs may not provide perfect hedges either.

Hedging Volumetric Risks

LSEs providing electricity service at regulated prices in restructured electricity markets are wary of both price and quantity risks. As the electricity markets are inherently incomplete, the quantity risk cannot be perfectly hedged. Commonly proposed hedging alternatives include the implementation of a minimal variance hedge through purchasing electricity forwards and the utilization of weather derivatives.

POWER TRADING MARKETS MODELS

A competitive electricity market should be supported by proper trading tools that take into account of special nature of electricity which is different from other commodities. A successful implementation of trading system in electric energy and its derivative markets could fulfill restructuring objectives, which include competition and customer choice and serve vital needs of electricity market participants. (Fig. 4.6)

Trading is an activity in which transactions take place directly between two participants or indirectly through an exchange. Electricity trading through an exchange started for the first time in 1996 in New York Mercantile Exchange (NYMEX). Electricity trading has two main components, i.e. physical trading and financial trading. In physical trading, supply is balanced against demand and price is either determined in advance of trading or after trading. In financial trading, financial contracts take place between traders as agreements that give certainty to traders. Physical trading is generally done through an energy spot market or power pool while financial trading is through a financial market or exchange such as NYMEX or Chicago Board of Trade (CBOT). Trading in an electricity market is a risky task because the electricity is much different from other commodities due to its special nature such as non-storable, generation-demand balance, limited demand elasticity, transmission constraints and electric price related with other volatile commodities.

Electricity trading arrangements in USA, UK, Australia and some Latin American countries has undergone a profound transformation in last two decades. India has also started power trading from last four years.

A. U.K. Electricity Market

UK has been one of the leaders in developing spot electricity market

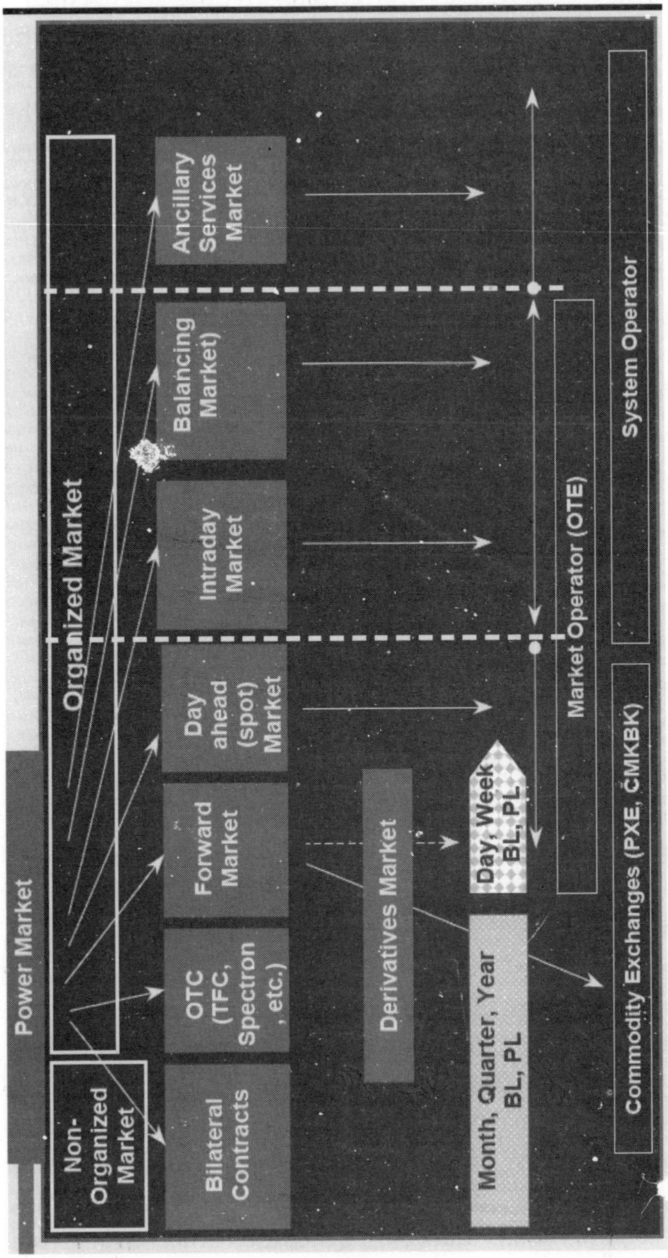

Figure 4.6: Organization of the Power Market—Types of Markets

trading system, which links the physical and financial domains. The initial competitive electricity market structure involved an electricity Pool for England and Wales. After a review, a new electricity trading arrangements (NETA) evolved slowly which provides the new structure and rules for the E&W electricity market. The transactions taking place within the NETA market are electricity price-quantity transactions on a half-hourly basis. The system operator (SO) and power exchanges (PX) are central to the functioning of the E&W electricity market under NETA. Major contractual relationship NETA electricity market is shown in Fig. 4.7.

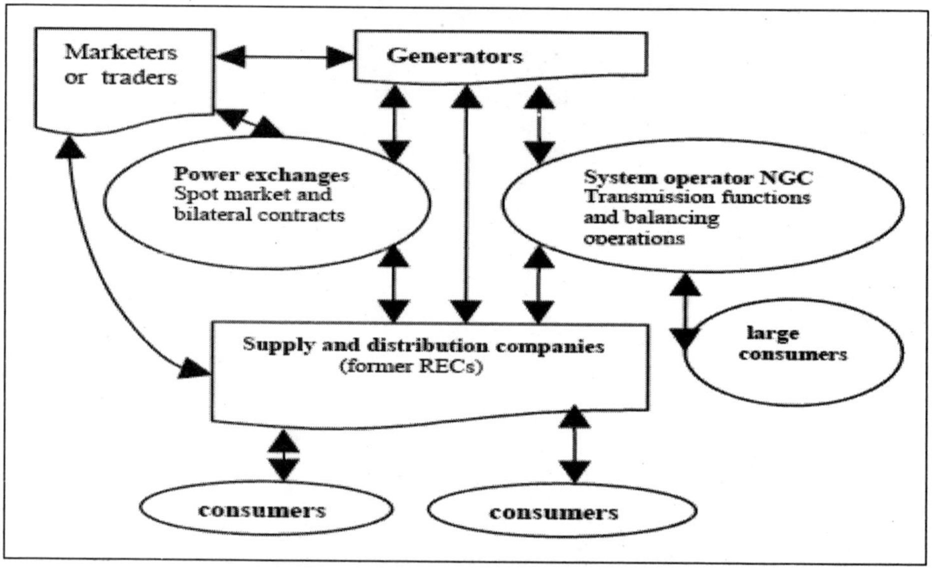

Figure 4.7: NETA Electricity Market - Major Contractual Relationships

PXs provide contracts that are 'cleared' giving a guarantee against default on a contract. Trading through brokers, over the counter (OTC) trading and other financial instruments (options and futures), also form the part of market trading. The SO for E&W, National Grid (NGC), currently has two functions: firstly the management of high voltage transmission system as transmission system operator (TSO) and secondly the supply of operational services. Generation forecasting, congestion management and provision of ancillary services are managed by NGC as SO. In addition the *balancing mechanism* allows the SO to maintain local and national balances of generation and consumption in real time, thus price and volume agreements within the balancing mechanism are made directly with the SO.

B. Nordic Electricity Market

Nord Pool, the Nordic Power Exchange, is the world's first international commodity exchange for electrical power. The Nordic power market which trades with neighboring countries and is dominated by hydropower, can be seen to be very different from that in E&W. Fig. 4.8 shows the Nordic electricity market's major contractual relationships.

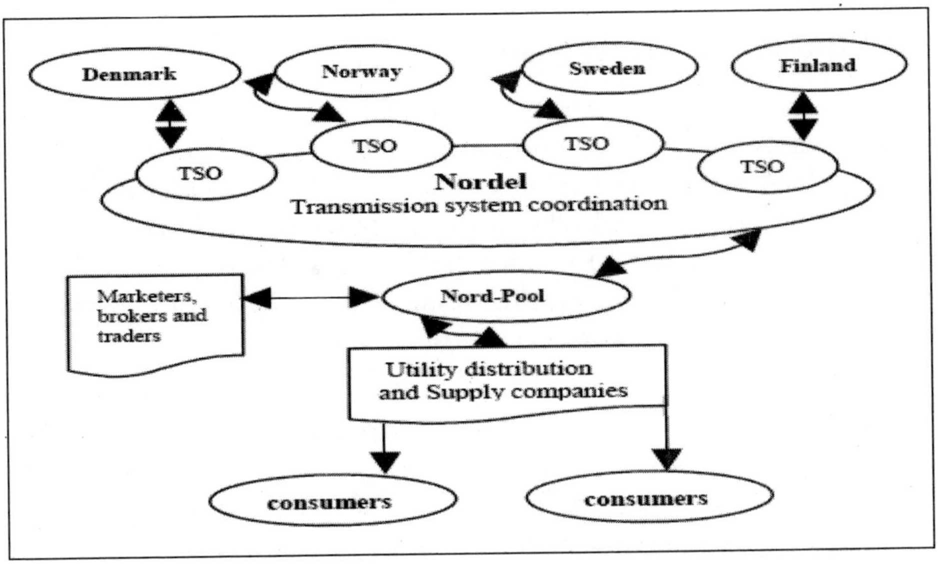

Figure 4.8: Nordic Electricity Market - Major Contractual Relationships

The existence of a transmission system linking Denmark, Norway, Sweden and Finland provides the basis for physical electricity exchanges organized on a national basis for these countries. The national transmission system operators (TSOs) are responsible for reliability and balance settlements. Nordel facilitates co-operation between these TSOs and deals with planning, operation and transmission pricing.

Nord Pool organizes trade in standardized physical and financial power contracts including clearing services to Nordic participants. The spot price for the Nordic electricity market is set by Nord Pool every hour. Elspot and Elbas are Nord Pool auction based spot market for trade in power contracts for physical delivery. On Elspot, hourly power contracts are traded daily for physical delivery in the next day's 24-hour period. On Elbas, continuous adjustment trading in hourly contracts can be performed until one hour before the delivery hour. New contracts are opened after the day-ahead Elspot prices have been set. Before 2 p.m. the remaining hours of the current day are tradable and then day-ahead contracts are open for trading.

The objective of Nord Pool financial market is to provide an efficient market, with excellent liquidity and a high level of security to offer a number of financial power contracts that can be used profitably by a variety of customer groups.

C. California Electricity Market

The competitive electric power market of California state began operation in 1998 with the California Independent System Operator (CAISO) and now bankrupt Power Exchange (PX) as the main operationally market facilitators. The market took off smoothly, and the prices were seemingly just and reasonable until May 2000, when the first signs of market crisis emerged. California's electricity crisis was the result of the collusion of a shortage of resources, poorly designed market and inaction by regulators or "regulatory failure".

The CAISO was originally designed to operate in conjunction with the PX, a day-ahead energy market that ceased to operate in January 2001. Without PX day-ahead market, all short-term balancing of supply and demand has been pushed into the more volatile real-time market. This is the result of flaws in original design and inconsistencies between the ISO's forward and real-time markets.

Now the CAISO is addressing these flaws through a comprehensive redesign effort known as Market Design 2002 (MD02). It allows the ISO to match buyers and sellers through a transparent day-ahead market that reduce reliance on the more volatile hour-ahead and real-time markets. Since the PX ceased operating there has been no transparent market for spot energy transactions to balance supply and demand ahead of real time. It also allows the ISO to manage congestion on the grid the day before, rather than in real time, thus enhancing real time reliability.

D. Indian Electricity Market

Principal Acts in the Indian Power Sector

In India, the power sector is the joint responsibility of state and central government and it is currently governed by three principal Acts:

- The Indian Electricity Act, 1910
- The Electricity (Supply) Act, 1948
- The Electricity Regulatory Commission Act (ERCA), 1998
- But in the near future these three Acts will be replaced by the Electricity Bill, 2001

Institutions in the Indian Power Sector

CEA (Central Electricity Authority)

The CEA is an agency of the central government, which was created under the Electricity (supply) Act, 1948. It is responsible for regulating investments in the power sector. So for example, till 1991 any scheme involving capital expenditure above Rs. 250 million, required approval from CEA for technical as well as economical aspects.

SEBs (State Electricity Boards)

The SEBs is state government owned integrated monopoly utilities which were established under the Indian Electricity (Supply) Act. SEBs has the monopoly over generation, transmission and distribution of power within the state. Except for cities like Mumbai, Kolkata and Ahmadabad, the entire distribution lies in the hands of these agencies.

CERC (Central Electricity Regulatory Commission)

The CERC was established by the Electricity Regulatory Commission Act, 1998. It consists of four members appointed by the central commission shall be guided by such directions in matters of policy involves public interest as the central government may give to it in writing. The CERC's aim is to promote competition, efficiency and economy in the electricity industry, encourage investment and safeguard the consumer interest.

The task of the CERC is:

- Regulation of tariffs of central government stations;
- Regulation of tariffs of electric power generated and sold across states in a composite packages;
- Regulation of inter-state transmission tariff;
- Regulation of inter-state transmission;
- In addition, the Act also gives the CERC an advisory role concerning

power and the environment, to advice government on issues relating to electricity, to electricity, to prepare and publish guidelines, and arbitrate on certain issues.

SERCs (State Electricity Regulatory Commissions)

The State Electricity Regulatory Commissions also are established under the Electricity Regulatory Commission Act, 1998. The SERCs consist of at most three members appointed by the state government.

The task of the SERCs is

- Determination of the tariff for electricity, wholesale, bulk, grid or retail;
- Determination of the tariff payable for the use of transmission;
- Regulation of power purchase and procurement process of the transmission utilities and distribution utilities;
- Promotion of competition, efficiency and economy in the activities of the electricity industry.

Power Corporations

In the late 1970's the government established corporation like the National Thermal Power Corporation (NTPC), the Bharat Heavy Electricals Limited (BHEL) and the power Grid Corporation of India (PGCIL). NTPC generates power from large pithead of the demand stations and sells it to various state utilities like the SEBs. So it satisfies about 25 percent of the demand for energy in India. BHEL and PGCIL on the one hand are responsible for manufacturing of electrical equipment like turbines, boilers or transformers and on the other hand for erection and maintenance of interstate transmission lines.

Independent Power Producers (IPPs)

Till 1991 more than 95 percent of distribution and above 98 percent of generation was under the government ownership. After 1991, because of severe foreign exchange crisis and a lack of capital for expanding power generation capacity, the Indian government allowed private foreign and Indian investment.

To attract investors, the government of offered concessions such as 100 percent foreign ownership, long-term purchase agreements and assured profits. In the first three-year period, state government and SEBs concluded about 240 contracts. The formation of contracts happened without competitive bidding and the states and SEBs did not care much about elementary norms of power planning, proper demand forecast and evolution of least cost plans based on comparative costing of different options for sites and fuels. The result was that only a fraction of these contracts contributed to increased power capacity. On account of this fact, central government enforced a competitive bidding route for acquiring new capacity.

Start of Privatization

The first state which started to restructure and privatizes the power sector was Orissa in the mid 1990s. Supported by the World Bank they started

(a) Un-bundling the integrated utility into three separate sectors of generation, transmission and distribution,

(b) Privatization of generation and distribution companies and,

(c) to establish independent regulatory commission to regulate these utilities. Soon afterwards, several other states like Haryana, Uttar Pradesh and Andhra Pradesh followed.

Power Trading Corporation of India Ltd. (PTC), the leading provider of power trading services, in India is trading power on a sustained basis since June 2002 through purchase from surplus utilities and sales to deficit State Electricity Boards (SEBs) at an economical price, providing best value to both the buyers and sellers and ensuring that the resources are utilized optimally.

PTC is a 'pure-play' trading entity, and does not own any generating units or transmission facilities. PTC acts as a single-window service provider that manages both financial as well as operational risks for the buyer and seller entities in its trading transactions. On the one hand timely payments are ensured to the sellers of power and on the other hand a definite quantum of power is delivered to the buyers of power in a reliable manner. For its services, PTC charges a predetermined amount of transaction charges, worked on a per unit (KWh) basis or as a percentage of the cost of power. The pricing and margin information is known to both the counterparties in a transparent manner. In some instances PTC has both bought and sold power from the same entity at different times of the day depending upon the load profile of the entity.

PTC catalyses the development of power projects by entering into multi-year contracts for future trading of power. These Power Purchase Agreements with PTC are being recognized by lenders as security for financial closure of power projects. Typically, the counterparty contracts for these projects or Power Sale Agreements are structured with multiple buyers, through which about 80% of the power generation from the project is tied up for long-term sale, and 20% is kept as reserve for the short-term market.

PTC has been identified as the nodal agency for cross border trading with neighboring countries: Bhutan, Nepal and Bangladesh, which are rich in hydro power resources. Utilities in Bhutan account for the nearly 24% trading volumes from cross-border sources. Being the pioneer in trading in India, PTC sees a developmental role for itself to increase the depth and breadth of the market under new Electricity Act, 2003. PTC also views an opportunity in alliances with emerging entities for setting up their operations in the manner that the business is recognized globally. In future, it intends to set up an online trading platform similar to a power exchange.

Though the power-trading scenario in India is at a nascent stage, it is growing at a rapid pace. The power market in India has evolved over the last four years and it is expected that it is likely to grow at a faster pace – with the reforms of SEBs and building up of transmission highways across the regions to increase Inter-regional power transfer capacity from currently available 8000 MW to 30,000 MW.

Electricity Market Experience

In the main, experience in the introduction of wholesale and retail competition has been mixed. Many regional markets have achieved some success and the ongoing trend continues to be towards deregulation and introduction of competition. However in 2000/2001 major failures such as the California electricity crisis and the Enron debacle caused a slow down in the pace of change and in some regions an increase in market regulation and reduction in competition. However, this trend is widely regarded as a temporary one against the longer term one towards more open and competitive markets.

Notwithstanding the favorable light in which market solutions are viewed conceptually, the "missing money" problem has to date proved intractable. If electricity prices were to move to the levels needed to incent new merchant (i.e. market-based) transmission and generation, the costs to consumers would be politically difficult. The increase in annual costs to consumers in New England alone were calculated at $3 billion during the recent FERC hearings on the NEPOOL market structure. Several mechanisms that are intended to incent new investment where it is most needed by offering enhanced capacity payments—but only in zones where generation is projected to be short—have been proposed for NEPOOL, PJM and NYPOOL, and go under the generic heading of "locational capacity" or LICAP (the PJM version under FERC review is called as the "Reliability Pricing Model", or "RPM"). There is substantial doubt as to whether any of these mechanisms will in fact incent new investment, given the regulatory risk and chronic instability of the market rules in US systems, and there are substantial concerns that the result will instead be to increase revenues to incumbent generators, and costs to consumers, in the constrained areas.

As the competitive but volatile electricity markets mature, generation companies, power marketers and Load Serving Entities (LSEs) seek certainty in their costs and revenues through hedging practices and contracting and active trading.

Chapter 5

Emission Trading

INTRODUCTION OF EMISSION TRADING

Emission Trading, the market based instrument used for environmental protection, has been adopted as one of the primary tools for international cooperation to reduce the green house gas emissions under Kyoto Protocol. However, emission trading is not new—tradable right for pollution control was proposed in 1968—and trading programmes have been implemented to reduce the emissions of oxides of sulphur and nitrogen, carbon dioxide and other pollutants

The challenge of the 21st century will be for human society to regain a healthy relationship with our 'living' earth. The signs are clear that right now we are failing in that task. Unless we change our ways, it is likely that comfortable civilization as we know it will disappear. Climate change is not just an environmental problem—it is a societal problem. The simple truth is that humanity is changing the atmosphere—every day we add around 70 million tonnes of invisible carbon dioxide, the very gas that we know controls the temperature of the planet.

Climate change is a critical threat to the continued existence of our civilization. The climate change that we are now seeing - also known as global warming—is caused predominantly by human activities. The largest single factor is the emission of carbon dioxide (CO_2) from the use of fossil fuels.

Directly or indirectly, every activity which uses fossil fuel energy will cause the generation of CO_2 emissions and thus contribute to climate change.

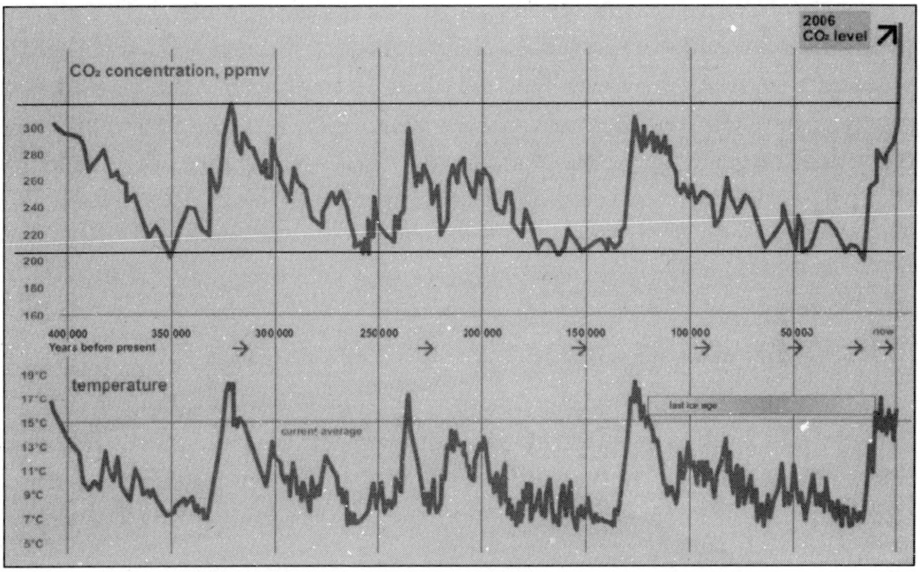

Figure 5.1: Relationship between CO_2 and Temperature

In principle emission trading is simple. However in practice applying the concept to different pollutants can become quite complex and term emission trading applies to the wide spectrum of the systems of different design.

Kyoto is a 'cap and trade' system that imposes national caps on the emissions of Annex I countries. On average, this cap requires countries to reduce their emissions 5.2% below their 1990 baseline over the 2008 to 2012 period. Although these caps are national-level commitments, in practice most countries will devolve their emissions targets to individual industrial entities. This means that the ultimate buyers of Credits are often individual companies that expect their emissions to exceed their quota (their Assigned Amount Units, Allowances for short). Typically, they will purchase Credits directly from another party with excess allowances, from a broker, from a JI/CDM developer, or on an exchange.

The Kyoto emissions trading scheme is a cap-and-trade scheme. In a cap-and-trade system parties are given an emissions allowance based on an emissions reduction target. In order to create scarcity a limited number of allowances are issued equal to the 'global' target below the business as usual emissions level for a particular period. In the Kyoto scheme each allowance is called an Assigned Amount Unit (AAU) which is equivalent to one tonne of carbon dioxide. At the end of a period each party must hold the equivalent number of AAUs equal to the amount of greenhouse gas it emitted. This allows parties to decide whether to reduce their emissions internally, or whether to buy credits from other parties, who may have been able to make an emission reduction more cheaply. Similarly, parties which have reduced their emissions below their target will be able to trade any surplus allowances they make to other parties who cannot, or who do not want to meet their targets internally. The rationale behind emissions trading is cost-effectiveness; that in theory, parties will choose the most cost-effective way to either make or buy their emission reductions.

The EU Emissions Trading Scheme (EU ETS) began in January 2005 and is the largest emissions trading scheme covering 12,000 installations in 25 countries. The trading units in this scheme are called EU Allowances (EUAs). Parties in this scheme can buy and sell EUAs, or they can purchase—within certain limits—CERs from the Clean Development Mechanism or ERUs under Joint Implementation.

Since Carbon Credits are tradable instruments with a transparent price, financial investors have started buying them for pure trading purposes. This market is expected to grow substantially, with banks, brokers, funds, arbitrageurs and private traders eventually participating.

Customers in the non-legally binding voluntary market are able to purchase both credits which originate from the compliance market and credits which originate from the voluntary market. When compliance market credits are used for voluntary offsetting they do not go towards assisting or meeting any legally-binding reduction targets.

It is primarily individuals who have to take steps to avoid and then reduce their own carbon emissions. In parallel to this, however, we believe that the voluntary carbon offset market does have a role to play both in reducing carbon emissions and raising awareness of climate change issues to the general public. Moreover it can provide a much-needed source of funding for the development of low carbon technologies and innovations in developing countries.

Problems with the voluntary carbon offset market fall broadly into two categories, those associated with the offset projects themselves, and those associated with offset provision to consumers. Many of the problems, particularly those relating to projects, apply both to those within the compliance market and the voluntary market. However, these problems often become more significant in the voluntary market as there are no overarching, enforceable standards by which to assess them or mitigate them.

How CER'S are Traded?

A transaction in CER trading involves buying of GHG emissions credits by entities (companies, Governments, etc.) from companies or Governments involved in projects related to carbon emission reduction in developing countries. The idea is to make developed countries pay for their wild ways with emissions while at the same time rewarding countries with good behavior in this regard. For example, a company in India can prove it that it has prevented emission of x-tons of carbon, it can sell this much amount of points or carbon credits to a company in say, the US which has been emitting carbon. This allows industries in developed countries to offset their emissions of carbon dioxide by investing in reforestation and clean energy projects in developing countries such as large-scale tree plantations as a lucrative alternative to reducing emissions. Planting 100,000 hectares of new forest can remove 1mn ton of carbon per year from the atmosphere.

Consider two companies, A and B, both of which emit significant quantities of a given pollutant. Their emissions may danger air quality, and relevant authorities may decide the emissions should be reduced by a given amount, say by 10%. At first glance the task seems simple: both A and B cut their emissions by 10%. But in real world this may impose different burden on both the companies. For example, company A, may by nature of its activities, be able to reduce its emissions by 10% or more at relatively low cost. Company B, on the other hand, might find it difficult and costly process. It is this potential difference in reduction cost between A and B that creates the market opportunity. It works as follows

Company A can reduce its emissions by a required amount at relatively low cost and can then make the affordable reductions. For Company B, the reduction cost is far greater and it would welcome the way of avoiding some of the outlay. Now what if Company A agrees to reduce some additional reductions instead of Company B, provided that Company B is ready to pay a price that is above the cost to A but below what it would cost Company B? in this situations emissions are cut overall by the required amount Company B saves the money and Company A earns the profit for its additional reductions and the total cost is reduced. In this simplified model of trading system, it makes no difference whether cuts are made by Company A or B; it's the overall amount that counts.

The current prices of EUAs does not reflect long term equilibrium price between supply and demand on the EU ETS: few entities are selling allowances, there are still large uncertainties over some national allocation plans, and weather and high oil prices have had an important impact on prices. Relatively thin volumes traded so far have also resulted in high price volatility.

What is Kyoto Protocol?

The Kyoto Protocol is an agreement negotiated as an amendment to the United Nations Framework Convention On Climate Change (UNFCCC, which was adopted at the Earth Summit in Rio de Janeiro in 1992). All parties to the UNFCCC can sign or ratify the Kyoto Protocol, while non-parties to the UNFCCC cannot.

The Kyoto Protocol, which was adopted at the third Conference of the Parties (COP_3) to the United Nations Framework Convention on Climate Change (UNFCCC) held in December 1997, came into force in February 2005. In order to assist the Parties to achieve their GHG emission reduction targets, the Protocol defines three innovative "flexibility mechanisms" to lower the overall costs to meet the targets. These mechanisms are comprised of the CDM, JI and Emissions Trading. Most of the industrialized countries have committed to reducing their aggregate emissions by 5.2 percent below 1990 levels during the first commitment period (2008–12); the United States and Australia have so far declined ratifying the protocol.

For each country with an emission commitment, the Kyoto objective is an "assigned amount" of emissions allowed over 2008-12, expressed in "assigned amount units" (or AAUs). The novelty of the Kyoto Protocol is that a country may trade its AAUs to another country, if its 2008-12 emissions are expected to be lower than its initial assigned amount.

The Kyoto Protocol introduced the following three flexibility mechanisms to supplement the domestic activities of the developed countries. The three flexibility mechanisms are:

- Joint Implementation (JI)
- Clean Development Mechanism (CDM)
- International carbon trading

The transfers of these emission reductions may take place through all three "flexibility mechanisms":

- by means of projects which reduce emissions within industrialized countries, in the case of JI;
- by projects which reduce emissions in developing countries, in the case of the CDM (which enables emission reductions achieved outside Annex I countries to be credited to these countries);
- by emission trading—which allows countries with binding commitments to trade AAUs.

Of these three, only the CDM is applicable between developed and developing countries that have ratified the protocol. The certified emission reductions (CERs) that result from CDM project activities have considerable economic use to both the host (developing) and investor (developed) countries. During the last few years the mechanisms have aroused worldwide interest in carbon investment and the carbon market, which is growing as companies and governments have started purchasing emissions credits through voluntary trading schemes, carbon investment funds, and government procurement tenders.

What is CDM?

The Clean Development Mechanism (CDM) is one of the innovative features of the Kyoto Protocol to the UNFCCC. It encourages investments in projects that provide sustainable development in developing countries, while at the same time limiting GHG emissions. The CDM was introduced in Article 12 of the Kyoto Protocol. Under this mechanism, legal entities in developed countries can invest in projects in developing countries that reduce GHG emissions. Once certified, these emission reductions can be used to meet the commitments made by the developed countries under the protocol. Although there are no immediate targets for the developing countries, it can be seen as an additional source of foreign direct investment into national mitigation projects, which would contribute to sustainable development and a decrease in worldwide GHG emission levels.

According to the Kyoto Protocol, project activities that qualify for the CDM are those related to specific GHG types and to the sources and sectors responsible for the majority of emissions, as established in Annex A of the Kyoto Protocol.

The Clean Development Mechanism (CDM) is a mechanism based on the provision of Article 12 of the Kyoto Protocol. It is a scheme for greenhouse gas (GHG) reduction through cooperation between developed countries (Annex I Parties to the United Nations Framework Convention on Climate Change (UNFCCC)), which are committed to certain GHG emission reduction targets in the Kyoto Protocol, and developing countries (non-Annex I Parties), which do not have any commitments to reduce GHG emissions. The purpose of the CDM is to assist to accomplish the GHG reduction targets of developed countries under the Kyoto Protocol, as well as to contribute to sustainable development of host countries. Under the CDM, Annex I Parties implement projects e.g. projects of landfill gas (methane) recovery with power generation resulting in reduction of greenhouse gas emissions within the territories of non-Annex I Parties. Annex I Parties are able to acquire all or parts of the credits (certified emission reductions: CERs) which result from the projects.

Under the Kyoto Protocol, the developing countries ratifying the protocol are eligible to participate in the CDM. India signed the protocol before COP 8 in 2002, which was hosted by the government of India in New Delhi. India offers a large potential for utilizing the CDM because of its inherent dependence on fossil fuels for development, its proactive government, and the enabling environment in place. Indeed, India is the most favoured destination for the CDM. India is a competitive supplier for cost-effective GHG offset projects. Recognizing the possible benefits derived from such investment flows to India, the government has placed the CDM at the top of its climate change agenda. The designated national authority (DNA) for CDM projects from India has been set up in the Ministry of Environment and Forests (MoEF).

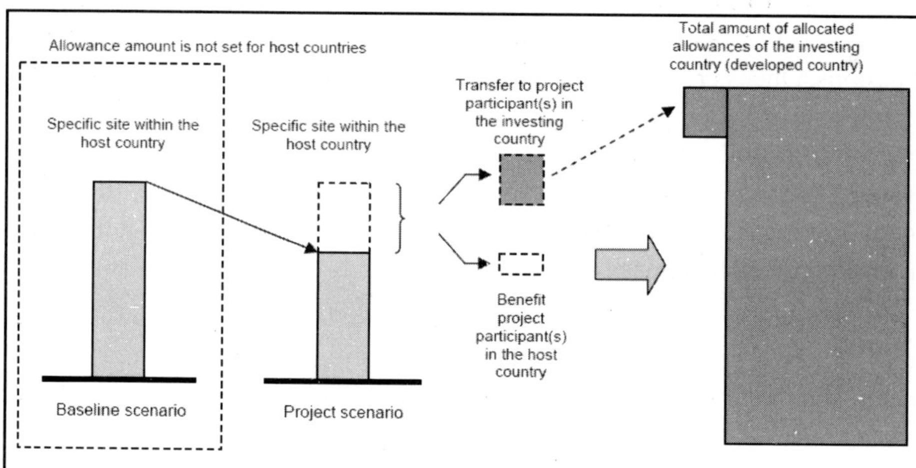

Figure 5.2

CDM Process

The Six Greenhouse Gases Addressed under the Kyoto Protocol

The six GHGs are not equal in terms of global warming potential (GWP), which measures the relative radiative effect of GHGs compared to CO_2. For example, one tonne of methane has a GWP as potent as 21 tonnes of CO_2.

Greenhouse gas	*Global warming potential*
1. Carbon dioxide (CO_2)	1
2. Methane (CH_4)	21
3. Nitrous oxide (N_2O)	310
4. Hydrofluorocarbons (HFCs)	140-11,700
5. Perfluorocarbons (PFCs)	6,500-9,200
6. Sulfur hexafluoride (SF_e)	23,900

Small-scale CDM Projects

Although the CDM is devised to foster the sustainable development of host countries, developing small-scale CDM project activities, which are known to be beneficial to the sustainable development of local communities, are often burdened with high costs for low returns. In order to leverage the development of small-scale CDM project activities, the UNFCCC introduced fast-track modalities and procedures with some preferential treatment. A project activity can be qualified as small-scale CDM if it meets one of the three following conditions

- Type I: renewable energy project activities with a maximum output capacity equivalent to up to 15 megawatts (or an appropriate equivalent).
- Type II: energy-efficiency improvement project activities which reduce energy consumption on the supply and/or demand side by up to the equivalent of 15 gigawatt-hours per year.
- Type III: other project activities that both reduce anthropogenic emissions by sources and directly emit less than 15 kilotonnes of CO_2 equivalent (CO_2e) annually.

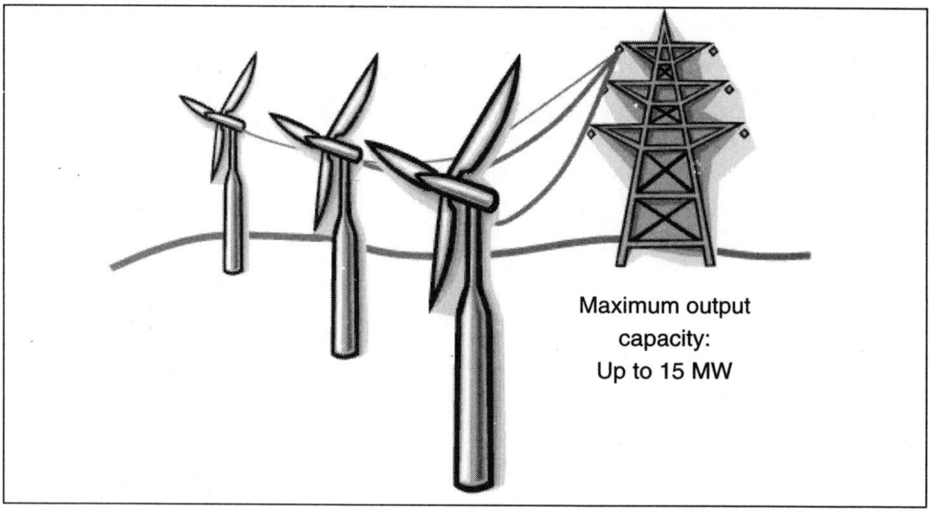

Figure 5.3: Renewable Energy Project Activity

Small-scale CDM project activities benefit from a number of privileges, which allows them to speed up their registration process. The details of the special treatment given to small-scale projects can be found in the overview of the CDM project cycle (section 3.7).

One special feature applicable only to small-scale CDM project activities is bundling and debundling. Bundling is to cluster projects that are too small to be attractive for investment, even with the additional CER revenues. By using the bundling scheme, small projects can become cost-effective and thus become sufficiently attractive with CER revenues. Many community-based projects (e.g., small hydropower), as well as projects for small- or medium-size enterprises, with significant contribution to local sustainable development often face difficulties in attracting sufficient interest for investment without a substantial level of public support. These projects can use the bundling scheme to improve their overall financial viability. Projects can be bundled into "sub-bundles" based on the small-scale project types (type I, II, or III) and project characteristics, such as technology types, emission reduction measures, location, and baseline methodologies.

Furthermore, bundling of one or more sub-bundles is possible and there is no limitation on the number of projects that can be sub-bundled, as long as the total size of the each sub-bundle cluster does not exceed the ceiling set for its small-scale project type While it is possible to bundle small projects together, however, large projects are not allowed to be debundled to smaller project sizes well within the range of small-scale CDM rules, in order to avoid anyone taking advantage of the CDM's fast-track and cost-effective scheme for small-scale CDM projects. While the bundling scheme may appear to be an ideal solution for small projects beneficial to sustainable development, there also exists a number of difficulties involved with the practice, for example, in developing a plan for monitoring all bundled project activities.

Key Concepts of CDM Project

(1) Baseline

Baseline is defined as "the scenario that reasonably represents the anthropogenic emissions by sources of greenhouse gases that would occur in the absence of the proposed project activity"

(2) Additionality

The concept of "additionality" is closely related to that of "baseline", and has to be paid particular attention to when setting up a baseline scenario and developing a methodology. It is defined in the "CDM project activity is additional if anthropogenic emissions of greenhouse gases by sources are reduced below those that would have occurred in the absence of the registered CDM project activity."

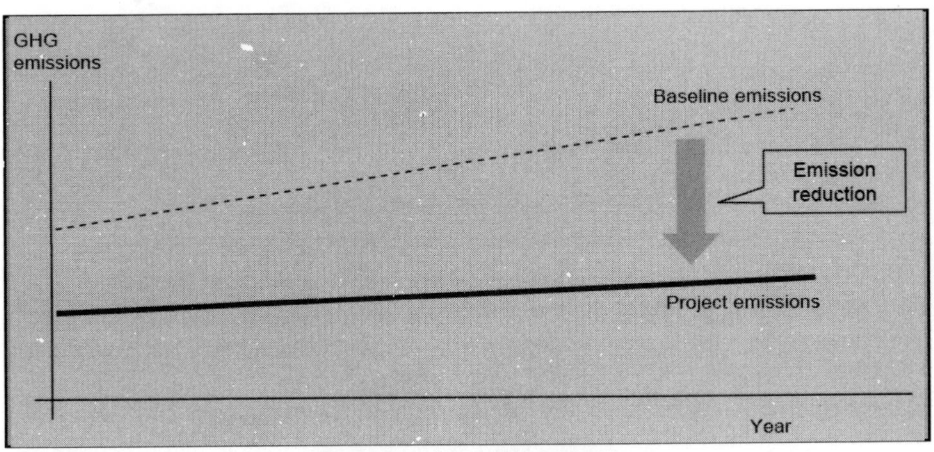

Concept of Additionality

Figure 5.4: CDM Project Cycle

CDM PROJECT CYCLE

The project cycle is common to all CDM project types, such as large scale, Small-Scale and A/R CDM activities.

1. Develop a CDM Project Activity

- Project participants develop a CDM project activity.
  - Consider various conditions associated with developing a CDM activity from the project planning stage.
  - Draft a Project Design Document (CDM-PDD) with all required elements.

2. Approval by the Host and Investing Parties

- Project participants obtain written approval of voluntary participation from the Designated national Authority (DNA) of each Party involved regarding the project activity that project participants wish to implement as a CDM project activity.
  - Project participants should confirm with the host and investing parties regarding the approval process.

3. Validation and Registration of the CDM Project Activity

- In order to go through validation, project participants should use the methodologies approved by the EB. If no approved methodology can apply to the proposed project activity, project participants must propose a new methodology for the project and have it approved by the EB.
- Validation is the process of independent evaluation of a project activity by a DOE, selected by the project participants, against the requirements of the CDM on the basis of the project design document (CDM-PDD)
- Registration is the formal acceptance of a validated project as a CDM project activity.

4. Monitoring of the CDM Project

- Project participants implement the CDM project activity and carry out proper monitoring necessary for calculation of GHG emission reductions, in accordance with the monitoring plan written in the PDD.

5. Verification, Certification and Issuance of CERs

- Project participants report to the DOE the results of monitoring of the CDM project activity and calculated emission reductions based on the results of monitoring activity.
- DOE verifies the results of monitoring and the resulting emission reductions.
- DOE certifies the emission reductions based on the results of verification.
- The EB issues CERs equal to the verified amount of GHG emission reductions.
- It is possible for a project activity, which met certain conditions, to have CERs issued for emission reductions starting as of the year 2000.

6. Distribution of CERs

- 2% of the CERs will be deducted as the share of proceeds to assist developing country parties that are particularly vulnerable to the adverse effects of climate change.
- The share of proceeds to cover administrative expensed to the CDM will be deducted.
- Remainders of the CERs are to be distributed among project participants.

Figure 5.5: CDM Project Cycle (as per Figure)

GLOBAL MARKETS

Major Buyers

The challenge of man-made climate change requires speedy and significant action across all fronts. While the principal need is to reduce emissions directly through changes in behavior or technological improvements, some emissions, at least in the short to medium term, continue to be unavoidable. Encouragement and assistance must be given to individuals, organizations and companies to offset because robust and credible offsetting can have a useful if limited role in mitigating current levels of, and projected short-term trends in, emissions.

The major buyers for the carbon credits are the Europeans, Japanese and Americans. But its difficult to find the exact number of the buyers in these three nations.

Cumulatively, Europe (EU, Iceland, Norway and Switzerland) has accounted for about two thirds of the CDM and JI market since 2006, while Japan has accounted for nearly one third. Private buyers accounted for 84% of European purchases of project-based assets in 2006 compared to about 80% and 70% in 2005 and 2004 respectively. For JI projects, the data shows that public buyers dominated with more than 90% market share. It has been estimated that EU and Japanese governments have only purchased about 22% of the assets identified for purchase from the flexible mechanisms (CDM, JI and AAUs). Since public buyers are likely to become more prominent in the market in the coming year or two.

Within Europe, the United Kingdom, led by the financial institutions located in the City of London, had a 43% market share of volumes transacted (up from 14% in 2005). Italy sharply increased its carbon acquisitions entering the market in 2005 (growing from 1% in 2005 to 15% so far in 2006). The UK has the opportunity to lead the international field in developing robust and helpful guidance and codes of practice at a national government level which will endorse meaningful offsets and assist people in choosing the best way to offset their emissions. The UK's financial and carbon markets have much to gain from a rapid growth in what is increasingly seen as a vital component of commercial activity and corporate responsibility. The international offset industry, if managed responsibly, will only grow over the short to medium

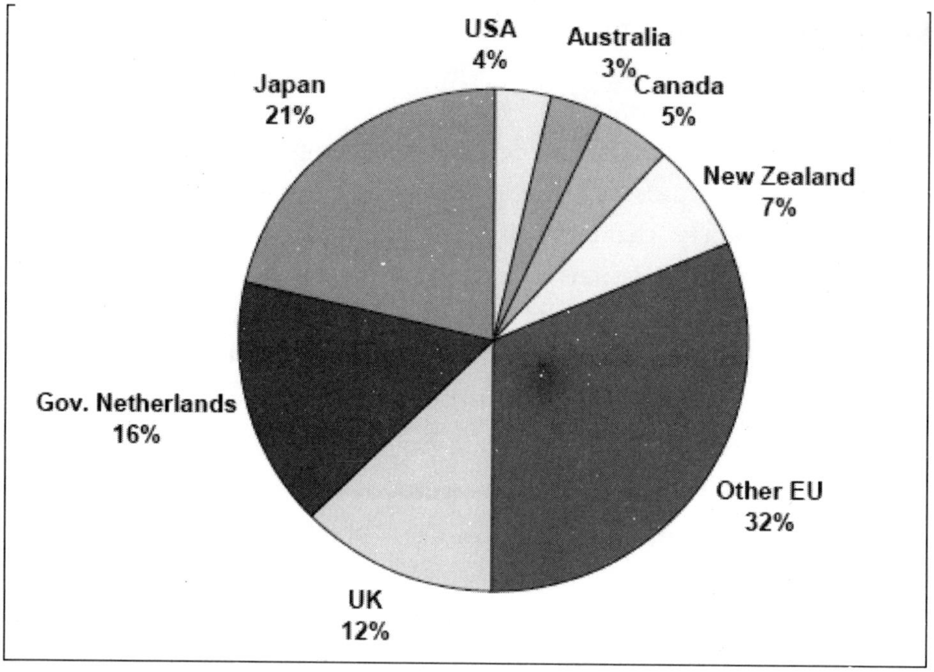

Figure 5.6: Share of Volume of ERs Purchased

term as many governments, like the UK Government, develop their own guidance or best practice or perhaps themselves move towards offsetting their own emissions, for their official travel or for their activities, as is the case in the UK.

European buyers sidelined Japanese buyers and picked up whatever assets they could find. Kyoto mechanisms are necessary for Japan to achieve the commitment of the Kyoto Protocol in cost-effective manner.

Strategy of Europe

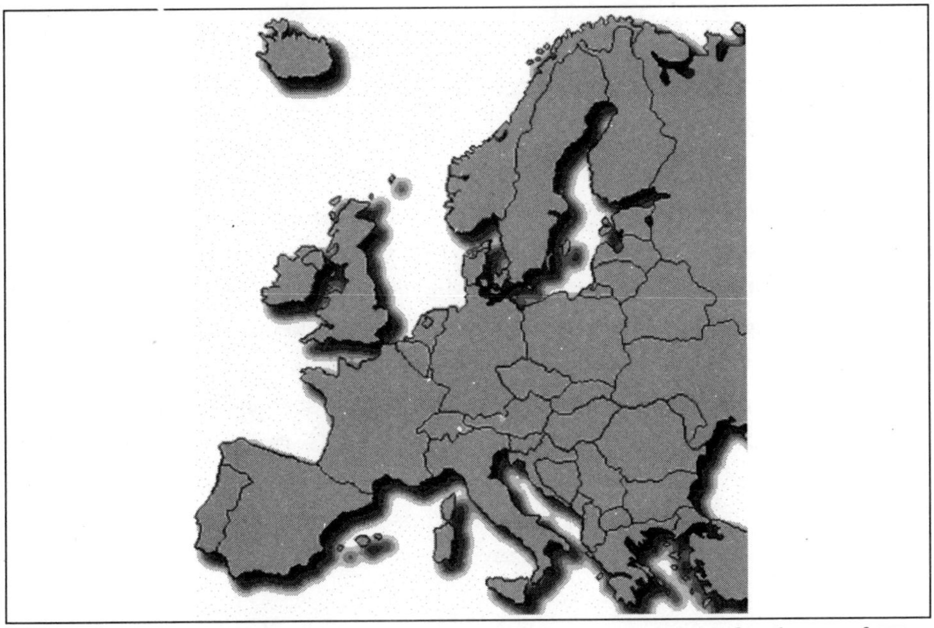

Private and Public entities in Europe represent 60% of volume of ER's are purchased through project based transactions against 21% for private and public entities in Japan and 4% for Canada.

Four active market for GHG allowance—EU ETS, UK emission trading system, the South Wales trading system and the Chicago Climate Exchange —of which EU ETS is largest

1. Price of EUA's VS Price of CDM/ER
2. There is wide gap between EUA's prices and CDM/JI prices

Reasons

- Delivery risk
- Weather and high oil prices

3. Government of Europe is the major buyer in Kyoto market the private sector appears to be the modest in Europe.
4. Main areas to capture are—Netherlands, Denmark, Sweden and Austria because of maximum industrialization
5. Europe main focus is to deal in HFC projects followed by CH_4 and N_2O (nitrous oxide).

The total European population estimated in 2007 is 809,624,686.

Ironically, some of the encouraging local programmes have been conducted in the Western and Central Europe. Meanwhile 284 mayors near about 50 million Europeans across the country have pledged 'to meet or beet' the goals of the Kyoto Protocol. They had targeted on the individual basis to reduce their carbon emissions by 25% by the end of 2025.

Germany is the most industrialized country as most of the business is taking place in the country that is wise it is quoted to use the German language. Germany is exploring ways to link up the European Union's carbon dioxide emissions trading scheme with the United States as it tries to broaden efforts to tackle climate change. Germany was also keen to ensure European companies were not at a competitive disadvantage because of the obligatory trading scheme although carbon markets are widely seen as a business-friendly way to squeeze emissions. In the past decade, Germany has reduced its emissions more than any other country in the EU. Since Germany signed the Kyoto Protocol in 1997, it has reduced its emissions of the six greenhouse gases by 19 percent. The target for Germany, set as part of a package with other EU countries, is 21 percent by 2012.

For emission reductions of -30% by 2020 and -80% by 2050, Germany's hypothetical ETS emissions target would be approx. 400 Mt CO_2e/a by 2020 (or 345 Mt CO_2e/a to meet the national -40 % target) and around 115 Mt CO_2e/a by 2050; the ETS-emission target of the UK would be around 200 Mt CO_2e/a in 2020 and roughly 55 Mt CO_2e/a in 2050, and the Netherlands's hypothetical ETS emissions target for 2020 would be about 55 Mt CO_2e/a by 2020 and some 15 Mt CO_2e/a by 2050.

The UK has the opportunity to lead the international field in developing robust and helpful guidance and codes of practice at a national government level which will endorse meaningful offsets and assist people in choosing the best way to offset their emissions. The UK's financial and carbon markets have much to gain from a rapid growth in what is increasingly seen as a vital component of commercial activity and corporate responsibility. The international offset industry, if managed responsibly, will only grow over the short to medium term as many governments, like the UK Government, develop their own guidance or best practice or perhaps they move towards offsetting their own emissions, for their official travel or for their activities, as is the case in the UK.

Strategy of Japan

Mostly Japanese private firms are the largest buyer of emission reductions

Example: Japan Carbon Finance ltd, a company who purchase the carbon credit on behalf of the other companies of Japan who are not able to achieve their targets.

Japan has the obstacles in order to have their own CDM projects

- Difficulties in obtaining necessary data to fill out PDD.
- Unreasonable request which hurts the project feasibility such as payment of waste water.
- So for these reasons Japan wants the proper appreciation for CDM projects development in host countries.

Japan mainly stress on the purchase of emissions reduction through Project based mechanism rather than Allowance based (Allowance based transactions under EU ETS have been conducted over the counter by brokers through some trading platform). In allowance based transactions information about prices is available online. So the project based is most favorable.

Japan is continuously promoting measures to shift socio-economy including urban/regional structure and public transportation infrastructure into low carbon one to shift Japan's energy demand and supply into low carbon type. Companies can promote systematic actions by industries and development and use of alternatives. (Green products)

The government will utilize the New Energy and Industrial Technology Development Organization (hereafter "NEDO") for obtaining credits (mainly for experts knowledge). Ministry of environment is imposing the global warming tax in Japan.

Japanese approaches in meeting the requirements of the Kyoto Protocol:

- Stable energy supply.
- Reduction of CO_2 under Kyoto protocol.
- Japan's nuclear policy in coming years.

Japan is failing for many reasons, but the primary explanation can be found in Japanese households. Although Japan's population is dwindling (the total population in 2007 is 127,433,494) the number of Japanese households is growing. More people are delaying or deciding against marriage, and instead live alone. Plus, each household is guzzling more energy than before. Energy savings gleaned from efficient new technologies are gobbled by the many appliances, gadgets, and air conditioners that fill Japanese homes. The same effect can be seen on Japan's roads. While the government introduced tough new rules requiring cars to get more miles from each gallon of gas, more Japanese people are driving instead of taking public transportation.

Japan Carbon Finance Ltd. is an organization formed on December 1, 2004 at Tokyo, Japan, whose business objective is to purchase the carbon credits (CERs and ERUs) generated until 2012 from CDM / JI projects. It made the fund known as "Japan GHG reduction Fund" of amount US $141.5 million. It provides the financial assistance for the project development also.

It is expected that even if the best possible efforts are made through domestic measures, there will still be a shortfall of 1.6%. In order for Japan to make utmost effort toward achievement of its Kyoto Protocol commitment, it is necessary for the public and private sectors to collaborate appropriately and effectively utilize a variety of methods to obtain credits through the Kyoto Mechanisms.

According to the protocol, Annex I countries have to achieve their imposed GHG reduction targets during the first commitment period of 2008 to 2012. In particular, in a severe situation is Japan since domestic measures would not be enough for Japan to achieve the reduction target. Therefore it will be inevitable for Japan to make use of the Kyoto mechanism. The Clean Development Mechanism (CDM), one of the Kyoto mechanisms, is an issue of the greatest concern of Japanese government. CDM will contribute to sustainable development of developing countries as well as reduction of greenhouses gas emissions. The following ministries in Japan are doing the work in the favor of global warming.

Ministry of the Environment

For achieving Japan's Kyoto Protocol commitment, the Ministry of the Environment, as a Deputy-Chief of the Global Warming Prevention Headquarters, will make independent efforts with regard to all aspects of promotion and utilization of the Kyoto Mechanisms by the government.

With a view to promoting efforts toward project formation by private businesses, etc., and contributing to the sustainable development of the host country through CDM/JI, etc. projects, among other aims, the Ministry of the Environment will make independent efforts for promotion and utilization of the Kyoto Mechanisms.

The Minister of the Environment, as a competent minister of NEDO's credit obtainment activities, will make independent efforts together with the Minister of Economy, Trade and Industry with regard to the obtainment of credit through NEDO.

Ministry of Economy, Trade and Industry

For achieving Japan's Kyoto Protocol commitment, the Ministry of Economy, Trade and Industry, as a Deputy-Chief of the Global Warming Prevention Headquarters, will make independent efforts with regard to all aspects of promotion and utilization of the Kyoto Mechanisms by the government.

With a view to promoting efforts toward project formation by private businesses, etc., disseminating Japan's energy and environmental technology worldwide, and alleviating energy use restrictions, among other aims, the Ministry of Economy, Trade and Industry will make independent efforts for promotion and utilization of the Kyoto Mechanisms.

The Minister of Economy, Trade and Industry, as a competent minister of NEDO's credit obtainment activities, will make independent efforts together with the Minister of the Environment with regard to the obtainment of credit through NEDO.

The Ministry of Economy, Trade and Industry will make independent efforts for promotion and utilization of the Kyoto Mechanisms utilizing ODA in conformity with international rules and on the premise of agreement of the recipient country.

Ministry of Foreign Affairs

With a view to complying with international treaties, the Ministry of Foreign Affairs will make independent efforts for achieving Japan's Kyoto Protocol commitment with regard to all aspects of promotion and utilization of the Kyoto Mechanisms by the government.

The Ministry of Foreign Affairs will make independent efforts with regard to coordinating negotiations and formation of agreements, etc. with foreign governments necessary for promoting and utilizing the Kyoto Mechanisms, building cooperative relations with foreign governments concerning the Kyoto Mechanisms, implementing the necessary studies, and promoting and utilizing the Kyoto Mechanisms through participation in international organizations, etc.

The Ministry of Foreign Affairs will make independent efforts for promotion and utilization of the Kyoto Mechanisms utilizing ODA in conformity with international rules and on the premise of agreement of the recipient country.

Ministry of Land, Infrastructure and Transport

The Ministry of Land, Infrastructure and Transport will make independent efforts for promotion and utilization of the Kyoto Mechanisms in the transport sector and the social capital development sector.

Ministry of Agriculture, Forestry and Fisheries

The Ministry of Agriculture, Forestry and Fisheries will make independent efforts for promotion and utilization of the Kyoto Mechanisms in the forest sector.

Ministry of Finance

The Ministry of Finance will make independent efforts for promotion and utilization of the Kyoto Mechanisms from the perspective of international financing. For example the ministry will support the vigorous activities of multilateral development banks and utilize the Japan Bank for International Cooperation.

The Ministry of Finance will make independent efforts for promotion and utilization of the Kyoto Mechanisms utilizing ODA in conformity with international rules and on the premise of agreement of the recipient country.

Who's Selling?

The largest seller of ERs is Asia (45% from January 2004 to April 2005). Latin America is second with 35% of the volume supplied. Projects in OECD countries, which include both JI projects in New Zealand and voluntary activities in the U.S., rank third with 14%, while transition economies rank fourth at 6%.

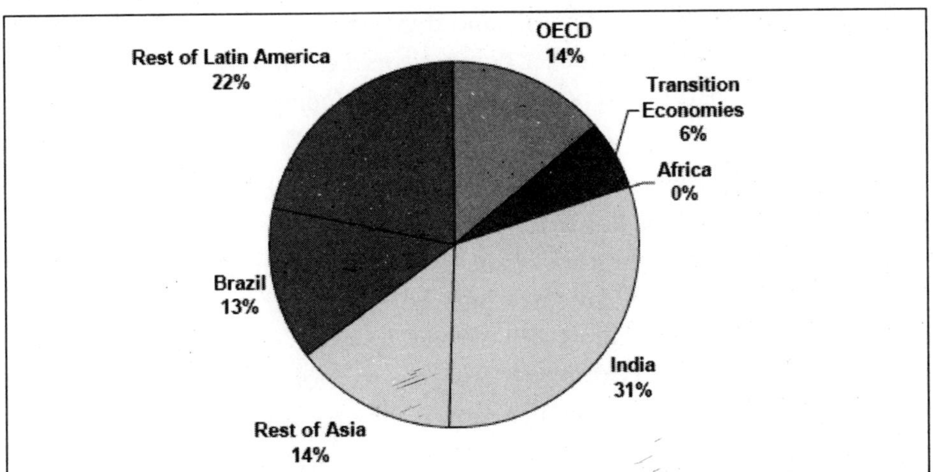

Figure 5.7: Share of Volume Supplied

DERIVATIVE AND OTC MARKET OF CARBON CREDITS

Emissions trading is the mechanism of trading between states or firms, the right (or similar object) related to gas emissions such as carbon dioxide, which are considered the cause of global warming. It was adopted by the Parties to the Third Session of the United Nations Framework Convention on Climate Change (December 1997), as a scheme to reduce greenhouse gas emissions efficiently using a market mechanism, and was incorporated into the Kyoto Protocol. Although the international trading of emissions under the Protocol will begin in 2008, in advance of this the movement to establish an original emissions trading market is becoming active in various countries. In this report significance of OTC market for emissions trading has been highlighted by taking Gensol in to reference.

The OTC market is a market where risk hedgers, risk takers, and brokers meet to deal directly in the trading of various derivative products based on various underlying assets such as interest rates, currency, equities, and commodities etc. The OTC market is also at the cutting edge of financial innovation, where new products are developed one after another based on the creativity and needs of unrestricted participants. It is believed that in the near future risk hedging techniques, such as medium-to-long term swaps, and options, will be dealt also in underlying related to emissions.

OTC market in which brokers are intermediary between the demand and supply of carbon credit as it is a success factors of OTC that is standardization, simplicity, liquidity and transparency – ultimately encourage the differentiation amongst other competitors i.e. their variety, flexibility, highly structured nature and occasionally extreme complexity in terms of risk and pricing.

In the United Kingdom (the UK), an emissions trading system open to unrestricted participation has already been in operation since April 2002, and, concurrently with the operation of the domestic system, the UK intends to implement laws necessary to carry out the EU enacted emissions trading system. Prime Minister Blair is also extremely active in seeking to increase emissions trading and is inviting positive participation from financial institutions without restriction, in order to enhance market liquidity.

DERIVATIVE MARKET

What is Derivative?

A derivative is a financial product. Its value is derived from the value of other financial product called bases or underlying asset in a contractual manner. Derivatives allow investors to transfer risk to others who could profit from taking the risk. The person transferring risk achieves price certainty but loses the opportunity for making additional profits when prices move opposite his fears. Likewise, the person taking on the risk will lose if the counterparty's fears are realized.

The most commonly used derivative contracts are:

- Forward contract
- Futures contract
- Swaps
- Options

Forward Contract

A forward contract is an agreement between buyer and seller parties for delivery of a specified quality and quantity of a good at an agreed date in the future at a specific price or at a price determined by formula at the time of delivery to the location specified in the contract.

Characteristics of Forward Contract

- Terms and conditions are negotiated
- Credit risk
- Unregulated market (not exchange-traded)

The specifications included in a forward contract are:

- Product
- Price—The price at which delivery will be made in the future.
- Quantity—Any number of units as mutually agreed.
- Quality—Type
- Future Delivery date
- Delivery Place—How and where delivery will be made at maturity

Future Contract

A Futures contract is an agreement between two parties to buy (long position) or sell (short position) an asset at a certain time in the future at a certain price. Future contracts are standardized exchange-traded contracts. The quantity of the underlying, quality of the underlying; the date and month of expiry and minimum price change are standardized. Like a forward contract, a futures contract obligates each party to buy or sell a specific amount of a commodity at a specified price. Unlike a forward contract, buyers and sellers of futures contracts deal with an exchange, not with each other.

Futures contracts are firm commitments to make or accept delivery of a specified quantity and quality of a commodity during a specific month in the future at a price agreed upon at the time the commitment is made. The buyer, known as the long, agrees to take delivery of the underlying commodity. The seller, known as the short, agrees to make delivery. Only a small number of contracts traded each year result in delivery of the underlying commodity. Instead, traders generally offset their futures positions before their contracts mature (a buyer will liquidate by selling the contract; the seller will liquidate by buying back the contract). The difference between the initial purchase or sale price and the price of the offsetting transaction represents the realized profit or loss.

Options

Options are derivative instruments that provide the holder with the right, but not the obligation, to, pay or receive some quantity of cash or commodity, at an agreed strike price. An option is a contract that gives the buyer of the contract the right to buy (a call or put option) or sell (a put or call option) at a specified price (the "strike price") over a specified period of time.

Swaps

Swaps is a purely financial (paper) transaction between two parties who agree to make regular payments to each other in the future

Swaps (also called contracts for differences) are the most recent innovation in finance. Swaps were created in part to give price certainty at a cost that is lower than the cost of options. A swap contract is an agreement between two parties to exchange a series of cash flows generated by underlying assets. No physical commodity is actually transferred between the buyer and seller. The contracts are entered into between the two counterparties, or principals, outside any centralized trading facility or exchange and are therefore characterized as OTC derivatives.

Futures and Forward Contracts of Carbon Credits

Most of the EUA trade is in forward and futures contracts, where the price is agreed now but allowances and payment don't change hands until a set date in the future. There is little trade in the 'spot' market (buy now, exchange immediately) relative to the forward market.

Companies that are covered under the EU ETS, so called 'compliance' buyers, buy and sell EUAs in an effort to manage their expected future needs of emissions permits based on their forward production plans of, for example, electricity, steel or cement.

Half or more of the trade in EUAs has up to now been 'over the counter' (OTC) in bilateral forward deals negotiated through brokers which may have varying terms and conditions. But there is growing trade in standardised futures contracts on various electronic energy and emissions exchanges such as the ECX, EEX, Nord Pool and Powernext.

The most-traded forward/futures contracts for EUAs in both the OTC and exchange markets have December maturities, that is, they are for delivery in December of upcoming years. This is because emissions targets are based around calendar years. Companies must reconcile their books for actual emissions and allowances, and demonstrate compliance with their annual target by March 31 of the following year.

Derivatives are traded both by professional and retail investor. Derivatives re used as risk management tool. That is, derivative can expose you to more or less risk depending on how you use them.

Currently futures contracts in carbon credits are actively traded in the European exchanges. A carbon futures contract is an agreement between two parties, either to buy or sell the carbon credit at a predetermined price and at a specified period. The underlying unit (carbon credit) that is being traded would be an electronic certificate bearing a unique serial number indicating the country of origin and sequestration year. Analysts advise companies operating in the Annex I countries to take a buy position (long position) in the current market for carbon futures to mitigate the possibility of increasing prices of carbon credits. In fact, many companies actively participate in this market to manage the price risks associated with the trading in carbon credits. The most prominent risk associated with carbon trading is the failure on the part of member countries with regard to compliance with Kyoto Protocol. The other risk is the uncertainty in the continuity of KP after the current commitment period of 2008-12.

Keeping in view the risks associated with futures contracts in carbon credits, trading in futures contracts in carbon allowances has now become a reality in Europe with burgeoning volumes. Currently there is active participation by public utilities, manufacturing entities, brokers, banks, and others. So with the prospective to capture the European carbon credit market. Multi Commodity of India Ltd. (MCX) entered into a strategic alliance with CCX in September 2005 to initiate futures carbon trading in India.

Price Influencing Factors

In Non-Annexure B countries (the developing countries) across the world, CER prices are influenced by various factors including EUA prices, crude oil prices, electricity, coal, natural gas, the level of economic activities across Annexure I countries, among others.

Some of the major price influencing factors:

- Supply-demand mismatch
- Policy issues
- Crude oil prices
- Coal prices
- CO_2 emissions
- Weather/Fuel prices
- European Union Allowances (EUAs) prices
- Foreign exchange fluctuations
- Global economic growth

Risks Associated with Carbon Credits

The coming into being and operation of the EU-ETS, the ECX futures exchange platform, revealed that there are market- and policy-related risks for CER producers, including the supply-side risks starting from the DNA approval risk to the CER issuance risk in a complete CDM approval cycle. Apart from these risks there are a host of other risks from both the supply and demand sides that the real market players confront with.

Most CDM projects by their very nature take a long time to generate the CERs and hence, face the aforesaid risks in large proportion, which if not hedged would lead to reduced realization. Under such a situation, the realization of CER generators at times may not even cover the investment put in to generate the CERs and thus, has the potential of even making a CDM project unviable in the long term. Given the long gestation period of CDM projects and the risks involved, it is rather inevitable that they pre-sell their potential credits in the futures market (preferably a domestic futures market, to avoid forex risk attached to participation in a foreign exchange) and thereby, cover their probable downside in the physical market.

Potential participants in carbon credits trading are as below:

- Hedgers
- Producers
- Intermediaries in spot markets

Ultimate Buyers

- Investors
- Arbitragers

Portfolio Managers

- Diverse participants with wide participation objectives
- Commodity financers
- Funding agencies
- Corporates having risk exposure in energy products

India as a Potential Supplier

India, being one of the leading generators of CERs through CDM, has a large scope in emissions trading. Analysts forecast that its trading in carbon credits would touch US$ 100 billion by 2010.

Currently, the total registered CDM projects are more than 300, almost 1/3rd of the total CDM projects registered with the UNFCCC. The total issued CERs with India as a host country till now stand at 34,101,315 (around 34 million), again around 1/3rd of the total CERs issued by the UNFCCC. In value terms (INR), it could be running into thousands

Various industries that have scope of generation of CERs:

- Agriculture
- Energy (renewable and non-renewable sources)
- Manufacturing
- Fugitive emissions from fuels (solid, oil and gas)

- Metal production
- Mining and mineral production
- Chemicals
- Afforestation and reforestation

Further, there has been a surge in number of registered projects in India. In 2007, a total of 160 new projects were registered with the UNFCCC indicating that more than half of all registered projects in India happened last year. It is expected that with increasing awareness this would go further up in the future. The number of expected annual CERs in India is hovering around 28 million and considering that each of these CERs is sold for around 15 euros, on an average, the expected value is going to be around Rs 2,500 crore.

Role of MCX

Multi Commodity Exchange of India Ltd. (MCX) entered into a strategic alliance with CCX in September 2005 to initiate carbon trading in India. The tie-up would provide immense scope and opportunity for domestic suppliers to realize better prices for their carbon credits. Further, the MCX-CCX alliance would also integrate the Indian market with its global counterparts to foster world-class best practices in the commodities futures market as related to emission trading. With MCX keen to play a major role on the emission front by extending its platform to add carbon credits to its existing basket of commodities with regard to commodities futures trading, the existing and potential suppliers of carbon credits in India have geared up to generate more carbon credits from their existing and ongoing projects to be sold in the international markets. With India supposed to be a major supplier of carbon credits, the tie-up between the two exchanges is expected to ensure better price discovery of carbon credits, besides covering risks associated with buying and selling.

FUTURE CONTRACTS

I. MULTI COMMODITY EXCHANGE OF INDIA LTD.

Contract Specifications of Carbon Credits ECXCFI Mini[SM]

Symbol	CFI
Description	CFIMMMYY
	Contracts available for trading
December 08 contract	1st Jan 2008 to 15th December of the contract year
December 09 contract	1st Jan 2008 to 15th December of the contract year
December 10 contract	1st Jan 2008 to 15th December of the contract year
December 11 contract	1st Jan 2008 to 15th December of the contract year
December 12 contract	1st Jan 2008 to 15th December of the contract year
	Trading
Trading period	Mondays through Saturdays
Trading session	Monday to Friday: 10.00 a.m. to 11.30 p.m. Saturday: 10.00 a.m. to 2.00 p.m.
Trading unit	200 tons of Carbon Credits (Carbon Emission Allowances)
Quotation/Base Value	Rs. Per ton
Maximum order size	10000 tons
Tick size (minimum price movement)	50 paise per ton
Daily price limits	4% (Exchange may revise this price limit to 5%, as prescribed by FMC, without cooling period)
Initial margin	6%
Special margin	In case of additional volatility, a special margin at such percentage, as deemed fit, will be imposed immediately on both buy and sale side in respect of all outstanding position, which will remain in force for next 2 days, after which the special margin will be relaxed.
Maximum allowable open position	For individual clients: 500,000 tons For a member collectively for all clients: Not more than 25% of the market's open position in a contract at any point of time
	Delivery
Delivery unit	200 tons of Carbon Credits (Carbon Emission Allowances)
Quality specifications	Carbon Credits (Carbon dioxide (CO_2) Emission Allowance). Each CO_2 Emission Allowance being an entitlement to emit one tonne of Carbon dioxide equivalent gases.

Delivery Option	Both Option
Special Delivery Provision	During the life of the futures contract, to the extent parties having open position on the exchange enter into bilateral physical trade as per their futures obligation and intimate the exchange, their respective futures position will be off-set by the exchange.
Final Settlement Price (DDR)	Price of ECX-CFI prevailing on European Climate Exchange for relevant contract on the date of expiry of MCX contract converted into Indian rupees.

Delivery and Settlement Procedure of ECX CFI Mini^{SM} Futures

Delivery logic	**Both Option**
****Special Delivery Provision**	During the life of the futures contract, to the extent parties having open position on the exchange enter into bilateral physical trade as per their futures obligation and intimate the exchange, their respective futures position will be off-set by the exchange.
Tender day	1st working day after expiry of contract by 6.00 p.m.
Tender and delivery period	1st to 3rd working days after expiry of the contract.
Buyer's and Seller's Intention	On the contract expiry day by 6.00 p.m. Seller will submit copies of relevant documents as a proof of holding carbon credits certificates at the time of giving his intention to the satisfaction of the Exchange and the buyer. The Exchange may specify additional documentation that may be required to make a secured delivery of carbon credit.
Mode of communication	Fax/Courier
Matching of Buyer's and Seller's intention	On the basis of intention received from the buyers and sellers, the Exchange will match the total quantity (units) offered by the sellers with that of the buyers and with respect to the matched quantity the allocation of delivery between the buyers and sellers will be done to the satisfaction of buyer and the Exchange. The unmatched quantity of open position will be closed out as per DDR and actual delivery will be effected only to the extent of matched quantity.
Dissemination of the information on delivery intention on TWS	On the contract expiry day by 7.00 p.m.
Delivery period margin	25% margin will be imposed during tender and delivery period on both buyers and sellers on matched quantity.

Exemption from delivery period margin	Delivery period margin is exempted if the Seller provides documentary proof of delivery of the carbon credit certificate.
Delivery allocation **- Date** **- Rate**	 On expiry date of the Contract At due date rate (DDR)
Delivery pay-in	On tender days
Delivery pay-out	E+3 working day by 11.00 a.m.
Pay-in of funds	E+2 working day by 11.00 a.m.
Pay-out of funds	E+3 working day by 11.00 a.m.
Penal provisions	After getting (matching) intentions from the buyer and seller to take or give delivery, if any of the party fails to honour his obligations, a penalty of 2.5% of the DDR will be imposed on him. Additionally, a replacement cost of 4% of DDR will be recovered from the defaulting buyer / seller. Out of the penalty, 2%(i.e. 80% of penalty amount) will be credited to IPF and 0.5% (i.e. 20% of penalty amount) will be credited to the counter party. While out of the replacement cost recovered 90% will be passed on to the counter party and 10% will be retained by the Exchange towards administrative expenses.
Taxes, Duties, Cess and Levies	UNFCC charges as applicable for change in holding will have to be borne by the seller which is currently at the rate of 2% of the units sold. All other charges, levies or Cess and taxes as applicable will be on account of buyer.
Close out of open positions	All outstanding positions on the expiry of contract where expression of interest for tendering delivery or receiving delivery has not been received and such positions where expression of intentions have been received but have not found the counter party for honoring the intentions, shall be closed out at due date rate and respective pay-in and pay-out of funds of such close out positions shall be effected on the following day of last day of trading by 11.00 a.m.
Due Date Rate (DDR)	Price of ECX-CFI prevailing on European Climate Exchange for relevant contract on the date of expiry of MCX contract. The ECX CFI settlement price will be converted at the Rupee – Euro rate as notified by RBI on that particular day (or last available).
Odd lot treatment	Not applicable
Delivery order	Along with tender notice, Carbon Credits delivery order will be submitted in specified format giving details of Members/ Registered Non-Members who shall perform delivery. The

	evidence of delivery shall be to the satisfaction of the buyer and the Exchange. Each delivery order issued shall be in multiples of minimum delivery lots and shall be designated for the specified delivery center. It will be accompanied with appropriate documents showing evidence of holding specified quantity of carbon credits. Order once submitted cannot be withdrawn or cancelled or changed unless so agreed by MCX in writing. Members tendering the delivery order shall clearly specify the project type and cannot be changed subsequently.
Delivery Procedure	On matching, the sellers are required to issue the relevant Carbon Credit certificates to the Exchange in the prescribed format to the satisfaction of the Exchange and the buyer.
Delivery Center	Mumbai (Member has to submit copies of relevant documents as a proof of holding carbon credits certificates at the Exchange)
Evidence of carbon credits in possession	At the time of issuing the delivery order, the seller must satisfy MCX that he holds carbon credits through appropriate documentation. The Exchange may seek additional protection to safeguard delivery from the seller.
Legal obligation	The member will provide appropriate tax forms wherever required as per law and as customary and neither of the parties will unreasonable refuses to do so.
Extension of delivery period	As per the Exchange decision due to a force majeure or otherwise.
Applicability of Byelaws, Rules, Business Rules of the Exchange	The general provisions of Byelaws, Rules and Business Rules of the Exchange and decisions taken by Forward Markets Commission, Board of Directors and Executive Committee of the Exchange in respect of matters specified above will form an integral part of this contract. The Exchange or FMC as the case may be further prescribe additional measures relating to delivery procedures, margining, risk management from time to time. (The interpretation or clarification given by the Exchange on any terms of this contract shall be final and binding on the members and others.)

***Note*: The format for intimating such bilateral physical trade will be informed to the market through a separate circular.

II. Chicago Climate Futures Exchange, LLC

Certified Emission Reduction Futures

Contract Size 1,000 Certified Emission Reductions ("CERs") representing 1,000 metric tons of carbon dioxide ("CO_2").

Quotation US dollars / metric ton CO_2

Minimum Tick Increment $0.01 per CER = $10.00 per contract

Symbol CER

Trading Hours 7:00 a.m. – 3:00 p.m. U.S. Central Time

Contract Listing Cycle Standard-cycle contract listings:

(a) Six consecutive quarterly contracts on a March, June, September, December cycle

(b) Front two serial calendar months; and

(c) Annual December contracts through 2012

CCFE may list additional annual December contracts and any other calendar month contract off the standard-cycle listing schedule through 2014.

Deliverable Instruments

CERs are transferable instruments issued by the Executive Board of the Clean Development Mechanism as operated under the Kyoto Protocol to the United Nations Framework Convention on Climate Change. (Temporary CERs (tCERs) are not acceptable for delivery. A tCER is a CER issued for an afforestration or reforestration project which expires at the end of the commitment period following the period during which it was issued.) Until such time as the United Nations' International Transaction Log is operational, the CER futures contract will be cash settled.

First Trading Day The first trading day of a standard-cycle contract is the first business day following an expiration day of standard-cycle contract.

Last Trading Day With the exception of the April contracts, the last trading day of a contract is the third-tolast business day of the expiration month. The last trading day for April contracts will be the fifth-to-last business day of the month in order to comply with the European Union Greenhouse Gas Emission Trading Scheme's (EU ETS) annual April 30th compliance deadline.

Physical Delivery Process Initially, clearing participants and parties trading the market must have accounts established within the United Kingdom's Department for Environment Food and Rural Affairs (UK DEFRA) emissions registry and be able to electronically transfer CERs. As additional national registries are linked to the International Transaction Log and become eligible to effect transfers, such registries may be added as eligible upon CCFE notification. Delivery is a three day process consisting of Position Day, Notice Day, and Delivery Day occuring over three consecutive business days.

Position Day

The first business following a CER futures contract's expiration day is the day that Clearing Members must report their long futures positions and tender delivery notices to the Clearing Service Provider.

Notice Day

On the business day after the Position Day, the Clearing Service Provider will make the appropriate delivery assignments. The seller clearing member provides to the buyer clearing member(s) a description of the underlying Certified Emission Reduction instruments to be delivered. The buyer clearing member(s) provides UK DEFRA registry account information to the seller clearing member. The information exchange is to be completed by 4:00 p.m. U.S. Central Time. The seller clearing member must ensure the appropriate CER instruments are on deposit in its or its customer's UK DEFRA registry account by 5:00 p.m. U.S. Central Time.

Delivery Day

CCFE CSP will issue payment instructions to the respective buyer clearing member for the full contract value based upon the expiration day's settlement price in a means and manner prescribed by the Clearing Service Provider. By 3:00 p.m. U.S. Central Time, the seller clearing member must ensure that it or its customer has electronically submitted the CER instrument transfer instructions.

Payment

The Clearing Service Provider will release the delivery proceeds to the seller clearing member upon receipt of the "CCFE Receipt of Delivery

Confirmation" from the buying clearing member.

Final Settlement Price For Cash Settled Product

Final contract settlement prices will be based on an Exchange conducted market price survey for guaranteed delivery and payment of CERs on the last business day of December 2008 for contract expirations occurring through calendar year 2008. For contracts expiring in years after 2008, the final contract settlement prices will be based on an Exchange conducted market price survey for guaranteed delivery and payment of CERs on the last business day corresponding to the year the contract expires.

Market participants will be surveyed between 5:00 p.m. and 5:15 p.m. London time (11:00 a.m. and 11:15 a.m. U.S. Central Time). The Exchange will survey a minimum of ten market participants. The final settlement price for an expiring contract will be determined by excluding the highest and lowest quotes and then calculating the simple

average of the remaining price quotes. In addition, final settlement prices for all listed futures contracts other than December will be derived using standard present valuation procedures, utilizing U.S. dollar LIBOR interest rates for the appropriate expiration period of the contracts. Results of the price survey will be posted at 6:00 p.m. London time (12:00 p.m. U.S. Central time).

Price Limits No daily price limits

Reportable Position Limits 25 contracts, equivalent to 25,000 CERs

Nearby Expiration Month

Speculative Position Limits

1,000 contracts, equivalent to 1,000,000 Certified Emission Reductions per each expiring contract. Contract specifications and related rules are subject to revision. If CCFE determines that revisions to the contract specifications and related rules are warranted, reasonable efforts will be taken to provide appropriate advance notification of such revisions. This document is a summary of the CCFE contract specification rules; see the CCFE Rulebook for complete contract.

Index